D0097657

AMC
Southern
New Hampshire
Trail Guide

2nd Edition

Welcome to the AMC

Founded in 1876, we are America's oldest conservation and recreation organization. We promote the protection, enjoyment, and wise use of the mountains, rivers, and trails of the Appalachian region. The AMC has twelve chapters from Maine to Washington, DC, comprised of tens of thousands of outdoor enthusiasts like you.

By purchasing this book you have contributed to our efforts to protect the Appalachian region. Proceeds from the sales of AMC Books and Maps support our regional land conservation efforts; trail building and maintenance; air- and water-quality research; search and rescue; and environmental education programs for school age children, at-risk youth, and outdoor enthusiasts.

The AMC encourages everyone to enjoy and appreciate the natural world because we believe that successful conservation depends on such experiences. So join us in the outdoors! We offer hiking, paddling, biking, skiing, and mountaineering activities throughout the Appalachian region for outdoor adventurers of every age and ability. Our destinations, such as our state-of-the-art Highland Center, are Model Environmental Education Facilities, demonstrating our stewardship ethic and providing a place for you to relax off-trail and learn more about local ecosystems and habitats, regional environmental issues, and mountain history and culture.

For more information about AMC membership, destinations, and conservation and education programs, turn to the back of this book or visit the AMC website at www.outdoors.org.

AMC
Southern
New Hampshire
Trail Guide

2nd Edition

AMC Guide to Hiking Mts. Monadnock,
Cardigan, Kearsarge, and the Lakes Region

Compiled and edited by
Gene Daniell and Steven D. Smith

APPALACHIAN MOUNTAIN CLUB BOOKS
BOSTON, MASSACHUSETTS

Front cover photograph: Eagle Cliff, Sandwich, NH © Robert Kozlow
Back cover photographs: Mt. Monadnock, from Jaffrey, NH © Robert Kozlow
Cover design: Belinda Thresher
Interior design: Eric Edstam
Cartography: Larry Garland

Distributed by the Globe Pequot Press, Guilford, CT.

Library of Congress Cataloging-in-Publication Data

Southern New Hampshire trail guide : hiking trails in southern New Hampshire /
compiled and edited by Steven Smith and Gene Daniell.
    p. cm.
  Includes index.
  ISBN 1-929173-60-1 (alk. paper)
  1. Hiking—New Hampshire—Guidebooks. 2. Trails—New Hampshire—Guidebooks.
3. New Hampshire—Guidebooks. I. Smith, Steven D., 1953- II. Daniell, Gene. III.
Appalachian Mountain Club.

 GV199.42.N4S68 2005
 917.4204'43--dc22

                            2005009773

The paper used in this publication meets the minimum requirements of the American
National Standard for Information Sciences—Permanence of Paper for Printed Library
Materials, ANSI Z39.48-1984. ∞

    Printed in the United States of America.
⊕ Printed on recycled paper using soy-based inks.

**Due to changes in conditions, use of the information
in this book is at the sole risk of the user.**

10 9 8 7 6 5 4 3 2 1   05 06 07 08 09

Contents

Locator Map

To Lincoln

To Conway

4.
THE LAKES
REGION

Squam Lake

West
Ossipee

25

2.
CARDIGAN &
KEARSARGE
REGION

Newfound
Lake

Lebanon

4

MT.
CARDIGAN

Meredith

16

M
A
I
N
E

Alexandria

104

93

Laconia

Lake
Winnipesaukee

VERMONT

11

89

MT.
KEARSARGE

4

5.
SOUTHEASTERN
NH

Rochester

Concord

4 202 9

Portsmouth

BEAR BROOK
SP

PAWTUCKAWAY
SP

9

202

293

Manchester

101

95

Keene

101

93

PISGAH SP

124

MT.
MONADNOCK

Jaffrey

3

Nashua

1.
MONADNOCK &
SOUTHWESTERN NH

MASSACHUSETTS

3.
THE MERRIMACK
VALLEY

Acknowledgments

A book like the *Southern New Hampshire Trail Guide* is the product of the efforts of many people, including those who have contributed to the 27 editions of its forerunner, the *White Mountain Guide,* over the period of 98 years since it was first brought into being. The editors constantly have in mind the enthusiastic mountain-walkers who trod the trails before us and created and preserved this magnificent tradition which is now our cherished responsibility. Properly recognizing everyone, past and present, who made some contribution to this book would require a small book of its own, but the editors would like to recognize a few people whose contributions were especially indispensable.

First, we would like to thank our families, and particularly our wives, Carol Smith and Debi Clark. Their contributions to this book, though not outwardly visible, were immense. Without their constant assistance, encouragement, and support, as well as companionship on many hikes—and tolerance for two husbands who are obsessed by the project of maintaining this book and could argue for half an hour the question of whether a particular trail segment is steep or merely rather steep—we would never have been able to give this book the time and energy we feel it deserves. Therefore we dedicate our part of the life of this venerable book to them, with love and gratitude.

Gene would like to dedicate his efforts in producing this book to the memory of his brother-in-law, Thomas Holt (1953–94). "Tom was my first and most beloved hiking companion, from our first hike together in the spring of 1970—the first "real" hike for either of us—when we lost a trail on North Pawtuckaway that was considerably less well marked than our guidebook seemed to indicate, and learned that if you had a map, a compass, and a modicum of common sense, you might be momentarily perplexed but you needn't be lost. (This trail remained hard to follow until 1986, when the late Vera Smith, my first *White Mountain Guide* co-editor, finally took the initiative to blaze it properly.) Tom had the purest, most passionate love of our forests and mountains of anyone I have ever known, and—though I feel his spirit with me whenever I go out into the woods—his premature passing left a void in my life that can never be filled."

Among the others who made unusually important contributions to this book, we wish to recognize the following:

First, we want to thank the staff of AMC Books, including Sarah Jane Shangraw, Belinda Thresher, and Laurie O'Reilly, as well as their associates and interns, including Eric Edstam, Mike Burdon, and Athena Lakri. Not only did they assume all the myriad (and frequently tedious) professional responsibilities of publishing this book so that we could concentrate on preparing the text, they managed to cope with the eccentricities and frailties of the editors without complaint, giving generous support and assistance even when we made their jobs harder.

Also, we want to thank Larry Garland, who turned our fantasy of bright, beautiful new computer-generated maps into a reality. His obsession with making things right is at least equal to our own, and as a result he has managed to digest a staggering amount of detail and overcome many difficulties inherent to such a pioneering effort in order to produce maps that will actually help hikers plan their trips and complete them successfully. Larry deserves more appreciation than we will ever be able to give him.

Then, we want to thank those who made other contributions to this book. For helping review sections of the manuscript or making numerous suggestions for improvements in details of both fact and style, we want to thank Hal and Peggy Graham of the Belknap Range Trail Tenders, Craig Sanborn of the Cardigan Highlanders, Julie Chappell of the AMC Cardigan Lodge, Geoff Jones of the Society for the Protection of New Hampshire Forests, Roioli Schweiker, Roy Schweiker, Richard Curry, Dave Roberts, Tom Curren and Kristen Clothier of the Lakes Region Conservation Trust, Dan Allen and Natalie Davis of the Sunapee–Ragged–Kearsarge Greenway Coalition, Mohamed Ellozy, Ruth Doan MacDougall, Peter Miller, Eric Savage, Scott Christensen, and Sandy and Lucille Stott, as well as the others too numerous to mention who helped in some way to make this a better, more accurate book. We also want to thank numerous personnel of the State of New Hampshire, including Bob Spoerl, the state's trail guru in the New Hampshire Bureau of Trails, and the supervisors and chief rangers of the individual state parks: Jeff Boucher of Pawtuckaway State Park, Andrew Zboray of Monadnock State Park, and Norma Repucci of Pisgah State Park.

Introduction

During the past two decades there has been a spectacular growth in the number and variety of trails available in New Hampshire south of the White Mountains. Recognizing that our *White Mountain Guide* could afford the space for only a small fraction of these trails, we inaugurated a guide to trails in southern and central New Hampshire in the late 1990s (the first edition of this book). Even this guide cannot include every trail that exists in this region, but it provides complete coverage to the trails on Mt. Monadnock, Mt. Cardigan, and Mt. Kearsarge—the three most prominent peaks in the region—as well as extensive coverage of the trail systems of the three largest state parks, Pisgah, Bear Brook, and Pawtuckaway. The guide also includes trails that offer qualities that most appeal to the hiker: views, climbs, summits, and interesting natural features, giving particular weight to the comparative importance of a given trail or feature relative to others in its vicinity. For somewhat less strenuous walks and hikes with an emphasis on nature, see *Nature Walks in Southern New Hampshire* and *Nature Walks in the New Hampshire Lakes Region,* both written by Julia Older and Steve Sherman and published by AMC Books.

Many trails that could not be included in this second edition merit consideration for inclusion in future editions. Some of these trails could not be included because agreements with landowners for their permanent routes have not been completed, while others have been excluded by time and space considerations. The editors of this book will gratefully accept suggestions from our readers concerning trails that should be considered for inclusion in future editions.

Trip Planning and Safety

Hiking is a sport of self-reliance. Its high potential for adventure and relatively low level of regulation have been made possible by the dedication of most hikers to the values of prudence and independence. This tradition of self-reliance imposes an obligation on each of us: at any time we may have to rely on our own ingenuity and judgment, aided by map and compass, to reach our goals or even make a timely exit from the woods. While the penalty for error rarely exceeds an unplanned and uncomfortable night in the woods, more serious consequences are possible. Most hikers find a high degree of satisfaction in obtaining the knowledge and skills that free them from blind dependence on the next blaze or trail sign and enable them to walk in the woods with confidence and assurance. Those who learn the skills of getting about in the woods, the habits of studious acquisition of information before the trip and careful observation while in the woods, soon find that they have earned "the Freedom of the Hills."

Plan your trip schedule with safety in mind. Consider the strength of your party and the general strenuousness of the trip: the overall distance, the amount of climbing, and the roughness of the terrain. Get a weather report, but be aware of the fact that most forecasts are not intended to apply to the mountain region; a day that is sunny and pleasant in the lowlands may well be inclement in the mountains. The National Weather Service in Gray ME issues a forecast for New Hampshire that includes a recreational forecast for the White Mountain region; it is broadcast on its short-wave radio station each morning and also carried on the National Weather Service telephone line (603-225-5191). Mountain weather information is also available on the AMC website (www.outdoors.org). Conditions on even the highest peaks of southern New Hampshire are usually considerably less severe than those in the high peaks of the White Mountains, but the recreational forecast may help to suggest lesser but still serious weather problems that may occur elsewhere in the state.

Plan to finish your hike with daylight to spare (remember that days grow shorter rapidly in late summer and fall). Hiking after dark, even with flashlights (which frequently fail), makes finding trails more difficult and crossing streams hazardous. Let someone else know where you will be hiking, and do not let inexperienced people get separated from the group. Many unpaved roads are not plowed in winter or are not passable during the spring mud season (which varies from place to place), so access to some trails may be much more difficult at these times.

Backcountry Hazards

Safe hiking means knowing how to avoid dangerous situations as well as being prepared to deal with problems when they do occur. The following section outlines the common hazards encountered in the northeast outdoors and discusses how to approach them. In emergencies, call the toll-free New Hampshire State Police number (800-525-5555).

Hypothermia

Hypothermia, the most serious danger to hikers in the New Hampshire woods, is the loss of ability to preserve body heat because of injury, exhaustion, lack of sufficient food, and inadequate or wet clothing. Although the mountain peaks in southern New Hampshire are not as high as those to the north, hikers must remember that weather conditions can change rapidly on exposed peaks. Hikers must be prepared to deal with varying conditions.

Many cases of hypothermia occur in temperatures above freezing; the most dangerous weather conditions involve rain, with wind, with temperatures below 50° F. The symptoms include uncontrolled shivering, impaired speech and movement, lowered body temperature, and drowsiness. In mild cases the victim should be given dry clothing and placed in a sleeping bag (perhaps with someone else in it to provide body heat), then quick-energy food and something warm (not hot) to drink. In severe cases only prompt hospitalization offers reasonable hope for recovery. It is not unusual for a victim to resist treatment and even combat rescuers. It should therefore be obvious that prevention of hypothermia is the only truly practical course. Uncontrollable shivering should be regarded as a sure sign of hypothermia; this shivering will eventually cease on its own, but that is merely the sign that the body has given up the struggle and is sinking toward death.

Much has been written about hypothermia, and some of the advice has been confusing, largely because a victim in an advanced state of hypothermia requires radically different treatment from one in the early stages of the illness.

Basically, chronic hypothermia—the form usually encountered in hiking situations—develops over the course of several hours when a person loses body heat faster than it can be generated. The body uses a number of means to prevent the temperature of vital organs from dropping to a level where proper functioning will be impaired; most important of these is the withdrawal of blood supply from the extremities of the body into the core. This is the reason that poor coordination of hands and legs is an important sign of a developing problem.

As the situation becomes more serious, the body goes into violent shivering, which produces a substantial amount of heat but consumes the body's last remaining energy reserves very rapidly. At this point rapid and decisive application of the treatments mentioned above may still save the victim's life. (Unfortunately, an exhausted hiker, or one who has not been eating or drinking properly, may not possess the energy reserves for violent shivering.)

A person who is shivering violently must be treated for hypothermia immediately and aggressively. Since victims do not always exhibit violent shivering, as a general rule it is safe to render this sort of treatment to anyone who is able to eat or drink voluntarily, perhaps with minor assistance. Once violent shivering has ceased, or when a victim is unable to eat or drink without exceptional assistance, the existence of a state of profound hypothermia must be assumed. The victim should be protected from further heat loss as much as possible and handled with extreme gentleness, and trained rescue personnel should be called for assistance unless the party is capable of providing an advanced litter evacuation themselves.

For those interested in more information, a thorough treatment of the subject is contained in *The Basic Essentials of Hypothermia* (2nd ed., 1999) by William W. Forgey, M.D., published by Globe Pequot Press, PO Box 480, Guilford, CT 06437 (www.globe-pequot.com).

Lightning

Lightning is another serious hazard on any bare ridge or summit. In other mountain ranges throughout the world, where thunderstorms are more common and shelter often much farther away, fairly elaborate advice is often provided for finding the least unsafe place to sit out a storm. In the areas covered in this guide, the best course of action is to avoid the dangerous places when thunderstorms are likely, and to go down the mountain to shelter in thick woods as quickly as possible if an unexpected "thumper" is detected. Most thunderstorms occur when a cold front passes or on very warm days; those produced by cold fronts are typically more sudden and violent. Weather forecasts that mention cold fronts or predict temperatures much above 80° in the low-lands and valleys should arouse concern.

Wildlife

The most risky part of hiking in the New Hampshire woods, in the opinion of many people, has always been the drive to the trailhead, and the recent rapid increase in New Hampshire's moose population has added a significant new hazard. During the first nine months of one recent year, for example, collisions between moose and automobiles caused the deaths of four people and more than 160 moose. The great majority of these collisions occurs in the period from early May to the middle of July, when the moose leave the woods to avoid the black flies and seek out the road salt that has accumulated in ditches near highways. Motorists need to be aware of the seriousness of the problem, particularly at night when these huge, dark-colored animals are both active and very difficult to see. Instinct often causes them to face an auto rather than run from it, and they are also apt to cross the road unpredictably as a car approaches. It is thus safest to assume that moose will behave in the most inconvenient manner possible. Otherwise they probably constitute little threat to hikers on foot, though it would be wise to give bulls a wide berth during the fall mating season.

Bears are common but tend to keep well out of sight. The last known case of a human killed by a bear in New Hampshire was in 1784—a 10-year-old boy in the town of Londonderry—and since that time many thousands of bears have perished from attacks by humans or their automobiles. Nevertheless, the bear is a large and unpredictable animal that must be treated with respect, though not fear. Several recent serious incidents have been unnecessarily provoked by deliberate feeding of bears, or by harassment by a dog leading to an attack on people nearby. Bears live mostly on nuts, berries, and other plants, and on dead animals, and rarely kill anything larger than a mouse. Since the closing of many of the town dumps in New Hampshire, where some bears routinely foraged for food, bears have become a nuisance and even a hazard at some popular campsites; any bear that has lost its natural fear of humans and gotten used to living off us is extremely dangerous.

The philosophy of dealing with bears has undergone some modification in recent years. Formerly the usual advice was that, if approached by a bear, one should throw down one's pack and back away slowly. This advice works, but unfortunately it teaches the bear that people have food and that very little effort and risk is required to make them part with it. The result is a bear that is likely to be more aggressive toward the next visitor, which may result in injury to the human (who may be you) and frequently results in a death sentence for the bear. Most hikers regard bears as an indispensable feature of wild country in New England, and preservation of the bears requires us to make sure that they remain wild, so feeding them either deliberately or through carelessness should be regarded as tantamount to bringing about their execution. Thus the current advice is that a hiker confronted by a bear should attempt to appear neither threatening nor frightened, and should back off slowly but not abandon food unless the bear appears irresistibly aggressive. A loud noise, such as one made by a whistle or by banging metal pots, is often useful. Careful protection of food at campsites is mandatory; it must never be kept overnight in a tent, but should be hung between trees well off the ground. For annual opening and closing dates of hunting season, see the New Hampshire Fish and Game Department website, www.wildlife.state.nh.us or call 603-271-3214.

Deer-hunting season (with rifles) is in November, when you'll probably see many more hunters than deer. Seasons involving muzzle-loader and bow-and-arrow hunters extend from mid-October through mid-December. Most hunters usually stay fairly close to roads, and, in general, the harder it would be to haul a deer out of a given area, the lower the probability that a hiker will encounter hunters there. In any case, avoid wearing brown or anything that might give a hunter the impression of the white flash of a white-tailed deer running away. Wearing hunter's-orange clothing is strongly recommended.

There are probably very few poisonous snakes in the southern half of New Hampshire. Mosquitoes and black flies are the woodland residents most frequently encountered by hikers. Mosquitoes are worst throughout the summer in low, wet areas, and black flies are most bloodthirsty from mid-May through early July; at times these winged pests can make life in the woods virtually unbearable. Fishermen's head-nets can be useful. The most effective repellents are based on the active ingredient diethyl-meta-toluamide, generally known as "DEET," but there are growing doubts about its safety. Hikers should probably apply repellents with DEET to clothing rather than skin where possible, and avoid using them on small children. Other effective repellents are available, and there is also a good deal of folklore and tradition on the subject: people who seek true solitude in the woods often employ the traditional creosote-scented recipes, reasoning that anything that repels fellow humans might have the same effect on insects.

Cars parked at trailheads are frequently targets of break-ins, so valuables or expensive equipment should never be left in cars while you are off hiking, particularly overnight.

Brook Crossings

Rivers and brooks are often crossed without bridges, and it is usually possible to jump from rock to rock; a hiking staff or stick is a great aid to balance. Use caution; several fatalities have resulted from hikers (particularly solo hikers) falling on slippery rocks and suffering an injury that rendered them unconscious, causing them to drown in relatively shallow streams. If you need to wade across a stream (often the safer course), wearing boots, but not necessarily socks, is recommended. Note that many crossings that may be only a nuisance in summer may be a serious obstacle in cold weather when one's feet and boots must be kept dry. Higher waters, which can turn innocuous brooks into virtually uncrossable torrents, come in the spring as snow melts, or after heavy rainstorms, particularly in the fall when trees drop their leaves and take up less water. Avoid trails with potentially dangerous stream crossings during these high-water periods. If you are cut off from roads by swollen streams, it is better to make a long detour, even if you need to wait and spend a night in the woods. Rushing current can make wading extremely hazardous, and several deaths have resulted. Flood waters may subside within a few hours, especially in small brooks. It is particularly important not to camp on the far side of a brook from your exit point if the crossing is difficult and heavy rain is predicted.

Drinking Water

The pleasure of quaffing a cup of water fresh from a pure mountain spring is one of the traditional attractions of the mountains. Unfortunately, the presence of cysts of the intestinal parasite *Giardia lamblia* in water sources is thought to be common, though difficult to prove. It is impossible to be sure whether a given source is safe, and all water sources in the southern half of New Hampshire should probably be regarded as contaminated, no matter how clear the water seems or remote the location. The safest course is for day hikers to carry their own water, and for those who use sources in the woods to filter the water before drinking it. The symptoms of giardiasis are severe intestinal distress and diarrhea, but such discomforts can have many other causes, making the disease difficult to diagnose accurately. The principal cause of the spread of this noxious ailment in the woods is probably careless disposal of human waste. Keep it at least 200 ft. away from water sources. If there are no toilets nearby, dig a hole 6 to 8 in. deep (but not below the organic layer of the soil) for a latrine and cover it completely after use. The bacteria in the organic layer of the soil will then decompose the waste naturally. Many people unknowingly carry the *Giardia* parasites, which have sometimes been present in municipal water supplies and frequently do not produce symptoms. Some authorities feel that the disease is more likely to be spread by party members to each other than by contaminated water. For this reason it would be advisable to be scrupulous about washing hands after answering calls of nature.

Camping

With a very few exceptions (as noted in individual descriptions), trailside camping (backpacking) is not permitted along the trails described in this book. In state parks, camping is allowed only in vehicle-accessible campgrounds. On private lands (including those owned by organizations such as the Audubon Society and the SPNHF) camping is permitted only with the permission of the landowner, which is very rarely given. Hikers also should never kindle wood campfires, even in places where others have obviously done so. Illegal camping and campfires are among the most common practices that may cause landowners to close trails.

What to Carry

Adequate equipment for a hike in the New Hampshire hills and forests varies greatly according to the length of the trip and the difficulty of getting to the nearest trailhead if trouble arises. If you are only strolling in to a pond or waterfall a mile or so from the road in good weather, then perhaps a light jacket, a candy bar, and a bottle of water will suffice. If, however, you are going above treeline and are not inclined to turn back at the first sign of questionable weather, you will need a good pack filled with plenty of warm clothing and food for emergency use, and other equipment. No determination of what one needs to take along can be made without considering the length of a trip and the hazards of the terrain it will cross.

   Good things to have in your pack for an ordinary summer day hike include guidebook, maps, water bottle (ordinary plastic soft-drink bottles, with or without original contents, work well), compass, knife (good-quality stainless steel, since ordinary steel rusts very quickly), rain gear, windbreaker, wool sweater(s), wool hat and mittens, waterproof matches, enough food for your usual needs plus extra high-energy foods in reserve (such as dried fruit or candy), first-aid supplies (including personal medicines, a non-prescription painkiller such as aspirin, acetaminophen, or ibuprofen, and adhesive bandages, gauze, and antiseptic), needle and thread, safety pins, nylon cord, trash bag, toilet paper, and a (small) flashlight or headlamp with extra batteries and a spare bulb.

Wear comfortable hiking boots. Lightweight boots, somewhat more sturdy than sneakers, are popular these days. Experienced hikers can often wear sneakers quite safely and comfortably on easy to moderate hikes. Unfortunately, most of the people who actually do wear sneakers on the trails are inexperienced and not accustomed to walking on rough trails, and have legs and ankles that are not trail-toughened. As a result, many leg injuries occur on short, relatively easy trails because of the large numbers of inexperienced hikers who wear sneakers when they need the support of boots.

Blue jeans, sweatshirts, and other cotton clothes are popular but, once wet, dry very slowly and may be uncomfortable; in adverse weather conditions they often seriously drain a cold and tired hiker's heat reserves. While such clothes are worn on summer trips by many hikers, people who are planning to travel to remote places or above treeline should seriously consider wearing (or at least carrying) wool or synthetics instead. Wool keeps much of its insulating value even when wet, and it (or one of several modern synthetic materials) is indispensable for hikers who want to visit places from which return to civilization might require substantial time and effort if conditions turn bad. Not only do hats, mittens, and other such gear provide safety in adverse conditions, but they also allow one to enjoy the summits in comfort on those occasional crisp, clear days when the views are particularly fine and the other hikers who snickered at one's bulging pack are driven from the magnificent vistas with terse greetings forced through chattering teeth.

Following Trails

In general, trails are maintained to provide a clear pathway while protecting the environment by minimizing erosion and other damage. Some may offer rough and difficult passage. Most hiking trails are marked with paint on trees or rocks, though a few still only have axe blazes cut into trees. In general, the color of blazing has no significance and may change without notice; therefore blazing color is sometimes not a reliable means of distinguishing particular trails from intersecting ones. Above timberline, cairns (piles of rocks) mark the trails. Where hikers have trodden out the vegetation, the footway is usually visible except when it is covered by snow or fallen leaves. In winter, signs at trailheads and intersections and blazes also are often covered by snow. Trails following or crossing logging roads require special care at intersections in order to distinguish the trail from diverging roads, particularly since blazing is usually very sparse while the trail follows the road. Around shelters or campsites, beaten paths may lead in all directions, so look for signs and paint blazes.

Hikers should be aware that some trails in this book (as noted in descriptions) are far less easy to follow than others; the presence of signs and blazes varies, and some trails are too new to have a well-beaten footway while others have received very little use. Inexperienced hikers should avoid trails that are described as being difficult to follow, and all trail users should observe and follow trail markings carefully. It cannot be emphasized too strongly that there is almost no trail that might not be closed unexpectedly or suddenly become obscure or hazardous under certain conditions. Trails can be rerouted or abandoned or closed by landowners. Signs are stolen or fall from their posts. Storms may cause blowdowns or landslides, which can obliterate a trail for an entire climbing season or longer. Trails may not be cleared of fallen trees and brush until late summer, and not all trails are cleared every year. Logging operations can cover trails with slash and add a bewildering network of new roads. In addition, even momentary inattention to trail markers, particularly arrows at sharp turns or signs at junctions, or misinterpretation of signs or guidebook descriptions can cause hikers to become separated from all but the most heavily traveled paths—or at least lead them into what may be a much longer or more difficult route. So please remember that this book is an aid to planning, not a substitute for observation and judgment.

As a consequence, all the trail-maintaining organizations, including the AMC, reserve the right to discontinue any trail without notice and expressly disclaim any legal responsibility for the condition of any trail. Most organizations give priority to heavily used trails, so lightly used trails quite often do not receive their share of attention and following them may require great care.

Distances, Times, and Elevation Gains

The distances, times, and elevation gains that appear in the tables at the end of trail descriptions are cumulative from the starting point at the head of each table. Elevation gains are given for the reverse direction only when they are significant, and are not cumulative—they apply only to the interval between the current entry and the next one (which will be the entry before the current one in the list). Elevation gains are not given for trails that are essentially level. Most of the trails in this book have been measured with a surveyor's wheel within the past few years. Minor inconsistencies sometimes occur when measured distances are rounded, and the distances given often differ from those on trail signs. Elevation gains are estimated and rounded to the nearest 50 ft.; some elevation gains can be determined almost to the foot, while others (such as where several minor ups and downs are traversed) are only roughly accurate. Elevations of places are estimated as closely as possible when not given precisely by our source maps. The USGS maps are used as the basis for all such information.

There is no reliable method for predicting how much time a particular hiker or group of hikers will actually take to complete a particular hike on a particular day. The factors that influence the speed of an individual hiker or hiking group are simply too numerous and too complex. Most hikers will observe that their own individual speed varies from day to day, often by a significant amount, depending on a number of factors, many of which—such as fatigue, weight of pack, and weather conditions—are fairly easy to identify. Hikers often forget to consider that a given segment of trail will usually require more time—perhaps much more—when encountered at the end of a strenuous day compared to what it might have required if encountered at the start of the day.

However, in order to give inexperienced hikers a rough basis for planning, estimated times have been calculated for this book by allowing a half-hour for each mile of distance or 1000 ft. of climbing. No attempt has been made to adjust these times for the difficulties of specific trails, since fine-tuning an inherently limited method would probably only lead to greater unjustified reliance on it. In many cases, as hikers gain experience, they find that they usually require a fairly predictable percentage of book time to hike most trails, but eventually they are almost certain to encounter a significant exception. Therefore, all hikers using this book should be well aware of the limitations of the time-estimating formula, and should always regard book times with a critical eye and check each trail description thoroughly for trail conditions that might render the given times misleading; these times may be very inadequate for steep or rough trails, for hikers with heavy packs, or for large groups, particularly those including inexperienced hikers. Average descent times vary even more greatly, with agility and the condition of the hiker's knees being the principal factors; times for descending are given in this book only for segments of ridgecrest trails that have substantial descents in both directions. In winter, times are even less predictable: on a packed trail travel may be faster than in summer, but with heavy packs or in deep snow it may take two or three times the summer estimate.

Using Maps

Hikers should always carry a map and compass and carefully keep track of their approximate location on the map. The Cardigan and Monadnock maps included with this guide are topographic maps (maps with the shape of the terrain represented by contour lines). Maps to all parts of New Hampshire, including the areas not covered by our Cardigan and Monadnock maps, are available from the United States Geological Survey (USGS). They are published in rectangles of several standard sizes called quadrangles ("quads"). All areas in the regions described in this guide are now covered by the recent, more detailed 7.5-minute quads—some in metric format—which have largely replaced the old 15-minute quads. Although topography on the newer maps is excellent, some recent maps are very inaccurate in showing the locations of trails. USGS maps can be obtained at a number of local outlets and from USGS Map Sales, Federal Center, Box 25286, Denver, CO 80225 (800-USA-MAPS). Index maps showing the available USGS quads in any state (specify states) and an informative pamphlet entitled "Topographic Maps" is available free on request from the USGS. USGS maps are now also available on compact disk from a number of sources; it is possible to obtain 7.5-minute quads for the entire state of New Hampshire on one compact disk, allowing one to print a map for any desired location.

This guide features two maps that were designed on a computer, using a variety of digital data. The most valuable source of data comes from global positioning system (GPS) technology. Every mile of trail on these maps was hiked and electronically recorded with GPS technology. The resulting maps accurately depict trail locations. Many previous maps, including USGS quadrangle maps, relied on less precise techniques to determine a trail's location. Universal Transverse Mercator (UTM) grid coordinates are included on the map sheets to facilitate the use of GPS receivers in the field. Additionally, a mileage scale runs around the outer frame of each map to help users estimate distance.

Although the original GPS data is very exact, certain features (including roads, streams, and trails) may have been approximated and/or exaggerated in order to show their proper relationships at map scale. We would appreciate your assistance by reporting corrections to: Southern New Hampshire Trail Guide, c/o AMC Books, 5 Joy St., Boston, MA 02108.

Extra copies of AMC maps may be purchased at the AMC's Boston, Pinkham Notch, and Highland Center retail locations, online at www.outdoors.org, or by calling 800-262-4455; as well as at bookstores and outdoor-equipment stores. Other maps of specific areas are mentioned in the relevant individual sections of this guide. Many of these are also available from the AMC.

The best compass for hiking is the protractor type: a circular, liquid-filled compass that turns on a rectangular base made of clear plastic. Excellent compasses of this type, with leaflets that give ample instructions for their use, are available for less than $10. Such a compass is easily set to the bearing you wish to follow, and then it is a simple matter of keeping the compass needle aligned to north and following the arrow on the base. More sophisticated and expensive compasses have features designed for special applications that are often not useful in the woods; they are normally harder to use and apt to cause confusion in an emergency situation. Directions of the compass given in the text are based on true north instead of magnetic north, unless otherwise specified. There is a deviation of approximately 16° between true north and magnetic north in the southern half of New Hampshire. This means that true north will be about 16° to the right of (clockwise from) the compass's north needle. If you take a bearing from a map, you should add 16° to the bearing when you set your compass. On the maps included with this guide, the black lines that run from bottom to top are aligned with true north and south.

If You're Lost

If you lose a trail and it is not visible to either side, it is usually best to back-track right away to the last mark seen and look again from there; this will be made much easier if you carefully note each trail marking and keep track of where and how long ago you saw the most recent one. Even when the trail cannot be immediately found, it is a serious but not desperate situation. Few people become truly lost in the New Hampshire woods; a moment's reflection and five minutes with the map will show that you probably know at least your approximate location and the direction to the nearest road, if nothing else. Most cases in which a person has become lost for any length of time involve panic and aimless wandering, so the most important first step is to stop and take a break, make an inventory of useful information, decide on a course of action, and stick to it. (The caution against allowing inexperienced persons to become separated from a group should be emphasized here, since they are most likely to panic and wander aimlessly. Make sure also that all party members are familiar with the route of the trip and the names of the trails to be used, so that if they do become separated they will have some prospect of rejoining the group.) If you have carefully kept track of your location on the map, it will usually be possible to find a nearby trail or road to which a compass course may be followed. Most distances are short enough that it is possible, in the absence of alternatives, to reach a highway in half a day, or at most in a whole day, simply by going downhill, carefully avoiding any dangerous cliffs (which will normally be found in areas where the map's contour lines are unusually close together), following a rough compass course—particularly in relatively flat areas—to avoid going in circles.

Winter Considerations

This book describes trails in the snowless season, which can vary considerably from year to year; higher elevations have much shorter snowless seasons. Trails in general are much harder to follow when there is snow on the ground, and deep snow requires ski or snowshoes and the skill to use them efficiently (although popular trails may be broken out through most of the winter). When ice is present, there is particular danger on mountains with steep open ledges, such as Monadnock, Cardigan, and Mt. Major. Accidents, some of them serious, are common on such lesser mountains when winter conditions prevail because of the ease of access for people who are unequipped and unprepared for the hazards they encounter. Do not underestimate the difficulty of these small mountains in adverse cold-weather conditions. Monadnock and Cardigan, especially, are high enough to have severe weather conditions. In spring, deep snowdrifts may remain on northern slopes even at lower elevations after all snow is gone on southern exposures. At this time of year, in order to avoid encountering deep drifts, hikers should be particularly wary of northern slopes as well as higher elevations.

No attempt is made to cover any kind of skiing (alpine, downhill, or cross-country), although several cross-country (ski-touring) trails are mentioned where they are open to hiking use in summer or happen to intersect hiking trails. Rock climbs are not described in this book, since they require special techniques and equipment and should be undertaken only by roped parties under qualified leaders, due to the high degree of danger to inexperienced or insufficiently equipped climbers or groups.

Landowner Regulations

Most of the trails in this book are located in public parks and forests or in the reservations of conservation organizations such as the New Hampshire Audubon Society and the Society for the Protection of New Hampshire Forests (SPNHF). Others—most prominently the Monadnock–Sunapee Greenway, the Sunapee–Ragged–Kearsarge Greenway, the Wapack Trail, and the Metacomet–Monadnock Trail—lie mostly on private land, but with the protection of formal agreements with landowners. On such trails hikers should exercise care to observe regulations that have been designed to protect the land itself and the rights of landowners. There are in addition a number of trails that cross private land with no formal permission from the landowner; the existence of such trails is supported only by a long tradition of public use. Some of these trails are among the most popular in southern New Hampshire—the trail to Mt. Major from NH 11 is an example—and despite many decades of public use and enjoyment these trails are subject to closure at the will of the landowner, so hikers should be particularly careful to respect the lands these trails pass over so as not to give the owners cause to consider closing them.

Many trails in the three largest state parks—Pisgah, Bear Brook, and Pawtuckaway—are multi-use trails, open to mountain bikes in summer and snowmobiles in winter. In most cases they have been much more heavily used for these purposes than for hiking in the past. Hikers, skiers, and snowshoers should be aware that they will be sharing the trails and should be prepared to extend trail courtesies to these other users.

Stewardship and Conservation

The trails that we use and enjoy are only in part the product of government agencies and public nonprofit organizations; there is ultimately no "they" responsible for providing the hiking public with a full variety of interesting, convenient, well-maintained trails. Many trails are cared for by one dedicated person or a small group. Funds for trail work are scarce, and unless hikers contribute both time and money to the maintenance of trails, the diversity of trails available to the public is almost certain to experience a sad decline. Every hiker can make some contribution to the improvement of the trails, if nothing more than pushing a blowdown off the trail rather than walking around it. They are our trails, and without our participation in their care they will languish. Write to AMC Trails, Pinkham Notch Camp, PO Box 298, Gorham, NH 03581, for more information regarding volunteer trail-maintenance activities, or see the AMC website, www.outdoors.org. Another group that is very active in trail maintenance in the southern half of New Hampshire is Trailwrights, PO Box 1223, Concord, NH 03302; email: trailwrights@pobox.com.

The AMC encourages hikers to heed basic backcountry ethics. Every hiker has an obligation to respect and care for the outdoor environment, so that it may be enjoyed by all who follow. As you hike, try to adhere to these rules of the outdoors:

- Carry out everything you carry in. Go a step further: Carry out any litter that you find.
- Don't pick the flowers, and avoid gathering wood. Even dead trees have their place in the ecosystem and should be left undisturbed. Do not light a campfire unless it is an emergency. If you are using a backpacking stove, do not leave it unattended.
- Stay on the trail, and try to avoid muddy places where foot traffic can cause erosion.
- Bury human waste at least 200 ft. from the trail and any water sources. The careless disposal of human waste is probably the principal cause of the spread of giardiasis.

- If you wish to listen to music, wear headphones. But it's much more interesting to listen to the sounds of the forest. Preserve the forest sounds for others to enjoy.
- Where dogs are permitted it is often with the stipulation they be leashed at all times. Respect and follow the rules regarding pets when hiking and be sure to control your pet so it won't be a nuisance to other hikers.
- On overnight trips, travel in small groups and practice low-impact camping. Use established campsites if available; if not, camp well away from trails and streams and avoid using sites that have been used previously by campers.

For more information, see the Leave No Trace appendix at the back of this book.

Section 1

Monadnock and Southwestern New Hampshire

**1.
MONADNOCK &
SOUTHWESTERN NH**

See AMC Southern New Hampshire Map 1: Mount Monadnock.

SUGGESTED HIKES

Easy Hikes

Pitcher Mtn. [lp: 0.8 mi., 300 ft., 0:35]. This small mountain along the Monadnock–Sunapee Greenway has excellent views from its open summit and fire tower.

Sharon Ledges [rt: 2.0 mi., 600 ft., 1:20]. From Temple Rd., follow the Wapack Trail north over a series of open ledges with good views; turn back where the trail re-enters the woods.

Gap Mtn. The north summit of this low peak along the Metacomet–Monadnock Trail has fine views of Mt. Monadnock and the Wapack Range. It is easily climbed from either the south trailhead **[rt: 2.6 mi., 650 ft., 1:40]** or the north trailhead **[rt: 2.8 mi., 750 ft., 1:45]**.

Bacon Ledge [rt: 2.2 mi., 600 ft., 1:25]. The Trout-n-Bacon Trail provides easy access to this open ledge in the SPNHF Peirce Reservation.

Bald Mtn. [lp: 2.3 mi., 900 ft., 1:35]. The Tamposi Trail passes two fine viewpoints on this peak in the dePierrefeu–Willard Pond Sanctuary.

South Pack Monadnock [lp: 2.8 mi., 850 ft., 1:50]. The Wapack Trail and Marion Davis Trail provide a loop hike over this open summit.

Moderate Hikes

Mt. Monadnock. A nearly limitless variety of routes can be used to ascend this impressively bare and overwhelmingly popular peak. The most-used route from the state park headquarters on the southeast side of the mountain is the White Dot Trail **[rt: 4.0 mi., 1800 ft., 2:55]**; this can be combined with the White Cross Trail for a loop **[lp: 4.2 mi., 1800 ft., 3:00]**. The Marlboro and Dublin Trails provide a fine route from the west **[rt: 4.4 mi., 1850 ft., 3:10]**.

Bald Rock [lp: 3.9 mi., 1250 ft., 2:40]. An interesting loop along less-used trails can be made over this open spur of Monadnock from the parking area on the south side; use the Old Toll Road, Parker Trail, Cliff Walk, Hedgehog Trail, Side Foot Trail, Do Drop Trail, and Old Halfway House Trail.

North Pack Monadnock [lp: 5.9 mi., 1350 ft., 3:40]. The recently opened Ted's Trail and Carolyn's Trail make a loop over this fine peak, with a variety of viewpoints.

Crotched Mtn. [rt: 3.6 mi., 850 ft., 2:10]. Shannon's Trail provides a scenic route from the Greenfield trailhead to the fine outlook near the summit. A longer and more challenging loop with several viewpoints can be fashioned from the Francestown trailhead using the Summit Trail and a side trip on Cindy's Trail **[lp: 6.8 mi., 1450 ft., 4:10]**.

Lovewell Mtn. [rt: 4.6 mi., 950 ft., 2:45]. The southern approach to this interesting peak on the Monadnock–Sunapee Greenway leads to several viewpoints.

Skatutakee and Thumb Mtns. [lp: 4.9 mi., 900 ft., 2:55]. The Harriskat, Thumbs Up, and Thumbs Down Trails provide a loop over these two peaks with good views of Mt. Monadnock.

Lake Solitude and White Ledge [rt: 5.6 mi., 1600 ft., 3:35]. The Newbury and Lake Solitude Trails lead to a picturesque pond and fine viewpoint on the south ridge of Sunapee Mtn. The trip can be extended to the ski area complex at the summit **[rt: 7.2 mi., 2150 ft., 4:40]**.

Kilburn Pond Loop [lp: 6.3 mi., 300 ft., 3:20]. A mostly gentle loop around scenic Kilburn Pond in Pisgah State Park.

Pisgah Viewpoints Loop [lp: 6.6 mi., 950 ft., 3:45]. This loop leads through fine hemlock forests and passes three good viewpoints. From the western trailhead for Pisgah State Park on NH 63, take the Davis Hill Trail, the Hubbard Hill Trail to Hubbard Hill's viewpoint and back, the Baker Pond Trail, and the Pisgah Ridge Trail to Parker's Perch, then return to the trailhead via a connecting trail and the Kilburn Loop.

Strenuous Hikes

Lucia's Lookout [lp: 8.8 mi., 1450 ft., 5:10]. For an extended backcountry hike from Pillsbury State Park, follow the Five Summers Trail, Monadnock–Sunapee Greenway (with a side trip to the excellent lookout), and Bear Pond Trail.

Mt. Monadnock via Pumpelly Trail [rt: 8.8 mi., 1950 ft., 5:25]. The longest, most scenic, and least used major route up Monadnock.

LIST OF TRAILS

LIST OF TRAILS

This section covers the southern part of the western New Hampshire hill country. Mt. Monadnock is by far the best-known and most popular peak in the area. The Metacomet–Monadnock Trail runs from Meriden, Connecticut, across Massachusetts to Mt. Monadnock, passing over Little Monadnock Mtn. and Gap Mtn. in its New Hampshire section. The Monadnock–Sunapee Greenway runs from Mt. Monadnock to Sunapee Mtn., passing over Pitcher Mtn. and Lovewell Mtn. The Wapack Trail follows the ridgecrest of the Wapack Range, including the Pack Monadnocks, Temple Mtn., and Barrett Mtn. Pisgah State Park in Chesterfield, Hinsdale, and Winchester, a relatively undeveloped park containing 13,000 acres, has a trail network of more than 60 miles.

Other mountains and areas covered in this section include Wantastiquet Mtn., Mine Ledge, Daniels Mtn., and the adjacent Madame Sherri Forest in Hinsdale and Chesterfield; Crotched Mtn. in Francestown; Skatutakee Mtn., Thumb Mtn., and other trails of the Harris Center in Hancock; and Sunapee Mtn. in Newbury. Other areas containing significant trails include Fox Research Forest in Hillsborough, the Pierce Reservation in Stoddard, the dePierrefeu–Willard Pond Wildlife Sanctuary in Antrim, Pillsbury State Park in Washington, and the Saint-Gaudens National Historical Site in Cornish.

Mount Monadnock

Mt. Monadnock (3159 ft.), also called Grand Monadnock, rises in the towns of Jaffrey and Dublin, about 10 mi. north of the New Hampshire–Massachusetts border. It is an isolated mountain that towers 1500 to 2000 ft. above the surrounding country, visible from most of the prominent viewpoints in central New England. Its summit commands exceptionally extensive and distant views; Mt. Washington is sometimes visible when it has snow cover. Two prominent southern crags are worthy of note: Monte Rosa (2510 ft.) on the southwest ridge, and Bald Rock (2628 ft.), signed as Kiasticuticus (literally "Skinhead") Peak, on the south ridge. Combining extremely rugged mountain scenery, a relatively short and easy ascent (compared to major peaks in the White Mtns.), and convenient access from the population centers of southern New England, Monadnock is reputedly (after Mt. Fuji in Japan) the second most frequently climbed mountain in the world; on one Columbus Day in the late 1970s, it was ascended by throngs estimated at nearly 10,000 people. The vast expanses of open ledge on the upper slopes, which provide the continuous vistas that make this mountain so attractive to visitors, can also be very slippery in wet or icy conditions, and hazardous in thunderstorms; trails must be followed carefully when visibility is poor, as hikers might encounter dangerous cliffs in the attempt to descend without trail. It would be wise to regard any water source on this mountain with extreme suspicion.

There are several major trails to the summit and a network of connecting and secondary trails on the east, south, and west sides of the main peak. This network deteriorated badly after a fire in 1954 destroyed the old hotel called the Halfway House, where many amateur trail builders had their base of operations, but most of these trails have been restored by the dedicated efforts of state park personnel. It is possible to ascend Monadnock in relative solitude on these attractive trails, particularly if you avoid weekends. The White Arrow Trail—the most direct route to the summit on this side—and many other trails begin near the Halfway House site, a starting point for many attractive circuit trips that is located on the west flank of Monadnock's south ridge at about 2100 ft. Direct routes to this site are provided by a foot trail—the Old Halfway House Trail—and by a former toll road, now closed to public vehicular use but open for hikers. The trail and road both leave a parking area on NH 124 near the height-of-land, 5.0 mi. west of Jaffrey and about 4 mi. east of Troy; the road climbs 1.2 mi. and 600 ft. in elevation to the old hotel site.

The upper 500 ft. of the mountain is open ledge, bared by a series of forest fires. Farmers frequently set fires to clear the lower slopes for pasture, and around 1800 a major fire of unknown origin burned for about two weeks, greatly damaging the forests on the upper part of the mountain. Subsequent fires and windstorms completed the devastation, creating an impenetrable maze of blown-down trees that was a natural lair for wolves that preyed on the sheep in the pastures. (During the first half of the nineteenth century, sheep were probably the most important agricultural product in the western New Hampshire hill country.) Sometime between 1810 and 1820, a fire set by farmers attempting to oust the wolves got out of control and burned with an intensity that consumed even the soil, reducing the upper part of the mountain to bare, sterile rock. Since then small plants, shrubs, and trees have lodged themselves in various cracks and crannies, creating small pockets of soil and beginning the process that, if left undisturbed, will restore the mountain forest in a few millennia.

Visitors from outside the immediate vicinity of the mountain began to arrive at about the same time as the last of the great fires, and by 1850 Monadnock was established as a major attraction for New Englanders. Due to the proximity of the mountain to Concord MA, where the Transcendentalist literary movement with its deep interest in nature developed around the figures of

Ralph Waldo Emerson and Henry David Thoreau, Mt. Monadnock attained the
status of something like a sacred mountain and was immortalized in the works
of these notable writers and others. Monadnock's slopes probably bear more
historic trails, former trails, ruins, and named minor features than any other
mountain in New England, including Mt. Washington. The *Monadnock Guide*,
published by the SPNHF (currently out of print), provides details of much of
this history as well as extensive information about the natural history of the
mountain.

The public reservation on the mountain now comprises about 5000 contigu-
ous acres cooperatively administered by the state, the town of Jaffrey, the Association to Protect Mt. Monadnock, and the SPNHF. At Monadnock State Park,
just off Poole Memorial Rd., the state maintains picnic grounds, a parking lot,
and a public campground (fees charged for each). Camping is not permitted
anywhere on the mountain, except at the state park campground. Dogs (or other
pets) are not allowed anywhere in the state park. The Monadnock trail system is
shown on the AMC Monadnock Map included with this book, and Monadnock
is covered by the USGS Monadnock Mtn. and Marlborough quadrangles.

Old Halfway House Trail (map 1: C1–D2)

This recently reopened trail parallels the western side of the Old Toll Road and
provides a more attractive, less heavily used approach to the Halfway House
Site from the Old Toll Road parking area on NH 124. Although not blazed, it is
easy to follow.

The trail bears left off the Old Toll Road just above the parking area, trail
kiosk, and gate, and parallels the road next to an old stone wall. It soon ascends
a short distance away from the road, follows a long level section, and at 1.1 mi.
crosses the Cart Path just below a house to the right. It passes through an overgrown field, swings right, and ascends a short distance to the Old Toll Road
less than 0.1 mi. below the Halfway House Site clearing.

Distance from the Old Toll Road parking area (1490')

    to Halfway House Site (2090'): 1.3 mi. (2.1 km.), 600 ft., 55 min.

White Arrow Trail (map 1: B3–C2)

One of the oldest and most heavily used routes to the summit, this trail continues along the north end of the toll road from the site of the Halfway House,

where numerous far less heavily used side trails also originate. It is marked by
painted white arrows. It follows the road, which soon ends at the old picnic
area on the left, where the Royce Trail (Metacomet–Monadnock Trail), Monte
Rosa Trail, and Fairy Spring Trail begin. From this point to the summit the
White Arrow Trail is part of the Metacomet–Monadnock Trail. It immediately
begins to climb rather steeply through the woods on a broad, rocky path past
Quarter-Way Spring. At 0.6 mi. the Amphitheater Trail enters from the right
and continues across the White Arrow Trail toward the Smith Summit Trail.
The upper end of the Side Foot Trail is about 100 yd. to the right (east) on the
Amphitheater Trail. The White Arrow Trail soon reaches the treeline, where it
bears left and starts to ascend the ledges in the open. Just below the summit a
side path on the right makes an interesting scramble up a narrow gully. The
main trail soon gains the summit plateau, where it meets the Dublin Trail, and
turns right in company with this trail to reach the summit in another 75 yd.

Distance from Halfway House site (2090')

> *to* Mt. Monadnock summit (3159'): 1.1 mi. (1.7 km.), 1050 ft., 1 hr. 5
> min.

Distance from Old Toll Road parking area (1490')

> *to* Mt. Monadnock summit (3159') via Old Halfway House Trail or Old
> Toll Road and White Arrow Trail: 2.3 mi. (3.7 km.), 1700 ft., 2 hr.

Dublin Trail (map 1: A2–B3)

This trail ascends Monadnock from the north; it is a link in the
Monadnock–Sunapee Greenway. From the flagpole in Dublin village, go west
on NH 101 (Main St.). At 0.4 mi. bear left on East Lake Rd., which becomes
Old Marlboro Rd. At 2.5 mi. go left downhill on Old Troy Rd., pass through a
crossroads, and continue to a small clearing on the right at 4.0 mi., where there
is parking space. (Beyond the houses at 3.4 mi. the road becomes narrow and
poor; it may be impassable when muddy.) The trail, marked with white Ds,
starts opposite the clearing and climbs to the tip of the ridge, passing an unreliable spring at 1.0 mi. It follows the ledgy ridge with occasional good views,
passes another unreliable spring at the foot of a rock at 1.8 mi., and emerges
above timberline. The Marlboro Trail enters on the right at 2.0 mi., just beyond
a prominent cap of rock, a false summit. The Dublin Trail continues upward to
meet the White Arrow Trail 75 yd. below the true summit.

Distance from Old Troy Rd. (1460')

   to Mt. Monadnock summit (3159'): 2.2 mi. (3.5 km.), 1700 ft., 1 hr.
    55 min.

Pumpelly Trail (map 1: A3 B3)

This is the longest, most strenuous, and most scenic direct route to the summit
of Monadnock. Follow NH 101 (Main St.) west from the flagpole in Dublin
village for 0.4 mi., then turn left on Lake Rd. (sign). The trail (no sign) leaves
the road left in another 0.4 mi., opposite a log cabin on the pond and 75 yd. east
of where the road reaches the shore.

    The trail follows a woods road for 120 yd., turns right into a narrow path
through a stone wall (small cairn and sign), then turns left onto a woods road
again at 0.2 mi. It crosses Oak Hill at 0.7 mi. and continues with gradual ups
and downs, becoming a footpath. At 1.8 mi. it turns sharp left and begins the
rather steep and rough ascent of the north end of the Pumpelly Ridge. The trail
zigzags up and emerges on the first semi-open ledges on the shoulder of the
mountain at 2.2 mi., almost exactly halfway to the summit. From here the trail
is rough and rocky, running near the ridgecrest with many minor ups and
downs, but offers many excellent views from bare ledges. At 3.0 mi. the Cascade Link enters on the left, ascending from the Monadnock State Park trail
network on the eastern slopes, and at 3.7 mi. the Spellman Trail also enters on
the left just below the Sarcophagus, a huge rectangular boulder in plain view.
From here onward the trail, marked by large cairns, runs mostly on open ledge
where many glacial striations are plainly visible. It soon passes a small alpine
meadow, and at 4.0 mi. the Red Spot Trail enters left. (This trail connects the
Pumpelly Trail with the Cascade Link on the lower east slope of the mountain,
and with the Smith Connecting Link on the upper east slope. The Smith Connecting Link runs across the White Dot and White Cross trails to Bald Rock,
linking the Pumpelly Trail with the complex of trails that radiate from the
Halfway House site.) The Pumpelly Trail soon passes through a little gap with
steep, ledgy walls, then comes completely into the open in another 80 yd. and
continues over the ledges to the summit.

    Descending, the trail runs nearly due east; look for a summit rock with
"Pumpelly Trail" and a large white arrow painted on it. There are few cairns for
the first 200 yd., and care must be taken to locate the first one. In several cases
the cairns are rather small.

Distances from Lake Rd. (1530')

   to   Cascade Link (2700'): 3.0 mi., 1300 ft. (rev. 100 ft.), 2 hr. 10 min.
   to   Mt. Monadnock summit (3159'): 4.4 mi. (7.1 km.), 1800 ft. (rev. 50 ft.),
         3 hr. 5 min.

White Dot Trail *(map 1: B3–C3)*

This trail starts at the parking area near the Monadnock State Park headquarters at the west end of Poole Memorial Rd. in Monadnock State Park. It begins
on a broad woods road, descends slightly, and crosses a small brook. At 0.5 mi.
the Spruce Link leaves left; this is a cutoff path 0.3 mi. long that joins the
White Cross Trail above Falcon Spring. The White Dot Trail then climbs gradually through woods to a jct. with the Cascade Link and White Cross Trail at
Falcon Spring at 0.7 mi. The White Cross and White Dot trails run roughly parallel from here and rejoin high up on the mountain; the White Dot Trail is
steeper, but only 0.2 mi. shorter than the White Cross, while views from the
White Cross are more interesting.

The White Dot Trail goes straight at the jct. just above Falcon Spring,
ascends the steep ridge, and emerges at 1.1 mi. on the semi-open plateau near
treeline. It passes the Old Ski Path, which runs right (north) 0.2 mi. to the Red
Spot Trail, then climbs on ledges through meager evergreens. At 1.6 mi. the
White Dot Trail crosses the Smith Connecting Link, which circles the east
side of the summit cone from Bald Rock to the Red Spot Trail, connecting the
Halfway House site to the Pumpelly Trail. The White Cross Trail rejoins on
the left at 1.7 mi., and the White Dot Trail continues up slanting ledges to the
summit.

Distance from Poole Memorial Rd. (1380')

   to   Mt. Monadnock summit (3159'): 2.0 mi. (3.2 km.), 1800 ft., 1 hr.
         55 min.

White Cross Trail *(map 1: B3–C3)*

This trail provides a less steep and more scenic alternative to the middle section of the White Dot Trail. Trail distances given in the text below are from the
state park parking area via the White Dot Trail. The White Cross Trail diverges
left from the White Dot Trail at the jct. just above Falcon Spring and angles
gradually uphill. At 0.9 mi. the Spruce Link enters on the left, and the White

Cross Trail turns sharp right and starts to climb at moderate grades over boulders left by an old slide. It passes through an old burn (good views back to the east and south across a ravine called Dingle Dell) and finally reaches the flat southeast shoulder. It soon emerges from sparse evergreens on the ledges. The Smith Connecting Link crosses at 1.8 mi., and the White Cross Trail rejoins the White Dot Trail at 1.9 mi., following the latter trail to the summit.

Distance from lower junction with White Dot Trail (1850')

> *to* upper junction with White Dot Trail (2850'): 1.2 mi. (2.0 km.), 1000 ft., 1 hr. 5 min.

Distance from Poole Memorial Rd. (1380')

> *to* Mt. Monadnock summit (3159') via White Dot Trail, White Cross Trail, and White Dot Trail: 2.2 mi. (3.5 km.), 1800 ft., 2 hr.

Harling Trail (map 1: C3–C4)

The Harling Trail is reached from Poole Memorial Rd. 0.2 mi. east of the entrance to Monadnock State Park; follow the Hinkley Trail, a connecting trail 0.6 mi. long, to its end. Here the Harling Trail begins, running west on an old woods road, and reaches the Cascade Link a short distance north of the Falcon Spring jct. From here, follow the Cascade Link right for the Red Spot, Spellman, and Pumpelly trails.

Distance from Poole Memorial Rd. (1300')

> *to* Cascade Link (1850') via Hinkley Trail: 1.3 mi. (2.1 km.), 550 ft., 55 min.

Cascade Link (map 1: B3–C3)

This trail runs between Falcon Spring jct. and the Pumpelly Trail, angling upward, south to north. Combined with the Pumpelly Trail, it is an interesting descent route from the summit to the state park. With either the Spellman Trail or the Red Spot Trail, it offers the most varied ascents from the east side of the mountain.

The Cascade Link starts at the Falcon Spring jct., reached by the White Dot Trail. It runs northeast, descends slightly, passes the Harling Trail on the right, and continues through spruce woods to a brook and the little cascades for which this trail is named. At 0.3 mi. it crosses the brook and climbs gradually along its east side, rising about 300 ft. before it leaves the brook and winds over ledges in thick woods. The Birchtoft Trail enters on the right at 0.5 mi., and the Red Spot Trail leaves left for Pumpelly Ridge and the Pumpelly Trail in another 30 yd., just before an old east-west stone wall. At 0.7 mi. the Spellman Trail leaves left, and the Cascade Link climbs close to the east bank of a small brook to where the brook rises, close to the boundary between Dublin and Jaffrey. From there, prominent cairns mark the Cascade Link over open ledges to a saddle on the Pumpelly Ridge (2700 ft.), where it ends at the Pumpelly Trail. (The Pumpelly Trail is a scenic route to the summit with many outlooks, marked with cairns.)

Distance from Falcon Spring (1850')

   to Pumpelly Trail (2700'): 1.4 mi. (2.3 km.), 850 ft., 1 hr. 10 min.

Spellman Trail (map 1: B3)

This trail leaves the Cascade Link 0.7 mi. from Falcon Spring and makes the steepest climb (700 ft. in about 0.6 mi.) on the mountain, up to the Pumpelly Trail just north of the Sarcophagus. The Spellman Trail is a good scramble in its middle section, with excellent views back to the east, including the skyline of Boston on a clear day. This trail is difficult to follow when snow covers the white dots that mark the route on the rocks because, in winding about to avoid the worst ledges, the trail does not always follow a clear line.

Distance from Cascade Link (2150')

   to Pumpelly Trail (2850'): 0.6 mi. (0.9 km.), 700 ft., 40 min.

Red Spot Trail (map 1: B3)

This trail, much less challenging than the Spellman Trail, provides a scenic alternative to the more heavily used trails on the east side of the mountain. It leaves the Cascade Link 0.5 mi. from Falcon Spring, 30 yd. beyond the Birchtoft Trail, and ascends somewhat roughly via long switchbacks. At 0.4 mi. the Old Ski Path leaves left for the White Dot Trail. At 0.7 mi. the Red Spot Trail emerges on ledges with good views, then passes the northern end of the Smith Connecting Link at 0.9 mi. and soon ends at the Pumpelly Trail 0.4 mi. below the summit.

Distance from Cascade Link (2150')

to Pumpelly Trail (2950'): 1.0 mi. (1.7 km.), 800 ft., 55 min.

Birchtoft Trail (map 1: B3–B4)

This trail begins near the state-owned Gilson Pond Area, located on Dublin Rd. 1 mi. north of Poole Memorial Rd. Follow the recreation area entrance road a short distance, then turn left on the first driveway and follow it 100 yd. to the shore of Gilson Pond. The trail (sign) skirts the east and south shores of the pond. At 0.1 mi. the east end of the Pond Loop Trail continues straight ahead as the Birchtoft Trail turns left, and at 0.2 mi. the west end of the Pond Loop Trail diverges to the right (north). (The Pond Loop Trail is a path 0.8 mi. long that runs around Gilson Pond, passing a spur path 0.3 mi. long, called the Ravine Trail, that leads into a hemlock ravine.) The Birchtoft Trail ascends by easy grades to end at the Cascade Link 0.5 mi. from Falcon Spring.

Distance from Gilson Pond (1210')

to Cascade Link (2150'): 2.1 mi. (3.3 km.), 950 ft., 1 hr. 30 min.

Marlboro Trail (map 1: B1–B2)

This is one of the oldest trails to the summit, dating to 1850 or earlier. Follow NH 124 west from Jaffrey, past the roads leading to Monadnock State Park and the Halfway House site. Take Shaker Farm Rd., the first dirt road on the right north of the Troy–Marlboro town line, 0.6 mi. north of Perkins Pond. Follow this road 0.7 mi. to a clearing on the left and an old cellar hole (parking). The trail follows a woods road for 0.9 mi. to a wall that runs east and west, then climbs up the nose of the ridge to the open ledges, marked with cairns and white Ms. At 1.3 mi. the Marian Trail leaves the Marlboro Trail on the right at the ledges known as the Rock House or Stone House (about 2450 ft.). The Marlboro Trail climbs to a shoulder where it ends at the jct. with the Dublin Trail, which comes up from the left and continues 0.3 mi. to the summit.

Distances from parking area, road west of Perkins Pond (1320')

to Dublin Trail (2950'): 1.9 mi. (3.1 km.), 1650 ft., 1 hr. 45 min.

to Mt. Monadnock summit (3159') via Dublin Trail: 2.2 mi. (3.5 km.), 1850 ft., 2 hr.

Halfway House Site Region Paths

An almost unlimited variety of good walks can be made starting at the old Halfway House site, reached from the Old Toll Road parking area in 1.2 mi. by either the Old Halfway House Trail or the Old Toll Road. A particularly rewarding round trip to the summit combines an ascent over Bald Rock via the Cliff Walk and the Smith Connecting, Red Spot, and Pumpelly trails with a descent on the Smith Summit Trail and one of the trails that lead down from Monte Rosa.

One of the finest scenic trails on Mt. Monadnock is the *Cliff Walk*, marked with white Cs, which begins on the Parker Trail 0.3 mi. from the Old Toll Road and runs 1.4 mi. along the south and east edge of the south ridge, from Hello Rock to Bald Rock, past splendid viewpoints—notably Thoreau's Seat, Emerson's Seat, and What Cheer Point—and historical points such as the Graphite Mine (left), which operated around 1850. Several paths lead up to the Cliff Walk from the Halfway House site. Three such trails are the Hello Rock Trail, the Point Surprise Trail, and the Thoreau Trail, which leave the Halfway House clearing at the southeast corner between the road and Moses Spring. The *Hello Rock Trail* trail ascends gradually 0.4 mi. through a fine forest to the Cliff Walk at Hello Rock. At 80 yd. above the Halfway House site, the *Point Surprise Trail* diverges left and ascends 0.3 mi. to the Cliff Walk, and the *Thoreau Trail* diverges farther left and climbs 0.4 mi. to the Cliff Walk at Thoreau's Seat.

Bald Rock is the bare peak on the south ridge of Monadnock; its highest point is a pointed boulder inscribed Kiasticuticus Peak. From Bald Rock, the *Smith Connecting Link*, marked with yellow Ss, descends a short distance, soon passes Coffee Pot Corner, and shortly reaches the Four Spots, a trail jct. The Smith Connecting Link goes right at this jct. and eventually crosses the White Cross Trail, then the White Dot Trail; it ends at the Red Spot Trail just below the Pumpelly Trail, a total of 0.7 mi. The trail that forks left at the Four Spots jct. is the eastern end of the *Amphitheater Trail*; it climbs with little grade to join the Side Foot Trail, which soon reaches the White Arrow Trail, after which the Amphitheater Trail continues west (no sign) to the Smith Summit Trail.

The *Side Foot Trail* is an excellent alternative to the lower part of the White Arrow Trail and avoids much of the very heavy traffic on that trail. To reach the Side Foot Trail, climb the bank at the left of the Halfway House clearing and follow a path a few yards into the woods to a trail jct. The Side Foot Trail leaves left and climbs 0.7 mi. to join the White Arrow Trail at Halfway Spring. Three trails in close succession—the *Do Drop Trail* (0.2 mi.), the *Noble Trail*

(0.3 mi.), and the *Hedgehog Trail* (0.3 mi.)—leave to the right of the Side Foot Trail and climb steeply to the Cliff Walk.

The *Monte Rosa Trail* leaves the tiny clearing of the former picnic grounds just past the north end of the Halfway House clearing, where the Royce Trail (a segment of the Metacomet–Monadnock Trail) enters from NH 124. The Monte Rosa Trail climbs to a jct. at 0.3 mi. where the *Fairy Spring Trail*, an alternate path that runs 0.3 mi. from the picnic grounds past the foundation of Fassett's Mountain House and Fairy Spring, enters on the right. In a few steps above this jct., the Monte Rosa Trail bears left (right is the *Smith Bypass*, leading directly to the Tooth), and ascends to the summit of Monte Rosa at 0.4 mi. The *Great Pasture Trail* leaves the jct. of the Marian and Mossy Brook trails, ascends to the summit of Monte Rosa and the Monte Rosa Trail at 0.3 mi. The *Smith Summit Trail* (marked by white dots) starts at the summit of Monte Rosa, descends steeply to the Tooth, a large pointed boulder, then circles gradually up the west side of the mountain 0.7 mi. to the White Arrow and Dublin trails just below the summit. The *Amphitheater Trail*, 0.4 mi. long, leaves the Smith Summit Trail on the right a short distance beyond the base of Monte Rosa and runs across the top of the Black Precipice, giving views into the ravine called the Amphitheater, then continues across the White Arrow and Side Foot trails to the Smith Connecting Link. The *Cart Path* leads west from the toll road about 0.3 mi. below the Halfway House site, crosses the Old Halfway House Trail and the Royce (Metacomet–Monadnock) Trail, and ends abruptly at 0.5 mi. at the jct. with the Mossy Brook Trail. The *Mossy Brook Trail* continues 0.3 mi. to the jct. with the Marian and Great Pasture trails. The *Marian Trail* leaves this jct., then turns sharp right near the Bear Pit, a depression to the west so named because a bear was once reputedly trapped in the quagmire, and continues 0.6 mi. to the Marlboro Trail at the Rock House (also known as the Stone House).

Parker Trail (map 1: C2–C3)

The Parker Trail begins at the picnic area at Monadnock State Park, on the west side of the outlet brook from the reservoir, and heads west across the south slope of the mountain to the Old Toll Road. It maintains a gentle grade and provides easy walking through mature woods. This trail has signs at both ends and is blazed with yellow paint. At 0.6 mi. the Lost Farm Trail diverges right for the upper part of the Cliff Walk, and at 1.2 mi. the lower end of the Cliff Walk is on the right. The Parker Trail joins the Old Toll Road 0.6 mi. above NH 124 and 0.6 mi. below the Halfway House site.

Distance from west side of reservoir outlet brook (1310')

   to   Old Toll Road (1720'): 1.5 mi. (2.4 km.), 400 ft., 55 min.

Lost Farm Trail (map 1: C3)

This trail branches right from the Parker Trail 0.6 mi. from the state park and leads in 1.1 mi. to Emerson's Seat on the Cliff Walk. A fine circuit walk from the park headquarters combines this trail with the Cliff Walk, the Smith Connecting Link, and either the White Cross Trail or the White Dot Trail.

Distance from Parker Trail (1510')

   to   Cliff Walk (2300'): 1.1 mi. (1.7 km.), 800 ft., 55 min.

Metacomet–Monadnock Trail and Vicinity

Metacomet–Monadnock Trail

The Metacomet–Monadnock Trail, 160 mi. long, begins in the Hanging Hills of Meriden CT, and runs north along the traprock ridge that borders the Connecticut River. It traverses Mt. Tom and the Holyoke Range, and passes over the Northfield Hills and Mt. Grace. The New Hampshire section, 18.5 mi. long, includes Little Monadnock Mtn. and Gap Mtn. and terminates at Grand Monadnock. (Previous to this section, the trail parallels the state line for some distance and runs just inside the New Hampshire border for a short distance in one section; this part is not described below.) The trail is clearly marked by white rectangular paint blazes. Space constraints prevent its full and detailed coverage by this guide; what follows is a brief account of the entire trail and a more detailed account of two of its more important features, Little Monadnock Mtn. (1900 ft.) and Gap Mtn. (south peak, 1900 ft.; north peak, 1840 ft.). For a more detailed description of the entire Metacomet–Monadnock Trail, the *Metacomet–Monadnock Trail Guide*, published by the Berkshire Chapter of the AMC, is available from New England Cartographics, PO Box 369, Amherst, MA 01004.

The best means of access to the south end of the New Hampshire section of the Metacomet–Monadnock Trail is from MA 32 0.5 mi. south of the Massachusetts–New Hampshire state line. The trail follows a woods road that passes south of the Newton Cemetery and descends moderately to cross Falls Brook at 0.7 mi. Here a spur path leads right about 100 yd. to the top of a waterfall. The main path swings left (north) and climbs, crossing the state line into New Hampshire at 1.1 mi. and continuing to Greenwood Rd. at 1.7 mi. It traverses to the north along a wooded ridge, then at 2.9 mi. turns right (east) onto an old road and bears left (northeast, then north) at a jct. at 3.1 mi. At 4.7 mi. the trail reaches NH 119 and follows it to the left (west).

At 5.0 mi. the trail turns right onto an unmarked dirt road and ascends gradually, then at 5.4 mi. It turns left onto a woods road in a clearing. It runs along the east slope of Grassy Hill until it descends to cross Tully Brook at 6.0 mi., then climbs to Old Troy Rd. at 8.0 mi. It follows this road downhill to the right for 150 yd., then turns left through a stone wall and ascends to the wooded summit of Little Monadnock Mtn. at 9.2 mi., then descends to the jct. at 9.5 mi. with the trail that ascends from Rhododendron State Park. The trail continues to descend past a fine north outlook, crosses a power line clearing at 10.0 mi., and turns right onto a dirt road at 10.8 mi. Continuing to descend, the road reaches homes and becomes improved gravel (Prospect St.) at 11.5 mi. At the bottom of the hill turn right onto Russell St., then left onto Depot St., and reach Troy village at 12.5 mi.

From Troy village the trail crosses the Ashuelot River and follows NH 12 south, then at 13.0 mi. turns left onto Quarry Rd. After crossing power lines, it continues straight on a woods road, then at 14.0 mi. leaves the road on the left. It then crosses Fern Hill in 100 yd. and descends across an area of old farmland with fields and stone walls, passing a yellow-blazed trail from the south trailhead for Gap Mtn. on the right at 14.3 mi. At 14.7 mi. it crosses a woods road near a gate and begins the serious ascent of Gap Mtn. At 15.1 mi. the unmarked side path to the south peak (the true summit) of Gap Mtn. leaves on the right, and the main trail continues to climb to the north peak of Gap Mtn., reaching the summit at 15.2 mi. Here, and along the ridge to the north, there are many excellent vistas featuring the impressive rocky crest of Mt. Monadnock, which rises about 1300 ft. higher only 6 mi. to the northeast. The trail descends across a succession of open ledges, passes a jct. at 16.1 mi. where a former route of the trail, now blazed in blue, leaves on the left. The trail crosses Quarry Brook and ascends across Old County Rd. (not maintained) at 16.3 mi., passes a short link path to the north trailhead for Gap Mtn. on the left at 16.6 mi., then runs through the woods above a swampy area to NH 124 at 17.3 mi. It enters Monadnock State Park at 17.6 mi. as the Royce Trail, and ascends across the Cart Path to meet the White Arrow Trail in the small clearing of the former picnic grounds at 18.7 mi. It then follows the White Arrow Trail to the summit of Monadnock at 19.6 mi.

Gap Mountain

This small mountain in the town of Troy (south peak, 1900 ft.; north peak, 1840 ft.) is named for its double-humped summit, which is a prominent feature of the view south from Monadnock. Most of the mountain is in the SPNHF Gap Mountain Reservation. It is crossed by the Metacomet–Monadnock Trail, with newly constructed trailheads providing easy access from north or south. The open ledges of the north peak provide excellent views in all directions, with especially fine perspectives on Monadnock and the Wapack Range. The higher south summit, reached by an obscure, little-used side path, affords a view to the northeast. Refer to the USGS Monadnock Mtn. quadrangle.

Gap Mountain North Approach (USGS Monadnock Mtn. quad). From NH 124, 0.8 mi. west of the Old Toll Rd. parking area for Mt. Monadnock and 0.5 mi. east of the jct. with Jaffrey Rd., turn south onto Bullard Rd. (formerly Old County Rd.). The trailhead is located on a short side road to the left, 0.5 mi. from NH 124. The trail passes a kiosk and in 60 yd. meets the white-blazed Metacomet–Monadnock Trail and turns right on it. At 0.1 mi. it crosses a stone wall and swings left up the slope (in the reverse direction, watch carefully for this turn), bears right through another stone wall, then descends to cross a woods road; avoid a path that forks left on the far side. It crosses Quarry Brook at 0.3 mi., then soon passes through a stone wall and turns sharp right to follow it. At 0.5 mi., where a blue-blazed path diverges right, it bears left (sign for Royce Trail) and climbs steadily by switchbacks to a small saddle. Here it turns left and ascends into an area of low growth, with increasing views north to Mt. Monadnock. It crosses a ledgy false summit, dips to a minor saddle, and ascends a short distance to the open north peak.

Distance from trailhead on Bullard Rd. (1190')

   to north peak of Gap Mtn. (1840'): 1.4 mi. (2.3 km.), 700 ft. (rev. 50 ft.), 1 hr. 5 min.

Gap Mountain South Approach (USGS Monadnock Mtn. quad). From NH 12, 1.5 mi. south of the Troy town center, turn left (north) onto Gap Mountain Rd. In 0.5 mi. this road bears right at a fork, and at 0.9 mi. from NH 12 it turns left and reaches trailhead parking on the left in another 0.1 mi. The yellow-blazed trail passes a kiosk and runs level, then slightly downhill to meet the white-blazed Metacomet–Monadnock Trail at 0.4 mi. (Descending, be sure to bear left here on the yellow-blazed trail.) The trail to Gap Mtn. turns right here, crosses a brook, and ascends through hemlocks and pines, crossing three stone walls. At 0.7 mi. it emerges in a meadow, turns left to follow its edge for 40 yd., re-enters the woods, and crosses a woods road. It passes a kiosk on the far side of the road and climbs through pines and old overgrown pastures, swinging to the left and becoming steeper higher up. At 1.2 mi. it begins a steep climb up ledges, passing an obscure side path on the right that leads about 0.2 mi. to the mostly wooded south peak. The main trail continues steeply to the open north peak.

Distance from trailhead on Gap Mountain Rd. (1270')

   to north peak of Gap Mtn. (1840'): 1.3 mi. (2.1 km.), 600 ft. (rev. 50 ft.), 55 min.

Little Monadnock Mountain (USGS Monadnock Mtn. quad)

This small mountain (1900 ft.) in the town of Fitzwilliam offers good views to the north from its northern ridge. It can be ascended by the Metacomet–Monadnock Trail from the north or the south, or by a path that ascends from Rhododendron State Park in Fitzwilliam, reached by following signs from NH 119 between Richmond and Fitzwilliam. A good loop hike can be made by ascending on the path from Rhododendron State Park, then following the Metacomet–Monadnock Trail south to Old Troy Rd., and returning to the starting point via Old Troy Rd. and Rhododendron Rd.

The trail from Rhododendron State Park begins by following the short Rhododendron Loop, then diverges and ascends to meet the Metacomet–Monadnock Trail 0.3 mi. north of the summit of Little Monadnock. For the summit, turn left here. The best viewpoint lies about 250 yd. downhill (to the right) from this jct.

Distances from Rhododendron State Park (1200')

   to Little Monadnock Mtn. summit (1900'): 1.2 mi. (1.9 km.), 700 ft., 55 min.

   to starting point by complete loop via Metacomet–Monadnock Trail, Old Troy Rd., and Rhododendron Rd.: 4.1 mi. (6.5 km.), 800 ft., 2 hr. 25 min.

Wantastiquet Mountain Area

Wantastiquet Mtn. (1388 ft.) is a bluff that rises more than 1100 ft. in 0.6 mi. from the Connecticut River directly across from Brattleboro VT. Refer to the USGS Brattleboro quadrangle. Excellent views across the Connecticut Valley are available from the flat summit of this mountain, which stands on the

Chesterfield–Hinsdale town line about 3 mi. west of Pisgah State Park. Local legend states that the mountain is the lair of many rattlesnakes; this was probably true at one time, but no reliable sightings of venomous reptiles have been made for many years and they are now officially considered to have been extirpated from the area. The summit and northeast slopes are part of the Madame Sherri Forest, named for the theatrical costume designer who once owned this land and built a castle (now in ruins) on it. A recently constructed network of trails now provides access to Mine Ledge (1365 ft.), East Hill (1115 ft.), and Daniels Mtn. (1230 ft.) to the east of Wantastiquet. Plans are underway to connect existing trails to complete a through trail from Wantastiquet Mtn. to Mt. Monadnock. Maps of the trails in this area may be found online at www.chesterfieldoutdoors.com.

Wantastiquet Mountain Trail (USGS Brattleboro quad)

For most of its length this trail is a gravel road that was cut to serve the quarries on the mountain. The trail begins on Mountain Rd., which leaves the north side of NH 119 just east of the bridge over the Connecticut River leading to Vermont; this is about 7 mi. west of the jct. of NH 119 with NH 63 in Hinsdale. There is parking about 0.2 mi. from NH 119. The trail passes between a pair of granite posts and ascends; avoid a lower road to the left that has a green gate. Almost immediately the trail passes through an orange gate, with a waterfall on a small stream on the right—avoid multiple side paths (except to view the waterfall or explore). The trail ascends past two switchbacks to another orange gate followed by a view to the west, then climbs by seven more switchbacks to a four-way intersection, where a side path turns right and climbs the last 50 yd. to the viewpoint at the north summit, marked by a monument to Walter H. Child. The road continues 0.1 mi. to a clearing near the communications tower at the slightly higher south summit. Here the Mine Ledge Trail (no sign) runs east to Mine Ledge and continues to the Ann Stokes Loop at Indian Pond.

Distance from parking area (280')

> *to* viewpoint near north summit of Wantastiquet Mtn. (1368'): 2.0 mi. (3.2 km.), 1100 ft., 1 hr. 35 min.

Ann Stokes Loop (USGS Brattleboro quad)

This trail, named for the landowner who donated this parcel of conservation land, provides a loop hike in the Madame Sherri Forest to secluded Indian Pond and two fine viewpoints on East Hill. It also provides access to the Mine Ledge Trail to Wantastiquet Mtn. and the Daniels Mountain Loop over Daniels Mtn. From the intersection of NH 9 and NH 63 in Chesterfield, follow NH 63 south for 1.6 mi. and turn right onto Stage Rd., then bear left onto Castle Rd. at 1.8 mi. At 2.8 mi. bear left onto Gulf Rd. and follow it to trailhead parking for Madame Sherri Forest on the left at 4.7 mi. If approaching from the west on NH 9, turn right onto Mountain Rd. 0.4 mi. east of US 5, then quickly bear left onto Gulf Rd. and follow it 2.2 mi. to the trailhead on the right.

The Ann Stokes Loop crosses a bridge over the outlet from a small pond and reaches a fork in 60 yd. The right fork leads 90 yd. uphill to the ruins of the Madame Sherri Castle. The main trail takes the left fork, runs along the shore of a marshy pond with one bypass to the right, and reaches the loop jct. at 0.2 mi. The loop is described in the counterclockwise direction. Turning right at the loop jct., the west branch of the loop climbs moderately to the jct. with the Mine Ledge Trail near the shore of Indian Pond at 0.6 mi. (The best viewpoint at the pond is found by following the Mine Ledge Trail 70 yd. to the right, then taking a side path 50 yd. left down to the shore.) The Ann Stokes Loop turns left at the jct., skirts the shrubby shore of the pond, and climbs steeply to a ledge overlooking the pond and Wantastiquet Mtn. at 0.8 mi. In another 0.1 mi. the summit of East Hill is reached; here a short side path leads left to a ledge with a good view east. The trail now descends to a low area with many large hemlocks, ascends easily, turns left just before reaching a ledge and runs over a knoll, then descends to its jct. with the south branch of the Daniels Mountain Loop on the right at 1.6 mi. Here the Ann Stokes Loop turns sharp left and descends 50 yd. to a jct. with the north branch of the Daniels Mountain Loop, also on the right. The Ann Stokes Loop again bears left and descends at mostly easy grades, with two bypasses to the left, and returns to the loop jct. at 2.2 mi. Continue straight ahead to return to the trailhead.

Distances from parking area on Gulf Rd. (640')

   to Mine Ledge Trail and Indian Pond (915'): 0.6 mi., 300 ft., 25 min.

   to Daniels Mountain Loop, south branch (900'): 1.6 mi., 550 ft. (rev. 250 ft.), 1 hr. 5 min.

   for complete loop: 2.4 mi. (3.9 km), 550 ft. (rev. 300 ft.), 1 hr. 30 min.

Mine Ledge Trail (USGS Brattleboro quad)

This trail provides a route from the Madame Sherri Forest to Mine Ledge, a prominent outcrop with a good view, and Wantastiquet Mtn. It is unblazed and rough in places but is fairly easy for experienced hikers to follow. It diverges right (sign) from the west branch of the Ann Stokes Loop, 0.6 mi. from the parking area on Gulf Rd. In 70 yd. a side path leads 50 yd. left to the shore of Indian Pond. The main trail ascends steeply to a ledge overlooking the pond at 0.2 mi. It continues up through oak forest, then meanders along a ridgecrest with minor ups and downs. At 0.7 mi. the main trail turns right; here a side path continues ahead 70 yd. to a ledge with a view west, then bears left and runs 80 yd. along a cliff edge to the best viewpoint at Mine Ledge, with views south and east. The main trail descends steeply to a saddle, where a trail diverges left for NH 119, climbs over a knoll and descends into a gully, then ascends briefly to a clearing near the south summit of Wantastiquet Mountain, just north of a communication tower, at 1.1 mi. To reach the viewpoint at the slightly lower north summit, follow an obvious old road 0.1 mi. west from the clearing, descending slightly, then take a side path 50 yd. left to the ledge and monument. In the reverse direction, the Mine Ledge Trail (no sign) leaves the northeast side of the clearing near the communication tower.

Distance from Ann Stokes Loop (915')

> *to* viewpoint near north summit of Wantastiquet Mtn. (1368'): 1.2 mi. (1.9 km.), 600 ft. (rev. 150 ft.), 55 min.

Daniels Mountain Loop

This trail loops over the wooded summit of Daniels Mountain, passing two fine viewpoints. It may be accessed from Gulf Rd. to the north via the Ann Stokes Loop or from Plain Rd. to the east via the Daniels Mountain Trail. The Daniels Mountain Loop is described here starting at its southern jct. with the Ann Stokes Loop (1.6 mi. from Gulf Rd. via the west branch of the Ann Stokes Loop) and running in the counterclockwise direction.

From its southern jct. with the Ann Stokes Loop, the south branch of the Daniels Mountain Loop leads south on an old road, crosses a wet spot, and descends gently, passing an older road that joins from the right (in the reverse direction, bear right here). It diverges left off the road at 0.3 mi. and climbs to a small saddle at 0.4 mi., where it swings right across a streambed and climbs along a slope of hemlocks. After a slight descent it climbs easily to a left turn at 0.8 mi., where a side path leads 20 yd. right to a ledge with a view south. The main trail now climbs north, crosses the south knob of Daniels Mtn., descends to a saddle, and ascends rather steeply to the true summit (no view) at 1.2 mi., where the Daniels Mountain Trail joins from the right. Here the Daniels Mountain Loop turns sharp left and descends moderately, passing a side path left to a limited view. It climbs over a knoll and swings left, then right to the Cook Ledges at 1.6 mi., where there is a view west to East Hill and Wantastiquet Mtn. The trail descends steeply from the outlook, turns sharp left onto an old road, and reaches its northern jct. with the Ann Stokes Loop at 1.8 mi. To the left, it is 50 yd. to the jct. with the south branch of the Daniels Mountain Loop. To the right, the Ann Stokes Loop leads 0.8 mi. to the Gulf Rd. parking area.

Distances from southern junction with Ann Stokes Loop (900')

> *to* Daniels Mtn. summit (1230'): 1.2 mi., 400 ft. (rev. 50 ft.), 50 min.

> *to* northern junction with Ann Stokes Loop (900'): 1.8 mi. (2.9 km), 400 ft. (rev 350 ft.), 1 hr. 5 min.

Distance for circuit of Ann Stokes Loop and Daniels Mountain Loop

> 4.2 mi. (6.8 km), 950 ft., 2 hr. 35 min.

Daniels Mountain Trail

This trail ascends Daniels Mtn. from the east, meeting the Daniels Mountain Loop at the wooded summit. It is lightly used and must be followed with care. From NH 119 in Hinsdale, follow Plain Rd. north, bearing right at 2.7 mi. The trail (small sign) begins on the left at 5.4 mi. there is limited parking on the opposite side of the road. It descends 25 yd. to cross a brook, climbs alongside a stone wall for 65 yd., turns sharp right onto an old road, then turns left off it after another 70 yd. It climbs steeply, swings right along another stone wall at 0.2 mi. and levels, then bears left again to climb steadily by switchbacks. It passes to the right of a rocky knoll at 0.5 mi., eases briefly again, and then climbs through a ferny area to the summit and the jct. with the Daniels Mountain Loop.

Distance from Plain Rd. (700')

> *to* Daniels Mtn. summit (1230'): 0.8 mi. (1.3 km), 550 ft., 40 min.

Pisgah State Park

Pisgah State Park, located in the southwest corner of New Hampshire in the towns of Chesterfield, Winchester, and Hinsdale, is the largest state park in New Hampshire, covering an area of about 13,000 acres. It is largely undeveloped, but has a network of about 60 miles of multi-use trails. The park office and visitor center are located on Old Chesterfield at the southeastern entrance. The park in general receives very light use, and is consequently a wilder place than might be expected—but also more satisfying for those looking for adventure and solitude. Significant hills reached by trails include Hubbard Hill (1381 ft.), which has excellent views to the west, and the wooded Mt. Pisgah (1329 ft.), which has two fine east-facing viewpoints on its north ridge. You may obtain winter and summer trail maps at the park or at www.nhstateparks.org.

Old Horseshoe Road

This historic dirt road heads southeast out of Chesterfield, loops around almost 180° like a horseshoe, and connects with the Old Winchester Road running northwest back into Chesterfield. The Horseshoe Rd. trailhead provides the major northern access to Pisgah State Park and the Old Chesterfield Road. Located at the birthplace of Harlan Fiske Stone (1872-1946), former attorney general and chief justice of the United States, the trailhead is situated on a scenic bluff overlooking the valleys and ridges of Pisgah State Park to the south. There is ample parking and an information board with maps available. It is reached by taking Old Chesterfield Rd. 0.3 mi. east from NH 63 in Chesterfield, then making a right onto Horseshoe Rd. (sign) and following it 1.4 mi. southeast to the parking area. A memorial for Harlan Fiske Stone is on the right.

The old road, lined with stone walls, descends past an orange gate. At 0.3 mi., the Old Horseshoe Road Connector follows the main road as it curves right and reaches the Old Winchester Road in an additional 0.3 mi., while the Old Horseshoe Road turns left onto an old grassy road signed "Habitat Trail." It enters a semi-open area filled with sumac trees, and soon the northwest fork of the South Woods Trail leaves on the left. The trail re-enters the woods and passes a small beaver bog and dam to the right. At 0.5 mi., it reaches a jct.with the Old Chesterfield Road (left) and also the Old Winchester Road, which enters descending from the right through an area flooded by recent beaver activity. Waterproof footwear may be advisable here, depending on the water level.

Distance from Horseshoe Rd. trailhead (1060')

> *to* Old Chesterfield Road/Old Winchester Road (910'): 0.5 mi. (0.8 km.),
> 0 ft. (rev. 150 ft.), 15 min.

Old Winchester Road

This historic dirt road was once part of a main highway that connected Chesterfield with Winchester. It descends a broad ridge into the valley through which runs the portion of the Old Chesterfield Road that is not open to automobiles, providing ample opportunities for various loops through the northwest section of the park. There is limited parking at this trailhead; for most longer trips, the Old Horseshoe Road trailhead with its large developed parking area should be used. To reach the Winchester Rd. trailhead, follow Winchester Rd. 1.3 mi. southeast of NH 63 in Chesterfield. Depending upon the road conditions and time of year, park as close to the locked gate as possible without obstructing the roadway or private drives.

The dirt road ascends straight ahead, enters Pisgah State Park (sign), and reaches the Hubbard Hill Trail (right) next to an information board and orange gate. It then descends, lined with stone walls. At 0.2 mi., the Old Horseshoe Road Connector follows the main road as it curves left and reaches the Old Horseshoe Road in an additional 0.3 mi., while the Old Winchester Road turns right onto an old woods road signed "Habitat Trail" and continues to descend. It skirts a semi-open area (left) filled with sumacs and enters a wet area created by recent beaver activity. Waterproof footwear may be advisable here, depending on the water level. The trail crosses stepping-stones through a particularly wet area next to a beaver dam (right) and meets the Old Chesterfield Road (straight ahead) and the Old Horseshoe Road (left) at a well-marked jct.

Distance from the Winchester Rd. trailhead (980')

> *to* Old Chesterfield Road and Old Horseshoe Road (910'): 0.6 mi. (1.0
> km.), 0 ft. (rev. 50 ft.), 20 min.

Dogwood Swamp Trail

This interesting and scenic trail connects Reservoir Road with the Old Chesterfield Road near Fullam Pond. It passes over a complex subsidiary ridge with several old ponds at various stages in their succession into marshy bogs. The trail is marked with intermittent blue blazes and requires concentration and care to follow, as there are many unexpected turns, which are poorly marked. Alert, experienced hikers should encounter few difficulties through this varied terrain; less experienced hikers may wish to take this trail with someone who has been over it before or may elect to take an alternative route. Difficult areas are highlighted in the description below. The trail begins on Reservoir Road, at a small parking area 1.5 mi. north of NH 119 via Reservoir Road itself (or 1.4 mi. north of NH 119 via the access trail from the designated trailhead parking area and Reservoir Road), just before the gated road switchbacks up the small ridge to Pisgah Reservoir.

The Dogwood Swamp Trail ascends through hardwoods on an old woods road marked with sparse blue blazes up a prominent ridge, heading generally northeast. It enters a hemlock forest, swings right near a small frog pond (right), and at 0.8 mi. reaches the first of several heights-of-land, beginning a series of undulating descents and ascents along the complex ridge top. At 1.3 mi. it passes the first open marsh (left), crosses a snowmobile bridge over an outlet brook at the southwest end of another marsh with a small beaver dam (left), and descends gradually. After passing yet another marshy area with a small frog pond (left), the trail swings sharp right and then sharp left in a hemlock forest. At this left turn do not descend straight on an old logging road, which leads 0.9 mi. downstream to Broad Brook Rd. near the western terminus of the Doolittle Trail. Watch for small arrows and blazes to guide the way through this section.

Almost immediately the trail crosses a snowmobile bridge over an outlet brook and swings left near a large marshy area (left). It follows the southern border of this open area along an undulating ridge and reaches the final height-of-land at 2.1 mi., where it begins the long descent toward Fullam Pond. It passes through a wet area and crosses several minor streams. After crossing a stream on a snowmobile bridge, the grade eases and the trail passes through an area with numerous blowdowns where the route should be followed with care. It passes through several wet areas past several large moss-covered boulders (left), joins a road coming from the left at a fork, and shortly thereafter reaches the Old Chesterfield Road at a point 1.1 mi. north of Broad Brook Rd. and 0.8 mi. south of the Chestnut Hill Trail and parking area.

Distances from Reservoir Road (620')

   to first height-of-land (920'): 0.8 mi., 300 ft., 35 min.

   to last height-of-land (1000'): 2.1 mi., 500 ft. (rev. 100 ft.), 1 hr. 20 min.

   to Old Chesterfield Road (680'): 3.3 mi. (5.3 km.), 500 ft. (rev. 300 ft.), 1 hr. 55 min.

Reservoir Trail

This old woods road connects Reservoir Road from the south to Old Chesterfield Road to the north, forming one of the major arteries through the center of the park. It intersects with many trails entering from the east and west, allowing for innumerable loops and circuits. It is scenic, with many fine viewpoints, and is easy to follow. It begins on Reservoir Road at the southeast corner of Pisgah Reservoir, 0.5 mi. north of the Dogwood Swamp Trail parking area.

The trail follows the eastern shore of Pisgah Reservoir with many unmarked paths leading left to the attractive shoreline. It swings right at an intersection (sign), passes through several wet areas, and at 0.9 mi. reaches the Chestnut Hill Trail (right) at Snowmobile Sign #16. It continues to parallel the eastern shore but at a greater distance, and at 1.5 mi. it reaches the northeast corner of the reservoir, where the Pisgah Ridge Trail leaves left across a small bridge. The Reservoir Trail swings right (arrow), crosses a snowmobile bridge over an inlet brook, and passes a small beaver pond (left). After crossing a dry stream bed on another snowmobile bridge, it swings right, then left, and at 1.9 mi. reaches the Parker Trail (right). The trail swings left (arrows), crosses a small brook on a snowmobile bridge, and begins a gradual ascent, crossing several small bridges. After reaching a small rocky ridge it swings right, and at 2.6 mi. the North Ponds Trail leaves right at Snowmobile Sign #17.

The Reservoir Trail swings left and descends, and in less than 0.1 mi. an unblazed spur leaves right and runs 0.2 mi. to the southwest shore of North Round Pond (small sign), a beautiful and seldom-visited body of water, far from the most popular attractions of the park. The main trail continues to descend by sweeping switchbacks, crosses two snowmobile bridges, and at 3.3 mi. reaches the Baker Pond Trail (left) at Snowmobile Sign #8. The Reservoir Trail now begins a persistent ascent through a hemlock forest along a small stream, crossing it several times. It reaches the height-of-land on a small ridge and begins a long gradual descent, passing through a clearing with a magnificent view northeast toward Mt. Monadnock and its surrounding hills. The trail descends past a group of small ledges and crosses several small streams, then swings right, then left, back into a hemlock forest. At 4.8 mi. it reaches the Old Chesterfield Road just past an orange gate. From here it is 0.1 mi. north on the Old Chesterfield Road to the jct. with the Old Winchester Road and Old Horseshoe Road.

Distances from Reservoir Road (890')

   to Chestnut Hill Trail (940'): 0.9 mi., 50 ft., 30 min.

   to Pisgah Ridge Trail (910'): 1.5 mi., 50 ft., 45 min.

to Parker Trail (940'): 1.9 mi., 100 ft. (rev. 50 ft.), 1 hr.

to North Ponds Trail (990'): 2.6 mi., 150 ft., 1 hr. 20 min.

to spur to North Round Pond (990'): 2.7 mi., 150 ft., 1 hr. 25 min.

to Baker Pond Trail (1090'): 3.3 mi., 250 ft., 1 hr. 45 min.

to Old Chesterfield Road (910'): 4.8 mi. (7.7 km.), 450 ft. (rev. 350 ft.), 2 hr. 40 min.

Lily Pond Trail

This trail provides a side trip from the Old Chesterfield Road to Lily Pond, a beautiful body of water, heavily used by beavers and waterfowl, located only 0.5 mi. from the Old Chesterfield Road. Unfortunately the trail is scantily marked with orange ribbons for most of its length and is difficult to follow. Alert and experienced hikers should be able to follow the trail from ribbon to ribbon; others will need extra time and care, backtracking carefully to the path if no traces of markings or footway are seen. Persistent walkers will be rewarded by an extremely scenic trail with two interesting small beaver ponds along the way. The trail leaves the Old Chesterfield Road 0.9 mi. north of the Fullam Pond gate and parking area and 0.7 mi. south of the jct. with the Old Winchester Road and the Old Horseshoe Road.

Leaving the Old Chesterfield Road, the Lily Pond Trail follows an old woods road through hemlocks to a small beaver pond (left) with a fine beaver lodge. From here, take extra care to find the way. The route skirts to the right of the pond and bears right uphill on an old woods road, crossing a small stream and ascending up a moderate slope to a flat area, where the trail swings left at the northeast corner of Lily Pond. From here it follows the eastern shore in a southerly direction. The pond is beautifully framed by larger hills to the west. With patience, beaver activity can be observed at the southern end of the pond near the large lodge. The trail swings left away from the pond at its southeast corner and descends with undulating grades. It passes by a wet area (left) before arriving at a small beaver pond (right). At the southeast corner of the pond, the trail ends at the green-blazed North Ponds Trail (no sign), 0.3 mi. from the Old Chesterfield Road (left).

Distances from Old Chesterfield Road (820')

to Lily Pond (960'): 0.5 mi., 150 ft., 20 min.

to North Ponds Trail at small beaver pond (690'): 1.1 mi. (1.8 km.), 150
ft. (rev. 250 ft.), 40 min.

to starting point (820') via North Ponds Trail and Old Chesterfield Road:
2.0 mi. (3.2 km.), 300 ft., 1 hr. 10 min.

Parker Trail

This trail connects the Chestnut Hill Trail with the Reservoir Trail and provides
a shortcut to points on the northern part of the Reservoir Trail from the Fullam
Pond gate and parking area on the Old Chesterfield Road. It ascends a large
complex subsidiary ridge that runs south to north through the center of the
park, and meets the Reservoir Trail south of its height-of-land on this ridge.
Although it is a narrow path for most of its length, it is well marked with yellow blazes and is fairly easy to follow as long as care is taken.

The trail makes a right turn onto an old woods road off the Chestnut Hill
Trail 0.4 mi. south of the Old Chesterfield Road, and ascends gradually
through mixed hemlocks for 0.2 mi., where the route narrows to a small footpath after crossing a small stream on a log bridge. Soon the path angles right
into a shallow gully surrounded by hemlocks, which it ascends, crossing a seasonal stream and passing a small marsh (left) in a beautiful hemlock and birch
forest. At 0.9 mi., the trail reaches the height-of-land and descends gradually to
the Reservoir Trail, at a point 0.4 mi. north of the Pisgah Ridge Trail and 0.8
mi. south of the North Ponds Trail.

Distance from Chestnut Hill Trail (750')

to Reservoir Trail (920'): 1.0 mi. (1.6 km.), 150 ft., 35 min.

Chestnut Hill Trail

This trail connects the Old Chesterfield Road at the Fullam Pond gate and
parking area with the Reservoir Trail at a point 1.0 mi. north of Reservoir
Road. It crosses a large complex subsidiary ridge, which runs south to north
through the middle of the park. It follows an old woods road for its entire
length, is marked with off-white blazes, and with a few exceptions is easy to
follow. The Fullam Pond gate and parking area is located 3.1 mi. north of the
south gate on Old Chesterfield Road and 1.6 mi. south of the jct. with the Old
Winchester Road and Old Horseshoe Road. This trailhead, the most northern
point that vehicles are permitted to drive to on the Old Chesterfield Road, may

be reached by motorized vehicles from the south during the dry season (late spring through autumn; inquire locally).

The trail ascends gradually on an old woods road in a generally south-southwest direction past an orange gate into a mixed hemlock forest. After several small stream crossings, the Parker Trail (pale yellow blazes) leaves right at 0.4 mi. for the Reservoir Trail. The Chestnut Hill Trail swings left and ascends gradually into a hemlock grove on a small ridge where several wet areas are crossed. The trail zigzags and ascends through a hardwood forest, descends briefly to a snowmobile bridge over a small stream, then ascends again to the height-of-land where there are interesting views during the colder months. The path then descends to the Reservoir Trail (Snowmobile Sign #16) at a point 1.0 mi. north of Reservoir Road and 0.5 mi. south of the Pisgah Ridge Trail.

Distance from Old Chesterfield Road at the Fullam Pond gate and parking area (690')

    to   Reservoir Trail (950'): 2.2 mi. (3.5 km.), 450 ft. (rev. 200 ft.), 1 hr. 20 min.

North Ponds Trail

This trail connects the Old Chesterfield Road with the Reservoir Trail near its height-of-land on a long, complex subsidiary ridge. It provides access to Lily Pond by the Lily Pond Trail and to North Round Pond by the Reservoir Trail and a short spur path. Both of these splendid ponds merit time to explore, as they are probably the least visited of the major bodies of water in the park. The trail follows an old woods road marked with pale green blazes for its entire length, and is easy to follow. It leaves the Old Chesterfield Road, 0.3 mi. north of the Fullam Pond gate and parking area and 1.3 mi. south of the jct. with the Old Winchester Road and Old Horseshoe Road.

The trail ascends gradually, passing a boggy area (left) and a boundary marker (left) that marks the Chesterfield–Winchester town line. The trail crosses a small stream and at 0.3 mi. reaches a double green blaze, just before a snowmobile bridge over an outlet brook that issues from a small beaver pond on the right. This is the southern terminus of the scantily marked Lily Pond Trail, which leaves to the right, marked only by several orange ribbons. Although Lily Pond (0.5 mi. north from here) is well worth visiting, this trail should be attempted only by experienced hikers who do not mind occasional improvisational walking.

Continuing straight across the bridge, the North Ponds Trail swings left, then right, and ascends the broad complex ridge, first through hemlocks, then through mixed forest. It crosses a small stream, reaches the height-of-land, and descends gradually to the Reservoir Trail (Snowmobile Sign #17). From here it is 0.3 mi. to North Round Pond by the Reservoir Trail and spur path, 2.6 mi. south to Reservoir Road, and 0.8 mi. north to Baker Pond by the Reservoir Trail and Baker Pond Trail.

Distance from Old Chesterfield Road (690')

   to Reservoir Trail (990'): 1.1 mi. (1.8 km.), 300 ft., 40 min.

Baker Pond Trail

This blue-blazed trail connects the Davis Hill Trail and Hubbard Hill Trail with the Reservoir Trail, passing by Baker Pond, an unspoiled, tranquil spot to observe waterfowl and beavers. From the jct. with the Davis Hill Trail and Hubbard Hill Trail, it descends gradually and swings left along the north shore of Baker Pond, where an unmarked path leads right to a scenic outlook across the length of the pond. The trail crosses a snowmobile bridge over an inlet brook, and swings right (south) along the eastern shore of the pond through a hemlock forest. Another unmarked path (right) leads to an outlook across the pond toward Davis Hill. At 0.4 mi. the orange-blazed Pisgah Ridge Trail diverges right in a small clearing. At 0.7 mi. the Baker Pond Trail turns sharp left (east) onto an old woods road and descends gradually to the Reservoir Trail (Snowmobile Sign #8) at a point 0.7 mi. north of the North Ponds Trail and 1.5 mi. south of the Old Chesterfield Road.

Distances from Davis Hill Trail and Hubbard Hill Trail (1200')

   to Pisgah Ridge Trail (1150'): 0.4 mi., 50 ft. (rev. 100 ft.), 15 min.

   to Reservoir Trail (1090'): 0.8 mi. (1.3 km.), 50 ft. (rev. 50 ft.), 25 min.

Hubbard Hill Trail

This historic road ascends from the Winchester Rd. trailhead along a ridge to the summit of Hubbard Hill, then descends to meet the Baker Pond Trail and Davis Hill Trail just above Baker Pond. The view from the summit of Hubbard Hill toward the Green Mtns. of Vermont is one of the finest in the park. The trail is marked with pink blazes and is easy to follow. The trailhead on

Winchester Rd. is located 1.3 mi. southeast of NH 63 in Chesterfield, just before the road enters Pisgah State Park at the gate. There is limited parking.

In a small clearing where the Old Winchester Road descends straight ahead, the Hubbard Hill Trail turns right onto an old woods road at an information board and ascends gradually past a chain-link gate, swings left (south) past an old cellar hole (left), and enters a partly cleared area at the site of an old farm. The road ascends sharply past two stone walls, then more gradually along a wooded ridge. After passing a spring (left), the road makes one long switchback (right, then left) up to the crest of the ridge at 1.2 mi. Here the north leg of a short loop path leads right 0.1 mi. to the summit of Hubbard Hill (1381 ft.), where there is a fine vista of the southern Green Mtns. Stratton Mtn., Mt. Snow, and Bromley Mtn. are visible over farms and pastures along the Connecticut River valley in the foreground. Once the view has been savored, hikers may either backtrack on the north leg of the loop or continue ahead 0.1 mi. on the south leg back to the main trail at a point about 70 yd. south of the beginning of the north leg. From the loop jct. the old road descends gradually, making one long switchback (right, then left), and at 1.6 mi. it ends at the jct. with the Davis Hill Trail and Baker Pond Trail.

Distances from Winchester Rd. trailhead (980')

> *to* Hubbard Hill summit loop path (1350'): 1.2 mi., 350 ft., 45 min.
>
> *to* Davis Hill Trail and Baker Pond Trail (1200'): 1.6 mi. (2.6 km.), 350 ft. (rev. 150 ft.), 1 hr.

Davis Hill Trail

This trail (white blazes) connects NH 63 at the Kilburn Road trailhead with the Hubbard Hill Trail and Baker Pond Trail at a point just north of Baker Pond, making possible a number of attractive loop hikes. The Kilburn Road trailhead is located on NH 63, 3.4 mi. south of Chesterfield and 3.9 mi. north of Hinsdale. There is an alternative snowmobile entrance on NH 63 0.3 mi. north of this trailhead.

The trail (sign) follows an old woods road in a northerly direction from a point near the trailhead (back near the entrance from NH 63). At 0.2 mi. it turns right onto another old road in a hemlock forest. The snowmobile entrance on NH 63 is 0.1 mi. to the left down this road. The trail ascends by several switchbacks, bears right at a fork, and descends to cross a stream on a snowmobile bridge. It then ascends again, passing the blue-blazed boundary markers at 0.9

mi. that signal the passage from Pisgah State Park into the Winchester Town Forest. At 1.0 mi. the height-of-land on Davis Hill is reached; here an unmarked path goes to the left, while the main trail descends through a hardwood forest and passes orange boundary markers (left) at 1.3 mi. as the trail re-enters Pisgah State Park in Chesterfield. The trail descends into a hemlock forest, swings to the right onto an old road, and crosses a small stream on a snowmobile bridge in an attractive glen. At 1.9 mi. the trail ends at the Hubbard Hill Trail (pink blazes) and Baker Pond Trail (blue blazes) at a point just north of Baker Pond and 0.4 mi. south of the fine western outlook on Hubbard Hill. From here, various circuits may be completed by taking either the Baker Pond Trail, Reservoir Trail, or Pisgah Ridge Trail and returning to the Kilburn Road trailhead via the Kilburn Loop.

Distances from Kilburn Road trailhead (1080')

  to height-of-land on Davis Hill (1410'): 1.0 mi., 350 ft., 40 min.

  to Hubbard Hill Trail and Baker Pond Trail (1200'): 1.9 mi. (3.1 km.), 350 ft. (rev. 200 ft.), 1 hr. 10 min.

Pisgah Ridge Trail

A ridge of small, craggy wooded peaks forms the backbone of Pisgah State Park, running south to north from Pisgah Reservoir to Baker Pond. Some of these hills offer excellent views of Mt. Monadnock to the east and the southern Green Mtns. to the west. The orange-blazed Pisgah Ridge Trail runs from the northern shore of Pisgah Reservoir over this chain, connecting with the Kilburn Loop (via a link path) and the Baker Pond Trail. Despite the low elevation of the summits, the trail is rugged, with several sharp ascents and descents, and takes longer than other trails in the park of comparable length. The hiker is rewarded, however, with several spectacular views and memorable moments that more than compensate for the effort involved.

The trail leaves the Reservoir Trail at the northeast corner of Pisgah Reservoir, 1.5 mi. north of Reservoir Road. It crosses a bridge over an inlet brook with a beaver dam and skirts the northern shore of the reservoir through a hemlock forest. At 0.3 mi. the route swings to the right away from the reservoir and ascends a boulder-strewn slope alongside a beautiful stream lined with moss. It swings away from the stream, then swings left, heading north onto the backbone of the ridge, passing a small clearing (right) with a view toward Mt. Monadnock and a striking view back toward the northern shore of the reservoir. Soon the trail descends into a small gully, then ascends toward Mt. Pisgah. This section is poorly blazed and should be followed with care. At 1.2 mi., the high point of Mt. Pisgah (1329 ft.), a wooded knob, is reached.

The trail descends to a small stream, then ascends scattered ledges, emerging onto an open crag with pines at 1.7 mi., where there is a magnificent view of Mt. Monadnock to the east and a vista toward southern Vermont to the west. This spot is known locally as Parker's Perch. The path descends steadily into a hemlock glen, then swings left into a small gully at 2.0 mi. (Here an unnamed, yellow-blazed connecting path signed "To Kilburn Loop" diverges left, descending past a small marsh (right) and moss-covered ledges (left), and crossing several small streams on snowmobile bridges. After passing a beaver bog and dam (left), it reaches the blue-blazed Kilburn Loop, 0.5 mi. from the Pisgah Ridge Trail; turn right to reach Kilburn Rd. in 0.3 mi. and the trailhead on NH 63 in 1.1 mi.)

From the jct. with the connecting path, the Pisgah Ridge Trail climbs out of the gully and ascends gradually north on a small ridge, then descends gradually by switchbacks into an interesting hemlock grove surrounded by boulder caves to the right and ledges to the left. It then ascends by switchbacks onto a ridge with an eastern lookout on semi-open ledges, swings left past a cellar hole (right), and at 2.6 mi. emerges onto an open ledge with a magnificent view of Mt. Monadnock and nearby hills to the east. The path descends through mixed softwoods scattered with mountain laurel to a small clearing and a jct. with the Baker Pond Trail, which leads left to Baker Pond and right to the Reservoir Trail.

Distances from Reservoir Trail (910')

   to Mt. Pisgah (1329'): 1.2 mi., 450 ft. (rev. 50 ft.), 50 min.

   to connecting path to Kilburn Loop (1170'): 2.0 mi., 600 ft. (rev. 300 ft.), 1 hr. 20 min.

   to Baker Pond Trail (1150'): 3.1 mi. (5.0 km.), 750 ft. (rev. 150 ft.), 1 hr. 55 min.

Kilburn Loop

One of the most popular hiking routes in the park, the Kilburn Loop provides an attractive overview of Pisgah State Park from an easily accessible trailhead. In a relatively short distance, the trail passes Kilburn Pond and its outlet brook, several marshy areas with small bogs, and attractive hemlock forests. The route is well blazed with blue diamond markers, well signed, and easy to follow. It is also a comfortable length to complete in half a day, making it an ideal family hike. The trailhead, which is shared with the Davis Hill Trail, is located on NH 63, 3.4 mi. south of Chesterfield and 3.9 mi. north of Hinsdale. There is ample parking.

The trail begins by following Kilburn Road, an old gravel road that heads east directly out of the parking area through two gateposts and past a mailbox to the right. It ascends gradually, swings right, begins a gentle descent, and enters the Kilburn Loop on the right at 0.6 mi. The loop is described here in a counter-clockwise direction. It follows an old woods road marked by blue diamond blazes and runs generally south. Almost immediately it passes within sight of Kilburn Pond, an attractive body of water lined with rocky outcroppings and hemlocks. The trail follows the western shore, passing numerous unmarked paths (left) leading to fine viewpoints overlooking the pond. Several of these spots by themselves justify a walk along this route and merit additional time. At 1.4 mi. the trail reaches the southwestern corner of the pond, where an old woods road leaves left. The trail bears right here, avoiding an old woods road (right), and descends parallel to a large outlet brook (left), crossing several small streams. At 1.9 mi. there are views to the left through the trees to a smaller pond (not shown on the park map). The trail passes this pond, then descends in earnest, crossing the outlet brook and a tributary stream on snowmobile bridges. The road makes a hard left where an old woods road leaves right to exit the park, then at 2.7 mi. begins the northward climb to complete the loop. The trail passes a smaller pond (left) that is seen through the trees, and shortly reaches red boundary blazes, which indicate the Hinsdale–Winchester town line. After passing a small spring (right) and swinging left onto a snowmobile bridge that crosses an outlet brook emerging from a small marsh (right), the Kilburn Loop leaves the old road and becomes a footpath in a hemlock forest.

The trail passes another pond that is seen through the trees to the left, crosses a small wet area, then ambles through a rock-strewn hardwood forest, ascending gradually into another hemlock forest. At 4.4 mi. the trail reaches its high point on a small ridge, then descends gradually by several switchbacks and at 5.2 mi. reaches a connecting path on the right that ascends 0.5 mi. and 100 ft. to the Pisgah Ridge Trail. At this jct., the Kilburn Loop merges with an old woods road coming from the left. The trail descends by one sweeping switchback, crosses a large inlet brook on a snowmobile bridge, then turns left (west) onto Kilburn Road at 5.5 mi. It passes an old woods road (left) and a small marshy area (right), and swings around the north shore of Kilburn Pond (left). It then ascends gradually, and at 5.7 mi. reaches the starting point of the Kilburn Loop (left), 0.6 mi. east of the trailhead.

Distances from the Kilburn Road trailhead (1080')

  to western end of Kilburn Loop (1030'): 0.6 mi., 50 ft. (rev. 100 ft.), 20 min.

  to southern end of Kilburn Loop (980'): 2.7 mi., 100 ft. (rev. 100 ft.), 1 hr. 25 min.

  to connecting path to Pisgah Ridge Trail (1080'): 5.2 mi., 200 ft., 2 hr. 40 min.

  to eastern end of Kilburn Loop (1050'): 5.5 mi., 200 ft. (rev. 50 ft.), 2 hr. 50 min.

  to Kilburn Road trailhead (1080') via complete loop: 6.3 mi. (10.1 km.), 300 ft., 3 hr. 20 min.

South Woods Trail

This trail connects the Old Horseshoe Road and Old Chesterfield Road with the Fullam Pond Trail. The central section is extremely difficult to follow due to a lack of blazes and an indistinct footway. It should be attempted only by experienced hikers who are willing to spend extra time locating the trail. The western end has two routes from separate entrances that come together after 0.5 mi. Both these paths coincide with part of the Habitat Trail, a self-guiding nature path with numbered posts keyed to an informational brochure that may be obtained from the park office. The southwest fork passes a beaver pond where water may flood the trail, so waterproof footwear may be desirable.

The northwest fork (the least wet approach) leaves the Old Horseshoe Road in an overgrown clearing filled with sumacs, 0.3 mi. south of the Horseshoe Rd. trailhead and 0.2 mi. north of the junction of the Old Chesterfield Road and Old Winchester Road. It enters the woods, passes a stone wall, and descends on an old woods road lined with stone walls to the point where the southwest fork comes in on the right at 0.5 mi.

The southwest fork leaves the Old Chesterfield Road just south of the convergence of the Old Horseshoe Road and Old Winchester Road. It descends gradually on an old woods road that coincides with the Habitat Trail, crosses two culverted brooks, and at 0.1 mi. makes a left onto an old grassy road signed "Wildlife Trail." The trail follows this road to the eastern shore of a large beaver pond in a beautiful open marsh, crosses the beaver dam (use caution) to the northeast corner of the pond, and heads into the woods bearing right onto another old woods road. This section of trail is extremely wet. The trail descends gradually past a stone wall and meets the northwest fork (left) at 0.4

mi. From here, the Habitat Trail turns left onto the northwest fork and ends at the Old Horseshoe Road.

The South Woods Trail turns right at this jct. (or continues straight if you are coming in on the northwest fork), crosses a stream on a snowmobile bridge past a large marshy area (left), crosses a brook on a log bridge, then crosses a small stream on a regular bridge. From here the route narrows to a trail and is extremely difficult to follow in places; it may require backtracking if the foot-way is lost. The route bypasses a small bog (left), crosses several small streams, then turns right onto an old woods road (no signs, arrows, or blazes). It skirts to the right of an open wetland area, re-enters the woods, and climbs over a small hill into a hemlock forest, where a large brook is crossed on a bridge. The old road follows the north bank of this brook downstream, recrosses the brook on a bridge, and at 1.6 mi. reaches a jct. where the trail forks again.

The trail bears left and ascends gradually to Fullam Pond Trail at a point just south of its jct. with the Nash Trail.

The former southeast fork of the trail has been abandoned.

Distances from the junction of the Old Chesterfield Road and Old Horseshoe Road (910')

> *to* convergence of northwest and southwest forks (840'): 0.5 mi., 0 ft. (rev. 50 ft.), 15 min.

> *to* Fullam Pond Trail (690'): 1.9 mi. (3.1 km.), 0 ft. (rev. 150 ft.), 55 min.

Old Chesterfield Road

Once the highway between Winchester and Chesterfield, this historic road is now the southeast-to-northwest artery through Pisgah State Park. The southern 3.3-mi. section may be used by motorized vehicles during the dry season (late spring through autumn; inquire locally for details) but is gated the remainder of the year. There are many historical exhibits and sites along the first 1.5 mi. as the road passes through the remains of an early-nineteenth-century farming and industrial community. An interesting 3.3-mi. loop, which includes many of the historical exhibits in the park, may be made by combining the Doolittle Trail with the northern section of the Broad Brook Road and the southern sec-tion of the Old Chesterfield Road. Accompanying literature may be obtained by contacting the state park office.

There is a small area for parking at the southern trailhead, 2.8 mi. northwest of Winchester. The road heads north, and in 0.2 mi. it passes an orange gate (locked during winter and early spring) and descends gradually on a well-graded gravel roadway, passing the park visitor center and office on the left. It passes the cider mill site (left, sign #1) shortly before reaching the Doolittle Trail (left) next to an old barn site (sign #2) at 0.4 mi. The road continues past the Benjamin Doolittle Homestead (right, sign #3), then a small pond (right), and ascends gradually past the Jediah Eaton Homestead (left, sign #4), the Ebenezer Hutchinson Homestead (left, sign #5), and a small parking area for the historic sites (right, signs #6 and #7). At 1.1 mi., the road reaches an orange gate that is locked during winter and early spring and at night during the rest of the year. Here John Hill Road leaves right and runs to Old Spofford Road.

The Old Chesterfield Road descends gradually to several culverted streams, passes the Nathan Field Homestead (right, sign #8), crosses a culverted brook, and ascends gradually. It passes Cheese Rock (right), a white pine stand (left, sign #10), and reaches the northern end of Broad Brook Road (left) at 1.5 mi. Heading generally northwest, the road passes an old woods road (left), and at 1.7 mi. the Snow Brook Trail comes in on the right at an orange gatepost next to an old woods road. The road descends gradually past a small clearing (left) into an open marshy area through which Broad Brook flows.

At 2.5 mi. the Old Chesterfield Road reaches the Nash Trail (right) at a small parking area, then swings left (west), crosses Broad Brook on a bridge and shortly reaches the Dogwood Swamp Trail (left) in a small clearing. The road curves several times through an open bog and at 3.1 mi. reaches the road to the Fullam Pond parking area (right), opposite Snowmobile Sign #13 (left). The Old Chesterfield Road continues straight ahead, passes through a small flooded area, and at 3.3 mi. reaches the Chestnut Hill Trail (left) at a small parking area. This is the northern limit of motorized travel permitted on this road.

The road now becomes a graded woods road and ascends gradually past a locked orange gate, passes the Winchester–Chesterfield boundary markers (right), and at 3.6 mi. reaches the North Ponds Trail (left) at Snowmobile Sign #14. The road descends gradually past a small beaver bog with lodge and dam (right), and at 4.2 mi. reaches the northern terminus of the Lily Pond Trail (left). The road continues through a wet area (left), crosses a culverted stream, and ascends gradually. At 4.4 mi. the road passes an unmarked woods road (right) that connects to the South Woods Trail near a beaver pond in 0.3 mi. The main road crosses several culverted streams, then descends gradually to the Reservoir Trail, which comes in on the left at an orange gate at 4.7 mi. The road then crosses a culverted stream and at 4.8 mi. reaches the southwest terminus of the South Woods Trail (right), which is a link to the Habitat Trail. The Old Chesterfield Road ends just beyond at an area of recent beaver activity, where the Old Winchester Road and Habitat Trail lead straight uphill 0.6 mi. to the Winchester Rd. trailhead and the Old Horseshoe Road leaves right uphill 0.5 mi. to the Horseshoe Rd. trailhead and parking area.

Distances from southern trailhead (880')

   to Broad Brook Road (710'): 1.5 mi., 50 ft. (rev. 200 ft.), 45 min.

   to Nash Trail (660'): 2.5 mi., 150 ft. (rev. 150 ft.), 1 hr. 20 min.

   to Chestnut Hill Trail and locked gate (680'): 3.3 mi., 150 ft., 1 hr. 45 min.

   to Old Winchester Road and Old Horseshoe Road (910'): 4.8 mi. (7.8 km.), 400 ft., 2 hr. 35 min.

Doolittle Trail

This short trail connects the Old Chesterfield Road with the Broad Brook Road. It descends into the Broad Brook valley through the remains of an early New Hampshire farming and industrial community with several numbered exhibits and sites scattered along the bank of the brook (accompanying literature may be obtained from the state park office). An interesting loop may be made by hiking the Doolittle Trail from east to west, heading north on the Broad Brook Road, then going south on the Old Chesterfield Road back to the starting point. The Doolittle Trail is generally easy to follow with the exception of a short segment near the eastern terminus where care must be taken.

The trail leaves the Old Chesterfield Road on an old grassy road, 0.2 mi. north of the southern gate and 0.7 mi. south of John Hill Road. It passes through an old orchard and overgrown field past several stone walls, then bears right off the old road into the forest (no sign). The trail turns left onto a footpath (sign) and ascends a small hill. This section should be followed with care as the footway is faint with few blazes or markings. The route swings right and then left, descends gradually, then turns left onto an old woods road (sign). From here on, the trail is easier to follow.

The trail passes over a small hill, descends through a hemlock forest to the Old Broad Brook Meadow (left, sign #23) at 0.7 mi., then swings right (north) and ascends through mixed woods. The trail crosses a stream on a snowmobile bridge and follows Broad Brook upstream, passes the Water Mill Dam Site (left, sign #22) at 0.9 mi., then swings left (west) and crosses Broad Brook and a tributary stream on two snowmobile bridges. Soon it meets the Broad Brook

Road, 1.0 mi. south of Old Chesterfield Road and 2.0 mi. north of the south gate and South Link Trail.

Distances from Old Chesterfield Road (910')

  to Broad Brook Road (590'): 1.1 mi. (1.8 km.), 0 ft. (rev. 350 ft.), 35 min.

  to starting point by complete loop via Doolittle Trail, Broad Brook Road, and Old Chesterfield Road: 3.3 mi. (5.3 km.), 400 ft. (rev. 50 ft.), 1 hr. 50 min.

Broad Brook Road

This is an extremely scenic and historic walk through the valley of Broad Brook, which was once the location of a thriving nineteenth-century farming and industrial community. The southern section of the road is open to hikers and snowmobiles only; it passes through attractive open marshes and flood plains. The northern mile passes through the remains of an early New Hampshire industrial settlement with foundations of mills, homesteads, schools, and water canals used to harness the streams to provide energy for the early mills. Motorized vehicles are allowed through this section from late spring through autumn (inquire locally). There are numbered exhibits and sites; accompanying literature may be obtained from the state park office.

There are several ways of access to Broad Brook Road. From late spring through autumn, hikers in vehicles may enter from the north by the Old Chesterfield Road, or from the south from the designated Reservoir Road trailhead on NH 119 by way of the South Link. Hikers on foot may also enter the road directly from NH 119 from the Broad Brook Road jct. (little parking available here). By any of these routes, this trail presents an interesting perspective on a former way of life that flourished well before the settlement of much of the rest of the United States.

From the designated Reservoir Road trailhead (on NH 119, 2.2 mi. east of Hinsdale), the access trail follows a woods road that leads uphill past an orange gate and crosses a power line clearing. At 0.2 mi. the route turns right and follows the Connector Trail, a snowmobile trail that passes through an attractive pine grove and reaches Reservoir Road at 0.4 mi. A short distance downhill to the right from here, at 0.5 mi., the South Link leaves on the left and ascends on an old woods road through hemlocks, then descends through mixed forest to reach the Broad Brook Road at 1.1 mi. from the parking area on NH 119. This point is 0.6 mi. north of NH 119 (at a point 3.2 mi. east of Hinsdale) and 0.1 mi. north of the locked south gate where Broad Brook Road enters Pisgah State

Park (parking very limited here). Distances given below are from the designated Reservoir Road trailhead.

From the jct. with the South Link, the Broad Brook Road leads gradually uphill past an open marsh and flood plains (right) and moss-covered ledges (left), and finally runs alongside Broad Brook itself (right). At 2.9 mi. it reaches the Historic Sites parking area and turnaround (left) which is the southern limit for motorized vehicle travel during the summer season. From here the road parallels Broad Brook through the remains of an early New Hampshire settlement with over a dozen historical exhibits on either side of the road. Included are the sites of steam mills, dams, barns, homesteads, water mills, a boarding house, and a school. At 3.0 mi. the road reaches the western terminus of the Doolittle Trail (right), which provides access to several other historical sites. In another half-mile the road crosses Broad Brook next to the site of the William King Water Mill and ascends gradually away from the brook, passing several historical sites, and reaches the Old Chesterfield Road 0.4 mi. north of John Hill Road and 1.6 mi. south of the Fullam Pond parking area.

Distances from designated Reservoir Road trailhead on NH 119 (390')

> *to* Broad Brook Road via connector trail and South Link (560'): 1.1 mi., 200 ft., 40 min.

> *to* Historic Sites parking area (590'): 2.9 mi., 200 ft., 1 hr. 30 min.

> *to* Doolittle Trail (590'): 3.0 mi., 200 ft., 1 hr. 35 min.

> *to* Old Chesterfield Road (710'): 4.0 mi. (6.4 km.), 350 ft., 2 hr. 10 min.

Snow Brook Trail

This scenic trail meanders in a westerly direction from the Old Spofford Road to the Old Chesterfield Road. It follows an old woods road for its entire length through attractive evergreen forests, along the bank of Snow Brook, and beside open marshlands. Although the route is longer and more serpentine than the park map indicates, it is easy to follow.

The eastern trailhead may be found by driving north on the Old Spofford Road, 4.8 mi. from Winchester, 3.5 mi. north of the road to Westport (see map), and 0.2 mi. north of John Hill Road. It has ample parking. The trail follows an old woods road through an orange gate into a mixed hemlock forest, swings right past a small marshy area (left), passes a stone wall, and begins a gradual descent, swinging left and then right into a beautiful mossy glen. After several more turns, it crosses Snow Brook on a snowmobile bridge, then continues to follow its course downstream. The road passes a small beaver bog (left), then swings left and re-crosses Snow Brook on another bridge. At 0.9 mi., an abandoned section of the Orchard Trail that formerly ran to Old Spofford Road, but has been closed by the landowner, is passed on the right (Snowmobile Sign #21). A short distance beyond, the Orchard Trail leaves left (Snowmobile Sign #21) for John Hill Road.

From here the trail swings right, crosses Snow Brook on a snowmobile bridge, ascends an embankment away from the brook, and skirts the south side of a large open marsh. It enters a pine forest and ascends to the Old Chesterfield Road, 0.2 mi. north of the Broad Brook Road and 1.3 mi. south of the Fullam Pond parking area.

Distances from Old Spofford Road trailhead (920')

   to   Orchard Trail (850'): 0.9 mi., 0 ft. (rev. 50 ft.), 25 min.

   to   Old Chesterfield Road (720'): 1.8 mi. (2.9 km.), 0 ft. (rev. 150 ft.), 55 min.

John Hill Road

This partly paved, partly gravel road connects the Old Spofford Road with the Old Chesterfield Road. It is suitable for hikers in all seasons, and is also used by all-terrain vehicles and snowmobiles. It is gated on both ends. To find out when the road is open to vehicles, consult the state park office. The road leaves the Old Spofford Road 0.2 mi. south of the trailhead for the Snow Brook Trail and 4.6 mi. north of Winchester. Hikers are encouraged to park at the trailhead for the Snow Brook Trail, where there is ample space.

The road descends through a wire gate with orange posts past a beaver pond (left), then ascends to a height-of-land at 0.4 mi. Here the road swings right and descends past a wet area. At 0.6 mi. an unmarked woods road (the Orchard Trail) leaves right (north) and runs to a turnaround in a small clearing. After passing another old road (right) and a small clearing with utility lines (right), John Hill Road swings left and descends to the Old Chesterfield Road at an orange gate, 0.4 mi. south of Broad Brook Road and 0.9 mi. north of the south gate.

Distances from Old Spofford Road (920')

   to   Orchard Trail (900'): 0.6 mi., 0 ft., 20 min.

   to   Old Chesterfield Road (750'): 1.2 mi. (1.9 km.), 0 ft. (rev. 150 ft.), 35 min.

Orchard Trail

This somewhat ill-defined trail travels north from John Hill Road to the Snow Brook Trail. A former section of the trail north of the Snow Brook Trail has been abandoned and the landowner forbids its use. The southern trailhead is located on John Hill Road at a point 0.6 mi. west of Old Spofford Road and 0.6 mi. east of Old Chesterfield Road.

The trail starts as an unmarked dirt road that almost immediately reaches a turnaround, where the trail bears right onto an old woods road (sign) and enters the woods. It passes two stone walls, descends gradually to a beaver bog, passes another stone wall, crosses a small stream, and at 0.6 mi. ends at the Snow Brook Trail, a woods road marked only with Snowmobile Sign #21.

Distances from John Hill Road (900')

   to Snow Brook Trail (850'): 0.6 mi. (1.0 km.), 0 ft. (rev. 50 ft.), 20 min.

Reservoir Road

This attractive trail from NH 119 to the south shore of Pisgah Reservoir uses a well-graded gravel road for most of its length. The trip may be extended to an 8-mi. loop by continuing on the Hinsdale Snowmobile Trail to NH 63 and walking south on NH 63 0.6 mi. to Hinsdale, then east on NH 119 for 2.2 mi. back to the trailhead. Some of the views from the shore of the reservoir are excellent.

There are now two approaches to Reservoir Road: one follows the access trail from the designated trailhead and parking area, 2.2 mi. east of Hinsdale on NH 119, and meets Reservoir Road, while the other follows the first part of Reservoir Road (no parking here), which begins 0.3 mi. east of the designated trailhead. Both are described below.

From the designated trailhead, a woods road (marked by blue diamonds) ascends past an orange gate and through a power line clearing. At 0.2 mi. the Connector Trail, a snowmobile trail, leaves right uphill and runs 0.2 mi. through an attractive pine grove to Reservoir Road. The main trail continues straight uphill on an old woods road, then quickly fades to a trail through mixed hemlocks and reaches Reservoir Road at 0.5 mi. Turn left here for Pisgah Reservoir (no sign).

From the base of Reservoir Road at NH 119 (no parking), the gravel road ascends past an orange gate and immediately enters Pisgah State Park (signs). There is a view of the paper mill on the Ashuelot River to the left. The road crosses a power line clearing and at 0.4 mi. reaches the South Link (right), which leads 0.6 mi. to Broad Brook Road at a point 0.1 mi. north of its southern gate. The main road leads straight 0.1 mi. to the Connector Trail, a snowmobile link that descends on the left 0.2 mi. back down to the access trail from the new trailhead at a point 0.2 mi. north of the new trailhead. The road then continues another 0.2 mi. to reach the access trail, which enters on the left (sign). Mileages in the text below are from the designated trailhead.

The Reservoir Road crosses a brook, passes two beaver ponds (right) in a marshy area, and at 1.4 mi. reaches the Dogwood Swamp Trail (right) across from a small parking area. The road now swings left, passes another orange gate with a mailbox (left), and begins a series of switchbacks up the side of a ridge. After a 0.5-mi. climb, the grade eases and the trail descends gradually to the Reservoir Trail (right), which serves as one of the major north–south arteries in the park. The road swings left around the south end of Pisgah Reservoir, passing several unmarked paths (right) that lead to the shore. At 2.2 mi., the road reaches a spillway at the southern end of the reservoir, where there are magnificent views north over the water toward Mt. Pisgah. On the other side of the spillway, the road continues as the Hinsdale Snowmobile Trail, which leads 2.8 mi. down to NH 63. Use caution if you cross the spillway; if the spillway cannot be crossed due to high water or winds, an unmarked bypass road to the left avoids the spillway and dam area.

Distances from the designated Reservoir Road trailhead (400')

   to Reservoir Road (560'): 0.5 mi., 150 ft., 20 min.

   to Dogwood Swamp Trail (620'): 1.4 mi., 200 ft., 50 min.

   to Reservoir Trail (940'): 2.0 mi., 550 ft., 1 hr. 20 min.

   to spillway at southern end of Pisgah Reservoir (890'): 2.2 mi. (3.5 km.), 550 ft. (rev. 50 ft.), 1 hr. 25 min.

Hinsdale Snowmobile Trail

This woods road is actively used in winter as part of one of the major snowmobile corridors through Pisgah State Park. An attractive loop can be made by combining this trail with the Reservoir Trail, a 0.6-mi. walk along NH 63 to Hinsdale, and a 2.2-mi. walk along NH 119 to the Reservoir Road trailhead. Hikers should be aware that there are few trail markings such as signs and blazes along this route, with the exception of a small number of snowmobile signs at major intersections. Take care to follow the route closely so that inadvertent wrong turns can be quickly corrected; a topographical map and compass would be particularly useful. There are several fine viewpoints along the shore of Pisgah Reservoir. Hikers wishing to attempt the complete loop should park their vehicles either in Hinsdale or at the designated Reservoir Road trailhead, since parking is not permitted at the start of this trail. From Hinsdale, follow NH 63 north on foot for 0.6 mi. to a small woods road over a small bridge on the right.

The trail ascends on this woods road, crossing the small snowmobile bridge, then swings hard left into the woods, bears left where an old woods road leaves right, and swings right. At 0.4 mi. the trail turns left at a three-way intersection, enters a power line clearing, bears left again, and ascends across the clearing back into the woods. There are several old woods roads on either side of the main road that should be avoided. The main road enters a hemlock forest, and at 1.3 mi. reaches an old camp on the left just before crossing a snowmobile bridge over a small beaver pond. The road passes through orange gateposts and enters Pisgah State Park (signs). The road makes the first of several crossings over a small brook as it follows the course of this stream uphill. It swings right through a semi-open area with evidence of old beaver activity and crosses the stream three times before entering a small open marsh on the left. The trail crosses the stream three more times in a fine hemlock forest, then leaves the stream behind as it climbs to higher ground.

At 2.1 mi. the trail reaches Snowmobile Sign #20 at a three-way intersection. To reach a beautiful cove on the western shore of Pisgah Reservoir, follow the unmarked road straight ahead. It leads 0.4 mi. over a small rocky ridge and then down to the shore of the reservoir.

The main route turns right at this intersection and continues on the unmarked road, heading generally southeast. It crosses a small stream on a snowmobile bridge, then passes over some corduroy in a wet area and swings right. At the height-of-land the road passes a stone wall, then descends gradually on a relatively flat ridge, swinging left to cross a long corduroy snowmobile bridge over a wet area, then another snowmobile bridge over a stagnant stream. The trail swings right and reaches Snowmobile Sign #19, where it swings left. After passing over yet another bridge, the trail emerges onto the southwest corner of Pisgah Reservoir at 2.8 mi. To reach the Reservoir Trail, cross a concrete barrier to a spillway on the southern shore of the reservoir. From here, there are good views north over the open water toward Mt. Pisgah. On the other side of the spillway, the road continues as the Reservoir Road, which leads 2.2 mi. via an access trail down to the designated Reservoir Road trailhead on NH 119, 2.2 mi. east of Hinsdale. Use caution if you cross the spillway; if the spillway cannot be crossed due to high water or winds, an unmarked bypass road to the right avoids the spillway and dam area.

Distances from NH 63 (330')

- *to* three-way intersection at power line clearing (590'): 0.4 mi., 250 ft., 20 min.
- *to* Pisgah State Park boundary (770'): 1.3 mi., 450 ft., 55 min.
- *to* spur trail to western cove of Pisgah Reservoir (890'): 2.1 mi., 550 ft., 1 hr. 20 min.
- *to* western cove of Pisgah Reservoir via spur trail (890'): 2.5 mi., 550 ft., 1 hr. 30 min.
- *to* Pisgah Reservoir spillway and Reservoir Road (890'): 2.8 mi. (4.5 km.), 550 ft., 1 hr. 40 min.
- *to* starting point (from any point) by complete loop via Reservoir Trail, Hinsdale Snowmobile Trail, NH 63, and NH 119: 7.8 mi. (12.6 km.), 900 ft., 4 hr. 20 min.

Old Spofford Road

This woods road runs south from the Beal's Road trailhead to the trailhead for the Snow Brook Trail. The southern half may be driven during the dry season from late spring through late autumn; however, parking is limited, and hikers are encouraged to use the designated trailhead parking areas. The northern half of this trail is extremely wet (particularly in spring) and may be flooded under a foot of water, making rubber boots or waders desirable. During the winter, the road is used by snowmobiles and may be well packed at times. The route is fairly obvious throughout its length despite the lack of signs or blazes. The Beal's Road trailhead can be reached by following Old Swanzey Rd. 1.8 mi. southeast from Tuttle Rd. Turn right onto a dirt road (sign) and follow it 0.6 mi. south to a small clearing with trail signs and limited parking.

The trail follows the unsigned dirt road south, passing a beaver pond to the right almost immediately. The woods road on the right at 0.1 mi. bypasses the wet areas that lie ahead, running on higher terrain, but is unblazed, unsigned, and difficult to follow. Shortly thereafter the main road passes through a boggy area, which may be flooded with a great deal of water. There is a stone wall to the right that may be used as a bypass if necessary. Several unmarked woods roads on either side should not be followed. At 0.5 mi. the trail passes through another extremely wet area with an old beaver lodge to the left. The road then enters a hemlock forest and becomes temporarily drier. A small brook is crossed at 0.8 mi. and, after a short descent, another significant wet, marshy area is crossed at 1.1 mi. Shortly, a small brook is forded and the Old Spofford Road ascends gradually to higher and drier ground.

A small parking area to the left marks the northern limit for motorized travel during the dry season. An attractive white pine grove on the right is followed by a small beaver pond with lodge and dam. At 1.9 mi., red-blazed boundary markers are passed as the road leaves Chesterfield and enters Winchester. Within a short distance, a small parking area appears on the left marked by a yellow ribbon, with an unmarked woods road to the right. (This is the abandoned northern end of the Orchard Trail. Due to negotiations between the landowner and the state park, there are no signs or blazes and hikers are currently forbidden to use the northern part of the trail that crosses private land; hikers are encouraged to use the section of the Orchard Trail from John Hill Road to the Snow Brook Trail only.) From here, it is 0.7 mi. south past several private homes to the trailhead for the Snow Brook Trail with its ample parking, and 0.2 mi. beyond to John Hill Road.

Distances from Beal's Road trailhead (980')

- *to* northern limit of motorized travel (890'): 1.2 mi., 0 ft. (rev. 100 ft.), 35 min.
- *to* Chesterfield–Winchester town line (950'): 1.9 mi., 50 ft., 1 hr.
- *to* Orchard Trail (980'): 2.1 mi., 100 ft., 1 hr. 5 min.
- *to* Snow Brook Trail trailhead (920'): 2.7 mi. (4.3 km.), 100 ft. (rev. 50 ft.), 1 hr. 25 min.
- *to* John Hill Road (920'): 2.9 mi. (4.7 km.), 100 ft., 1 hr. 30 min.

Nash Trail

This trail connects the Old Chesterfield Road with the Fullam Pond Trail. It parallels the eastern shore of Fullam Pond with a connecting spur leading down to the Fullam Pond Dam and the southern terminus of the Fullam Pond Trail. It is not blazed but is well signed and easy to follow throughout its length.

Leaving the Old Chesterfield Road at a small parking area just south of the bridge over Broad Brook, the trail follows an old grassy road in a northerly direction past two wooden gateposts. After a short distance, Broad Brook, which drains Fullam Pond and runs south to the Ashuelot River, may be seen on the left in a small clearing. At 0.4 mi. a red boundary marker is reached as the trail passes from Winchester into Chesterfield and swings right. Shortly thereafter, a connecting spur leaves left downhill on an old grassy road. In 0.1 mi. the spur reaches the southern terminus of the Fullam Pond Trail, crosses Fullam Pond Dam on a grated walkway, and ends 0.1 mi. beyond at the eastern shore of Fullam Pond.

The main trail swings right and then left, passes a stone wall, crosses a small stream on a snowmobile bridge, swings left again, and ends at the Fullam Pond Trail just north of the South Woods Trail. From here it is 0.6 mi. south to the Fullam Pond Dam by the Fullam Pond Trail, 0.6 mi. north to Beal's Road by the Fullam Pond Trail, and 2.0 mi. northwest to the Horseshoe Rd. trailhead by the South Woods Trail and the Old Horseshoe Road.

Distances from Old Chesterfield Road (660')

- *to* spur to Fullam Pond Dam (690'): 0.5 mi., 50 ft., 15 min.
- *to* Fullam Pond Dam and Fullam Pond Trail via spur (680'): 0.6 mi., 50 ft., 20 min.
- *to* Fullam Pond Trail and South Woods Trail (690'): 1.2 mi. (1.9 km.), 50 ft., 40 min.

Fullam Pond Trail

This old road runs south from Old Swanzey Rd. to Fullam Pond, 50 yd. east of the Fullam Pond Dam at the Nash Trail Spur. Although the road is wide and easy to follow, the northern end has virtually no signs or blazes, so the trail is easier to follow from south to north. It crosses the small northeast arm of Fullam Pond on a small causeway—the park map makes it appear that the trail does not cross the pond—then leads directly to the short spur that runs from the Nash Trail to the Fullam Pond Dam at its southeast corner. The trail (no signs or blazes) leaves Old Swanzey Rd. 1.2 mi. southeast of Tuttle Rd. between a large white house (right) and a log cabin home (left) on an unmarked woods road with a chain-link gate. Permission should be requested from the owners of the white house before leaving cars here.

The trail follows the old road generally south into Pisgah State Park (signs) at 0.2 mi. Swing left, then right at an unmarked intersection where care should be made not to turn left onto one of several old roads. The route ascends gradually to a height-of-land at 0.8 mi. and shortly thereafter passes a beaver pond (left) in a wet marshy area. The road then descends gradually, following an enlarging stream (which eventually becomes an inlet brook for Fullam Pond), crossing it several times. Shortly after a snowmobile bridge over this stream, Beal's Road is reached (left) at 1.6 mi., marked only by Snowmobile Sign #1 in a hemlock forest.

The trail continues to descend, making several crossings of the same stream, which has now enlarged to a small brook. The Nash Trail (left) and the South Woods Trail (right) are reached at 2.2 mi. Shortly after crossing another snowmobile bridge, the abandoned southeast fork of the South Woods Trail (right) is reached. The trail now follows a large inlet brook south as it enters the northern cove of Fullam Pond. At 2.5 mi. the road crosses the northeast corner of Fullam Pond on a causeway with a small spillway in the center. The trail re-enters the woods, with numerous unmarked paths (right) leading to the eastern shore of Fullam Pond. The trail ends at the unmarked Nash Trail Spur, 0.1 mi. west of the Nash Trail and 50 yd. east of the Fullam Pond Dam and the pond's eastern shore.

Distances from Old Swanzey Road (1030')

> *to* Pisgah State Park boundary (1030'): 0.2 mi., 0 ft., 5 min.
>
> *to* beaver pond at height-of-land (1050'): 0.9 mi., 50 ft., 30 min.
>
> *to* Beal's Road at Snowmobile Sign #1 (790'): 1.6 mi., 50 ft. (rev. 250 ft.), 50 min.
>
> *to* Nash Trail and South Woods Trail (690'): 2.2 mi., 50 ft. (rev. 100 ft.), 1 hr. 10 min.
>
> *to* spillway at northeast corner of Fullam Pond (680'): 2.5 mi., 50 ft., 1 hr. 15 min.
>
> *to* Nash Trail spur, just east of Fullam Pond Dam (680'): 2.8 mi. (4.5 km.), 50 ft., 1 hr. 25 min.

Beal's Road

This historic road ascends from the Beal's Road trailhead along the southern side of Beal's Knob and descends past a historic eighteenth-century graveyard on its way to the Fullam Pond Trail. It is well signed at its trailhead and easy to follow; however, it is designated only by Snowmobile Sign #1 at its jct. with the Fullam Pond Trail. Beal's Road trailhead may be reached by following Old

Swanzey Rd. 1.8 mi. southeast from Tuttle Rd. Turn right onto a signed dirt road and follow it 0.6 mi. south to a small clearing with trail signs and limited parking.

From the trailhead, the route passes an orange gate and follows an old grassy road, almost immediately reaching the lower junction of the Beal's Knob Trail (right). Both trails are marked with blue diamond blazes as part of the Beal's Knob Cross-Country Ski Loop over the summit. The road passes the northern shore of a significant beaver pond with its lodge (left) and ascends 0.4 mi. to a height-of-land and the upper junction of the Beal's Knob Trail (right), which leads in 0.4 mi. to the summit of Beal's Knob with its fine view of Mt. Monadnock.

No longer marked by blue blazes, Beal's Road descends into the forest and passes the Latham Beal Cemetery (1790) with its weathered stone markers. The road swings right, enters a mixed softwood forest, and descends gradually to the Fullam Pond Trail (Snowmobile Sign #1), 1.6 mi. south of Old Swanzey Rd. and 1.1 mi. north of the Fullam Pond Dam.

Distances from Beal's Road trailhead (990')

   to Beal's Knob Trail, upper junction (1080'): 0.4 mi., 100 ft., 15 min.

   to Latham Beal Cemetery (840'): 0.7 mi., 100 ft. (rev. 250 ft.), 25 min.

   to Fullam Pond Trail at Snowmobile Sign #1 (790'): 1.1 mi. (1.8 km.), 100 ft. (rev. 50 ft.), 35 min.

Beal's Knob Trail

This trail, marked with blue diamond cross-country ski blazes, ascends Beal's Knob, an attractive lookout with fine views east toward Mt. Monadnock. It leaves the Beal's Road just beyond the orange gate at the Beal's Road trailhead and ascends a grassy road around the north side of the Beal's Knob. At 0.3 mi. the trail swings left (south) through a hemlock forest and reaches a three-way jct., where a spur trail leaves left 0.2 mi. to the summit of Beal's Knob with its fine view. The main trail bears right, passes a stone wall, swings left onto an old road, passes two more stone walls, and ascends gradually to the Beal's Road at its height-of-land. From here it is 0.7 mi. right (west) to the Fullam Pond Trail and 0.4 mi. left (east) back downhill to the Beal's Road trailhead.

Distances from Beal's Road trailhead (990')

   to spur path to Beal's Knob summit (1100'): 0.4 mi., 100 ft., 15 min.

   to Beal's Knob summit via spur path (1180'): 0.6 mi., 200 ft., 25 min.

to Beal's Road at height-of-land (1080'): 0.6 mi. (1.0 km.), 100 ft., 20 min.

to starting point by complete loop to Beal's Knob summit via Beal's Knob Trail, spur path, and Beal's Road: 1.4 mi. (2.2 km.), 200 ft., 50 min.

Wapack Trail and Vicinity

Wapack Trail (Wapack Trail map by Friends of the Wapack; USGS Ashburnham, Peterborough South, Peterborough North, and Greenfield quads)

This trail follows the ridge of the Wapack Range, running mostly along the skyline for more than 21 mi. from Watatic Mtn. in Ashburnham MA over Barrett and Temple mountains and across the Pack Monadnocks in New Hampshire. There are many open ledges with fine views, and the spruce forest found in several places is similar to that of a more northern region. Refer to the USGS Ashburnham, Peterborough South, Peterborough North, and Greenfield quadrangles. The trail is blazed with yellow triangles and marked by cairns on open ledges. An organization named Friends of the Wapack (PO Box 115, West Peterborough, NH 03468, www.wapack.org) has been established to protect and maintain the trail; this group publishes a detailed guidebook and map to the Wapack Trail.

Section 1. Watatic Mountain. The southern end of the Wapack Trail begins in a small parking area off MA 119, about 1.5 mi. west of its jct. with MA 101 northeast of Ashburnham and 1.5 mi. east of the Massachusetts–New Hampshire border. The first part of the trail coincides with the Mid-State Trail. It passes a small pond and ascends to a jct. where it turns right; here the State Line Trail continues straight for 1.0 mi. and rejoins the Wapack Trail at the state line. The Wapack Trail climbs past two viewpoints to a shelter (Camp Gardner) in poor condition, then swings left and reaches the site of the former fire tower at the summit of Mt. Watatic (1836 ft.) at 1.2 mi., where there is a sweeping view. Here the old route of the Wapack Trail leaves on the right and makes a steep 0.6-mi. descent on a heavily used and badly eroded path along the power and telephone lines to MA 119, 0.7 mi. west of its junction with MA 101 northeast of Ashburnham (0.8 mi. east of the current trailhead of the Wapack). The Wapack Trail turns left and descends northwest across old ski trails and through spruce woods that are a state bird sanctuary, then crosses overgrown pastures on Nutting Hill, passing the summit, a ledgy area in a clearing, at 2.0 mi. The Wapack Trail then descends to a jct. near cellar holes (obscured by bushes) that mark the Nutting Place, settled by James Spaulding just before the American Revolution and continued by his son-in-law, Jonas Nutting, until about 1840. Here the Mid-State Trail turns left and joins the State Line Trail in a short distance.

From the Nutting Place jct. the trail continues north on a long-abandoned road into beech woods, and at 2.4 mi. it crosses a wall that runs east-west on the Massachusetts–New Hampshire border, where the Mid-State Trail and State Line Trail end on the left. A few yards west of the trail, close to the wall, are two stone survey monuments, one erected in 1834. Recent logging may cause sections of the trail between the state line and Binney Hill Rd. to be obscure. The trail continues north past the old woods roads and cellar holes of long-deserted farms, and reaches Binney Hill Rd. at 3.5 mi. This part of Binney Hill Rd. is no longer maintained, and it is possible to drive in from NH 119 for only about 0.3 mi. to an area where parking is limited because of private residences. The trail turns left (west) on this road and follows it for 0.2 mi. to the point where the Barrett Mtn. section of the Wapack Trail turns to the right off the road.

Section II. Barrett Mountain. The Barrett Mtn. section of the Wapack Trail runs from Binney Hill Rd. to the site of the former Wapack Lodge on NH 123/124. Recent logging may cause sections in the Binney Pond Rd. and Binney Ponds area to be obscure. Shortly after leaving Binney Hill Rd. at 3.7 mi. (sign, "Pond Trail"), the trail crosses a small brook, then skirts the Binney Ponds near their west shores. (Flooding from beaver dams may require a detour here.) The trail traverses the ridge of Barrett Mtn., nearly 3 mi. long and partly wooded, with four summits (the highest is 1885 ft.) and numerous outlooks. Two private trails intersect the Wapack Trail along this ridge, so hikers should be especially careful to identify the Wapack Trail at any junctions. In the saddle between the third and fourth summits, the trail crosses the location of one of the oldest roads from Massachusetts to the hill towns, the Boston Road, built in 1753. After descending from the northern end of Barrett Mtn., the trail enters an area where it encounters several ski trails, ascends an outlying knoll, then descends to the site of Wapack Lodge, which was located near NH 123/124 on the site of a house built in 1776 by Deacon John Brown of Concord MA.

Section III. Kidder Mountain. The Wapack Trail next crosses the lower western slopes of Kidder Mtn. (1805 ft.). From the Wapack Lodge site it crosses the highway at 9.1 mi. and enters a dirt road opposite the lodge driveway, and soon enters the woods. At 9.7 mi. the trail turns left on an old grassy road with bordering stone walls and crosses under a power line 150 yd. beyond. (A blue-blazed side trail leads right from here along the power lines, then left into the woods through a recently logged area to the summit of Kidder Mtn. at

0.9 mi., where there are good views) The Wapack Trail descends to a jct. with a gravel road from the left at a pond on the right. Here it turns right onto a woods road, crosses the pond outlet, and ascends gradually to the Wildcat Hill–Conant Hill saddle, where there is an old homestead site to the right. The trail descends gradually, still on the old roadway, and crosses the outlet of a beaver pond on the right. It then bears left onto Todd Rd. at 11.0 mi. and continues to Nashua Rd. (the road from Temple to Jaffrey) at 11.4 mi.

Section IV. Temple Mountain. The trail crosses Nashua Rd. and continues straight ahead along Temple Rd. for 0.4 mi., bears right at a fork, then turns right 30 yd. beyond to follow a dirt road for a short distance before entering the woods. (From Temple Rd. north, the trail passes through private land known as Avelinda Forest. Please observe the No Fires—No Smoking rules posted in the forest.) The trail then ascends the south end of Temple Mtn., which has several bare summits, though the highest summit, Holt Peak (2045 ft.), is broad, wooded, and viewless, while the southern summit, Burton Peak (2010 ft.), has limited views in several directions. At 12.1 mi. the trail emerges on the open Sharon Ledges, with intermittent views for the next 0.7 mi. At 13.2 mi., a short distance south of Burton Peak, the Berry Pasture Trail leaves left and descends 0.9 mi. through an abandoned pasture and down an old woods road to end at Mountain Rd., at a point 0.6 mi. northeast of the Sharon Arts Center on NH 123.

Shortly before reaching Holt Peak, the trail crosses a stone wall, then turns sharp left and parallels the wall a short distance before climbing to the summit at 14.3 mi. (An alternate route, used mostly as a ski bypass and marked by old red blazes, continues straight ahead beyond the wall, swings to the east of the summit, and rejoins the main trail 0.3 mi. north of the summit.) The trail follows the ridge, which has wide views, especially toward Grand Monadnock. Stone monuments mark the Sharon–Temple town line, which also follows this ridge. From the north summit the trail descends through the Temple Mountain Ski Area to NH 101 in Peterborough Gap at 16.2 mi., a few yards east of the road up South Pack Monadnock, which leaves NH 101 at the height-of-land.

Section V. Pack Monadnock. This extended ridge culminates in two open peaks, Pack Monadnock (2290 ft.), usually called South Pack Monadnock, and North Pack Monadnock (2276 ft.); pack is an Indian word meaning "little." The mountain stands between the towns of Peterborough and Temple and is a well-known landmark in southern New Hampshire and eastern Massachusetts. On the summit of South Pack is a small state reservation, General James Miller Park. (To reach the park, drive up the road that starts at the parking lot located just off NH 101, about 100 yd. west of the Temple Mtn. parking lot.)

The Wapack Trail crosses NH 101 just east of the state park sign, enters the woods, and reaches a trail jct. 25 yd. east of the parking area (sign, "Foot Trails," at the east end of the parking area). The blue-blazed trail on the right is the former route of the Wapack Trail, now the Marion Davis Trail.

Marion Davis Trail. This trail, 1.4 mi. long, angles up the east side of the mountain, then climbs moderately, passing near two radio towers, and reaches the automobile road at the summit just to the right of a small shed. It may be used to provide a convenient loop to the summit of South Pack Monadnock. The official Wapack Trail is more scenic but also somewhat more difficult than the Marion Davis Trail, particularly for descent.

The Wapack Trail continues north from the trail jct. near the parking area, crosses the automobile road, and immediately scrambles up a steep ledge. Turning northwest, it skirts the crest of ledges with views southwest and passes two crevice caves. The trail turns east through woods and over ledges, crosses a hollow, then runs north, angling upward parallel to the automobile road through a beautiful hemlock forest to the Summit Loop Trail, which enters on the right and continues straight ahead, making a loop around the summit 0.5 mi. long. The Wapack Trail then turns sharp right and ascends, coinciding with the Summit Loop Trail, to the fire tower on the summit of South Pack at 17.6 mi. Here the Summit Loop Trail diverges and descends into the woods to the left of the shed where the Marion Davis Trail also leaves the summit area. The Wapack Trail continues north from the north end of the summit road to the left of a stone lean-to (sign, Wapack) and descends gradually over ledges, crossing the Summit Loop Trail. A short distance to the left on the Summit Loop Trail is the upper end of the Raymond Trail. A new path, the Spruce Knoll Trail, runs east from the summit 0.3 mi. to a dead-end loop around a wooded, ledgy knoll.

Raymond Trail. This white-blazed trail ascends the west slope of the mountain 1050 ft. (rev. 100 ft.) in 1.6 mi. from East Mountain Rd. at a point 1.2 mi. northwest of the Miller State Park lower parking area via East Mountain Rd., Old Mountain Rd., and NH 101. The upper part of this trail is steep in places but offers several good views.

The Wapack Trail leads down the wooded north slope past a spring, ascends over the knoll sometimes called the Middle Peak, and reaches the jct. with the Cliff Trail on the right at 19.3 mi.

Cliff Trail. This blue-blazed trail is a longer and rougher but more scenic alternative route from here to the summit of North Pack. It descends sharply downhill for 0.3 mi., then swings north and ascends several rocky knolls with excellent views toward the southern Wapack Range and Grand Monadnock. At

0.7 mi., at the top of the South Cliff (the best viewpoint), a connecting path leads right 0.1 mi. to Ted's Trail. The Cliff Trail swings right and the grade eases as the trail follows an undulating ridge. It passes a jct. with Ted's Trail on the right at 1.0 mi., and rejoins the Wapack Trail at the summit of North Pack at 1.2 mi.

The main Wapack Trail ascends directly to the summit of North Pack at 20.0 mi. This ledgy peak provides fine views of central New Hampshire, the Contoocook River valley, and, on a clear day, Mt. Washington and other White Mtn. peaks. The trail descends north, northwest, then north again through overgrown pastures (take care to distinguish the trail from other paths), and ends at Old Mountain Rd., 2.6 mi. west of NH 31 (via Old Mtn. Rd. to Russell Station Rd.). In addition to the route provided by the Wapack Trail, two new trails (Ted's Trail and Carolyn's Trail, described below) make possible a loop hike to North Pack Monadnock (2276 ft.) from the north, with views from several ledges along the way.

Distances from MA 119 (1250')

- *to* Watatic Mtn. summit (1836'): 1.2 mi., 600 ft., 55 min.
- *to* Binney Hill Rd. near Binney Ponds (1360'): 3.7 mi., 800 ft. (rev. 700 ft.), 2 hr. 15 min.
- *to* Barrett Mtn., south summit (1826'): 5.1 mi., 1500 ft. (rev. 200 ft.), 3 hr. 20 min.
- *to* Barrett Mtn., north summit (1850'): 7.5 mi., 1950 ft. (rev. 450 ft.), 4 hr. 45 min.
- *to* NH 123/124 (1450'): 9.1 mi., 2050 ft. (rev. 500 ft.), 5 hr. 35 min.
- *to* Nashua Rd. (1240'): 11.4 mi., 2250 ft. (rev. 400 ft.), 6 hr. 50 min.
- *to* Temple Mtn., main summit (Holt Peak, 2045'): 14.3 mi., 3250 ft. (rev. 200 ft.), 8 hr. 45 min.
- *to* NH 101 (1480'): 16.2 mi., 3350 ft. (rev. 700 ft.), 9 hr. 45 min.
- *to* South Pack Monadnock summit (2290'): 17.6 mi., 4200 ft., 10 hr. 55 min.
- *to* North Pack Monadnock summit (2276'): 20.0 mi., 4850 ft. (rev. 650 ft.), 12 hr. 25 min.
- *to* Old Mountain Rd. (1310'): 21.6 mi. (34.8 km.), 4850 ft. (rev. 950 ft.), 13 hr. 15 min.

Ted's Trail (Wapack Trail map, USGS Greenfield quad)

From NH 31 at the blinking light in Greenfield, go south 2.8 mi. and turn right (west) onto Russell Station Rd. In 0.8 mi. turn right onto Mountain Rd., and at 1.4 mi. from NH 31 the trail (sign, yellow blazes) begins on the left, with parking for several cars on the right. The trail runs level through a wet area, crosses a brook on a bridge at 0.2 mi., and ascends easily to a jct. at 0.5 mi. where Carolyn's Trail diverges right. Here Ted's Trail bears left, crosses a skid road and a bridge over a brook, and meanders through a beautiful stand of red pine. It swings right and crosses two small brooks, then a larger brook on a bridge at the foot of a waterfall at 1.0 mi. It turns sharp left and climbs to the top of the waterfall, where a connector trail diverges right, leading 0.2 mi. to Carolyn's Trail. Ted's Trail climbs alongside the brook, passing several more waterfalls and skirting a logged area. At 1.5 mi. it enters the Wapack National Wildlife Refuge, and at 1.8 mi. it swings to the right, up the slope and away from the brook. In 200 yd. it crosses a stone wall and turns sharp left, then ascends through spruces and ledgy areas, passing a view back to the north at 2.2 mi. In another 120 yd. the trail turns left where a connecting path ascends 0.1 mi. right to Carolyn's Trail.

At 2.4 mi. Ted's Trail turns sharp right on a ledge with a view east and climbs over ledges with occasional views southeast toward the Boston skyline. It turns right again at 2.6 mi. where a branch trail diverges left. The branch trail traverses 0.1 mi. through an open area to the Cliff Trail at the top of the South Cliff, which offers a 180-degree panorama—the best view on the mountain. From the jct., Ted's Trail ascends north along the east side of the ridge, crossing a ledge with a view east at 2.8 mi. In another 50 yd. Carolyn's Trail joins from the right, and Ted's Trail turns left and climbs steeply for 0.1 mi. to the blue-blazed Cliff Trail. To the right, the Cliff Trail ascends easily over ledges and reaches the summit of North Pack in 0.2 mi. Ledges around the summit area provide views west, north, and east. Descending, there is no sign for Ted's Trail where it diverges left from the Cliff Trail; but there is a sign for the Cliff Trail opposite the jct.

Distances from Mountain Rd. (950')

   to Cliff Trail (2200'): 2.9 mi. (4.7 km.), 1250 ft., 2 hr. 5 min.

   to summit of North Pack Monadnock (2276') via Cliff Trail: 3.1 mi. (5.0 km.), 1350 ft., 2 hr. 15 min.

Carolyn's Trail (Wapack Trail map, USGS Greenfield quad)

This yellow-blazed trail links the lower and upper ends of Ted's Trail, providing a more direct route to North Pack. It diverges right from Ted's Trail, 0.5 mi. from Mountain Rd. At 0.1 mi. it turns left on a relocated section around a swamp. At 0.2 mi. it turns right where a connecting path diverges left, leading 0.2 mi. over a low ridge to Ted's Trail. Carolyn's Trail ascends at easy grades, passing through a stone wall at 0.4 mi. At 1.0 mi. the grade increases, and at 1.3 mi. the trail enters a beautiful spruce forest. At 1.7 mi. a connecting path diverges left, descending 0.1 mi. to Ted's Trail. Carolyn's Trail continues ahead and climbs up open ledges to its upper jct. with Ted's Trail, 0.3 mi. below the summit of North Pack.

Distance from lower junction with Ted's Trail (1000')

    to upper junction with Ted's Trail (2150'): 1.8 mi. (2.9 km.), 1150 ft., 1 hr. 30 min.

Distance from Mountain Rd. (950')

    for loop hike to North Pack Monadnock (2276') via Ted's Trail, Cliff Trail, and Carolyn's Trail, including side trip to South Cliff: 5.9 mi. (9.5 km.), 1350 ft., 3 hr. 40 min.

Crotched Mountain

Crotched Mtn. (2066 ft.) is in Francestown and Bennington, with a south spur in Greenfield. There are excellent views from various ledges along the ridgecrest, though none at the summit itself, where there are communications towers and abandoned buildings. The ski trails of the recently reopened Crotched Mountain Ski Area are on the north slopes of the mountain. In recent years the hiking trail system has been greatly expanded, with a major new trailhead in the Crotched Mountain Town Forest in Francestown. Refer to the USGS Greenfield, Peterborough North, Hillsboro, and Deering quadrangles.

Shannon's Trail (USGS Greenfield and Peterborough North quads)

This new yellow-blazed trail has largely superceded the older, unmarked Greenfield Trail as the preferred and more scenic route from the trailhead near the Crotched Mountain Rehabilitation Center. From NH 31 0.9 mi. north of Greenfield, turn onto Crotched Mountain Rd. Pass Gilbert Verney Drive on the right 1.4 mi. from NH 31 and park on the side of the road 0.1 mi. farther where there is a gated road and kiosk with trail map on the left. Do not block the gate. The trail enters the woods to the right beyond the kiosk and in 100 yd. ascends along the left edge of a meadow with views to the east and Crotched Mtn. in sight ahead. It re-enters the woods, crosses a gravel road at 0.2 mi., and ascends easily to an open grassy knoll at 0.5 mi. with fine views in all directions. (This knoll can also be reached by following the gravel road.) The trail passes to the right of radio towers and enters scrubby woods. At 0.6 mi. the well-worn footway of the Greenfield Trail (which starts on the gravel road from the trailhead and then follows a series of woods, roads, and footpaths) joins from the right, and at 0.8 mi. Nancy's Trail diverges right. Shannon's Trail descends slightly, then contours the slope and crosses a brook at 1.2 mi. It ascends moderately, and at 1.4 mi. it turns right where the upper section of the Greenfield Trail (sign, "To Bennington Trail") diverges left and ascends 0.1 mi. to the Bennington Trail. From this jct. Shannon's Trail climbs steeply over ledges, passing a connecting path leading 80 yd. left to the Bennington Trail at 1.5 mi. It continues to ascend, crossing two ledges with good views south, and scrambles up the left side of a large open ledge just below the summit, with excellent views south and west. The trail ends behind the top of the ledge, where it meets Cindy's Trail. From here a rough path climbs 125 yd. to the viewless, unattractive summit.

Distances from Crotched Mountain Rd. (1300')

> *to*   grassy knoll (1510'): 0.5 mi., 200 ft., 20 min.

> *to*   Cindy's Trail at open ledge near summit (2040'): 1.8 mi., 800 ft. (rev. 50 ft.), 1 hr. 20 min.

Bennington Trail (USGS Greenfield and Peterborough North quads)

From NH 31, 1.6 mi. south of the flashing light in Bennington, turn east onto Mountain Rd. (sign for Bennington Trail). At 0.4 mi. from NH 31 bear to the far right onto a dirt road at a three-way fork. The trail (sign) begins on the right 0.2 mi. up this somewhat rough road; there is limited parking at the trailhead, or one may park beside the road on the left just beyond the last house. The trail turns sharp right off the dirt road and follows an old woods road to a double cairn and sign, where it turns left. Follow it with care. It crosses several brooks, passes a spring, then begins to climb more steeply to its jct. with the Greenfield Trail at 1.2 mi. Here it turns sharp left, while a connecting path runs ahead 80 yd. to

Shannon's Trail. The Bennington and Greenfield trails now coincide, climbing rather steeply to a side path right to the large open ledge at the upper terminus of Shannon's Trail. The main trail continues another 100 yd. to the summit.

Distances from trailhead on dirt road (1000')

>   *to* Greenfield Trail (1750'): 1.0 mi., 750 ft., 55 min.

>   *to* Crotched Mtn. summit (2066'): 1.4 mi. (2.3 km.), 1050 ft., 1 hr. 15 min.

Summit Trail (USGS Greenfield quad)

This trail makes a loop over the eastern half of Crotched Mtn.'s ridgecrest (though it does not go to the true summit), offering views from a number of ledges. From NH 136, 1.9 mi. north of Greenfield and 2.5 mi. south of Francestown, turn west onto Farrington Rd. and immediately bear right into the parking area for the Crotched Mountain Town Forest, where there is a kiosk with a trail map. Follow the Link Trail to the left of the kiosk. This connecting path bears left at 0.1 mi., crosses a footbridge over a flooded area, and runs at easy grades through logged areas to Bullard Rd. (a gravel road on which vehicle access is restricted) at 0.7 mi. The Summit Trail (sign) starts across the road. Various segments of the Summit Trail were previously known as Miki's Trail, Cindy's Trail, and Randy's Trail; these names may still appear on signs at some jct. Mileages given below include the approach on the Link Trail. From Bullard Rd., the yellow-blazed Summit Trail soon bears right and comes to a fork at 0.8 mi. The loop is described in the counterclockwise direction, taking the right (east) fork for the ascent. The trail crosses a brook at 1.2 mi. and skirts the edge of a beaver pond. It then runs along the left edge of a field for 75 yd., re-enters the woods at a yellow-painted stake, and swings right to cross a woods road where the white-blazed Scot's Trail joins from the left. The two trails coincide for 60 yd., then the Summit Trail turns left as Scot's Trail diverges right. At 1.6 mi. Nancy's Trail diverges left at the edge of a beaver swamp. The Summit Trail runs along the edge of the swamp, climbs through a grove of large pines and hemlocks, and at 2.1 mi. crosses a woods road (signed "Old Mt. Road."). It climbs steeply along the base of a talus slope and at 2.3 mi. swings left to ascend the ridge; to this point, the trail was formerly called Miki's Trail, and the next section was a part of Cindy's Trail. After a short steep climb a side path leads 50 yd. left to a ledge with a view east. The main trail ascends past another outlook and reaches open ledges with views south at 2.6 mi. It meanders along the crest with minor ups and downs, soon crossing a ledge with a view north. At 2.9 mi. it emerges on a rocky knob with more views, then descends to a col and makes a winding climb to the next knob. It descends past a southeast viewpoint to a jct. at 3.3 mi. Here Cindy's Trail continues ahead 0.5 mi. to the ledge near the true summit, while the Summit Trail (from here back to the loop junction formerly known as Randy's Trail) turns left and makes a steep, rough descent for 0.2 mi., passing a cut view toward Mt. Monadnock. It continues down at a moderate grade, crossing Nancy's Trail at 4.0 mi. At 4.2 mi. the white-blazed Scot's Trail joins from the left just before a brook crossing, then soon diverges right; the two trails merge and diverge three more times in the next 0.4 mi. The Summit Trail passes by a marsh with a view up to Crotched Mtn. and reaches the loop jct. at 5.0 mi. Turn right to reach Bullard Rd. in 0.1 mi. and the parking area via the Link Trail in another 0.7 mi.

Distances from Crotched Mountain Town Forest parking area (915')

> *to*   beginning of Summit Trail (960') via Link Trail: 0.7 mi., 50 ft., 25 min.
>
> *to*   junction with Cindy's Trail via east loop of Summit Trail(1970'): 3.3 mi., 1200 ft. (rev. 150 ft.), 2 hr. 15 min.
>
> for loop back to parking area via west loop of Summit Trail and Link Trail: 5.8 mi. (9.3 km.), 1200 ft., 3 hr. 30 min.

Cindy's Trail (USGS Greenfield quad)

This short trail provides a link between the Summit Trail, at the point where it descends off the ridgecrest, and Shannon's Trail at the outlook ledge just below the true summit. Leaving the Summit Trail, it contours westward along the south side of the ridgecrest, descends, then climbs along the base of wooded ledges to meet Shannon's Trail at the back of the outlook ledge.

Distance from Summit Trail (1970')

> *to*   Shannon's Trail (2040'): 0.5 mi. (0.8 km.), 150 ft. (rev. 100 ft.), 20 min.

Nancy's Trail (USGS Greenfield quad)

This trail runs along the southern base of the mountain, linking Shannon's Trail with the west and east loops of the Summit Trail. Along with these trails and Cindy's Trail, it makes possible a loop over the entire ridgecrest from the Crotched Mountain Town Forest parking area. At its east end it leaves the east loop of the Summit Trail 1.6 mi. from the parking area, descends to a low spot beside a stone wall, then ascends to cross the west loop of the Summit Trail at

0.6 mi. It crosses a brook and switchbacks up the side of a ridge, then turns left at a cairn and meanders across the flat crest to meet Shannon's Trail at 1.2 mi.

Distance from east loop of Summit Trail (1200')

   to Shannon's Trail (1600'): 1.2 mi. (1.9 km.), 550 ft. (rev. 150 ft.), 50 min.

Distance from Crotched Mountain Town Forest parking area (915')

   for complete loop over Crotched Mtn. ridge via Link Trail, east loop of Summit Trail, Cindy's Trail, Shannon's Trail, Nancy's Trail and west loop of Summit Trail: 7.2 mi. (11.6 km.), 1350 ft., 4 hr. 15 min.

Fox Research Forest

This 1,455-acre preserve in the town of Hillsborough features a network of about 20 mi. of nature trails and multi-use trails. The environmental center, where an informational brochure with a map of the trail system can usually be obtained, is located about 2 mi. from the center of Hillsborough on Hillsborough Center Rd. (which leaves US 202/NH 9 in Hillsborough village roughly opposite NH 149). Refer to the USGS Hillsboro Upper Village and Hillsboro quadrangles. There are few distant views, except for the cleared view south to Monadnock from the observation tower on the side of Monroe Hill, but there are almost unlimited possibilities for short, medium, and even long woods walks by stringing together trail sections according to the desires of the visitor. The Ridge Trail, 10 mi. long, is the central artery circling through Fox State Forest and connecting with most of the other trails. Short nature walks are available on the popular Tree I.D. Trail and Mushroom Trail, while Mud Pond and Black Gum Swamp offer somewhat longer walks. Black Gum Swamp, which supports a stand of black gum (also known as tupelo) trees—quite rare in New Hampshire—is of particular interest to students of the New Hampshire woodlands. Mud Pond, whose name fails to suggest the beauty of this small pond surrounded by quaking bog with many interesting plant species, is the jewel of the area.

Skatutakee and Thumb Mountains

Skatutakee Mtn. (1998 ft.) and Thumb Mtn. (1978 ft.), located in the town of Hancock, offer interesting views, particularly to the south, from their open ledges. Refer to the USGS Marlborough quadrangle. The trails on these mountains, as well as a number of other trails nearby, are maintained by the Harris

Center for Conservation Education, which is the focal point of a 7000-acre tract of land that is maintained primarily as wildlife habitat by the cooperative effort of the Harris Center, the New Hampshire Audubon Society, the Society for the Protection of New Hampshire Forests, the New Hampshire Fish and Game Department, the town of Hancock, and a number of private landowners. To reach the Harris Center follow NH 123 west from its jct. with NH 137 for 2.2 mi.; turn left at a small Harris Center sign and follow Hunt Pond Rd. for 0.4 mi.; then turn left on King's Highway and follow it another 0.5 mi. to the Harris Center's parking lot. A trail map is usually available at the center when it is open. From here the Harriskat Trail leads to the summit of Skatutakee Mtn., which has the best views; on the return a loop hike may be made by taking the Thumbs Up Trail from Skatutakee Mtn. to Thumb Mtn., then descending to the parking lot via the Thumbs Down Trail. The Cadot Trail (formerly Bee Line Trail) ascends Skatutakee Mtn. from the south. These trails are not heavily blazed and must be followed with care. Finding the correct trail at the summit of Skatutakee also requires a bit of care. Near the large cairn on the highest ledge a double-ended light-blue arrow is painted on the ledge. Follow the arrow away from the cairn. In a short distance the Harriskat Trail (sign, "Harris Center") leaves on the right; a bit farther on the Thumbs Up Trail (sign, "Thumb"; marked by white plastic triangles) also leaves on the right; and the Cadot Trail (light blue blazes) continues ahead.

Harriskat Trail (USGS Marlborough quad)

This white-blazed trail begins on King's Highway (sign) opposite the main building of the Harris Center, just northwest of a sign for the Briggs Preserve. At 0.2 mi. it turns sharp right onto an older route of the trail (descending, turn sharp left off the old route). It crosses a wet area with several large boulders and at 0.6 mi. reaches the jct. with the Thumbs Down Trail to Thumb Mtn. The Harriskat Trail bears left uphill, then soon swings left onto a broad ridge and climbs across a stone wall, ascending with alternating moderate climbs and nearly level sections on the contour. At 0.9 mi. the trail runs level across a small boulder field, and at 1.2 mi. an unmarked, unsigned side trail enters on the left at a sharp right turn where the main trail is signed "Harris Center" for the descent. The trail now runs mostly through stands of conifers, and high up it passes a narrow outlook left through trees to Crotched Mtn. It climbs on ledges, then runs level across more ledges and reaches the summit, which is the highest of several jumbled ledges in an extensive open area. Here there are good views of Crotched Mtn., the Wapack Range, and Monadnock. The Cadot (formerly Bee Line) Trail enters here; the Thumbs Up Trail to Thumb Mtn. leaves the Cadot Trail on the right about 40 yd. from the summit.

Distances from King's Highway (1290')

   to Thumbs Down Trail (1400'): 0.6 mi., 100 ft., 20 min.

   to summit of Skatutakee Mtn. (1998'): 1.6 mi. (2.5 km.), 700 ft., 1 hr. 10 min.

   to starting point by complete loop via Harriskat Trail, Thumbs Up Trail, and Thumbs Down Trail: 4.9 mi. (7.9 km.), 900 ft., 2 hr. 55 min.

Thumbs Up Trail (USGS Marlborough quad)

This trail connects the summits of Skatutakee Mtn. and Thumb Mtn. From the summit of Skatutakee; descend on the Cadot Trail for about 40 yd., then turn right (sign, "Thumb"). The trail is well marked with white plastic triangles, though the footway is not always well beaten. The trail descends through a dark coniferous forest and, at the foot of the descent from Skatutakee Mtn. at 0.3 mi., makes a very sharp left turn, then soon leaves the dark coniferous forest and winds about a great deal on a fairly level ridge. At 1.0 mi. the trail reaches the jct. where the Thumbs Down Trail (marked by yellow blazes) enters on the right. The Thumbs Up Trail now ascends steeply to the summit of the first knob of Thumb Mtn., where it levels, descends slightly, crosses a stone wall, and resumes a moderate ascent to the summit of Thumb Mtn. at 1.3 mi. The trail continues 50 yd. to a ledge with views to Monadnock and the Wapack Range.

Distances from summit of Skatutakee Mtn. (1998')

   to junction with Thumbs Down Trail (1820'): 1.0 mi., 50 ft. (rev. 250 ft.), 30 min.

   to summit of Thumb Mtn. (1978'): 1.3 mi. (2.0 km.), 200 ft., 45 min.

Thumbs Down Trail (USGS Marlborough quad)

This trail descends from the Thumbs Up Trail at a jct. 0.3 mi. east of the summit of Thumb Mtn., completing the Skatutakee–Thumb loop. Since this loop is described in this guide for the clockwise direction, the Thumbs Down Trail is described here for the descent. Marked by yellow blazes, it descends from the jct. at the foot of Thumb Mtn. across several stone walls and reaches the north shore of Jacks Pond at 0.6 mi., at a point where a side path descends to the right

20 yd. to the edge of the pond. In another 100 yd. the trail makes a 90° turn to the left and follows a woods road downhill, crossing the outlet brook from Jacks Pond. At 1.0 mi. the trail bears to the right off the road, crosses a good-sized brook, and runs to the jct. with the Harriskat Trail 0.6 mi. from the Harris Center. If you are ascending by the Thumbs Down Trail, bear right (slightly downhill) at this jct.

Distance from junction with Thumbs Up Trail (1820')

   to junction with Harriskat Trail (1400'): 1.1 mi. (1.8 km.), 0 ft. (rev. 400 ft.), 35 min.

Cadot Trail (USGS Marlborough quad)

This trail (formerly called the Bee Line Trail) ascends Skatutakee Mtn. from the south. The trailhead is located on Old Dublin Rd. 1.1 mi. southwest of its jct. with King's Highway (this jct. is 0.7 mi. southeast of the Harris Center). Loop hikes can be made in combination with the direct trails from the Harris Center by means of the 1.8-mi. walk along King's Highway and Old Dublin Rd., both country gravel roads with little traffic.

   The trail (light blue blazes) ascends moderately on an old woods road lined with stone walls and furnished with rock culverts. At 0.3 mi. the trail levels and then climbs at gentle to easy grades. At 0.9 mi. it turns to the right off the road in an overgrown pasture and (now marked with light-green blazes) descends slightly to cross the bed of a small brook. It then begins a fairly steep ascent and crosses a stone wall. The grade becomes moderate, and the trail passes boulders with a limited outlook. The terrain becomes ledgy, and at a ledge—where there is a 5-ft.-high conical boulder about 10 yd. ahead in a level section—there is a fine view in the downhill direction of Monadnock framed by trees. At 1.4 mi. the trail crosses a stone wall on a ledge, and the grade becomes easy as the trail wanders around the summit ledges. The Thumbs Up Trail to Thumb Mtn. diverges left (sign, "Thumb," which is hard to see in ascending direction) about 40 yd. before the trail reaches the summit of Skatutakee Mtn., where there are good views of Crotched Mtn., the Wapack Range, and Monadnock.

Distance from Old Dublin Rd. (1160')

   to summit of Skatutakee Mtn. (1998'): 1.5 mi. (2.5 km.), 850 ft., 1 hr. 10 min.

Harris Center Trails

The Harris Center maintains several other trails that provide interesting walks, mostly over fairly easy terrain. T*he Dandelyon Trail* (yellow blazes) runs from the Harris Center, crossing the Boulder Train Trail twice. (The second [farther] crossing is not a true crossing; the Boulder Trail enters the Dandelyon Trail from the left, coincides with it for a while, then leaves on the right—this is not shown correctly on the Harris Center trail map.) It ends at a collection of erratic boulders at 0.5 mi. The *Boulder Train Trail* (blue blazes) is a loop 1.1 mi. long, with numbered stops keyed to an informational booklet available at the Harris Center. It involves more ascent and descent relative to its length than the other trails. It crosses the Dandelyon Trail twice, making possible an easy 0.2-mi. side trip to the boulders reached by that trail. The *Channing Trail* (red blazes) leaves the northeast corner of the Boulder Train Trail and makes a big 1.9-mi. loop back to King's Highway 0.7 mi. northwest of the Harris Center. The *Babbitt Trail* (red blazes) makes a 1.4-mi. loop in the woods northeast of NH 137. There is a connector trail, 0.2 mi. long, that runs between the trailhead of the Babbitt Trail on NH 137 and the Channing Trail at a point 1.4 mi. from the Harris Center via the Dandelyon Trail and Boulder Train Trail.

Two trails recently cut by the Harris Center but located at some distance from the main buildings offer interesting views. The *Cobb Hill Trail* leaves the end of the maintained section of Jacquith Rd., 0.6 mi. west of Old Dublin Rd. (parking on left, sign for Sydney Williams Woods), continues up the road for 0.6 mi., then turns left (sign) and follows a path up Cobb Hill marked by Harris Center trail markers to a cleared view of Mt. Monadnock at 1.3 mi. (550-ft. elevation gain). The upper section of the path is signed the "Jane Greene Trail." The *Kulish Ledges Trail* leaves the end of the regularly maintained section of Brickyard Rd. in Nelson, 0.7 mi. from Tolman Pond Rd. (parking on right just past private drive, sign for Harris Center). It continues up the road (recently improved for logging), diverges right on an old woods road at 0.4 mi. (no sign), takes the right fork at 0.6 mi. (Harris Center trail markers begin), climbs to the crest of a ridge, then descends slightly and rises to a ledge at 1.1 mi. (500-ft. elevation gain) with a restricted but attractive vista southeast toward Spoonwood Pond, Lake Nubanusit, and Thumb Mtn.

Peirce Reservation

Peirce Reservation comprises almost 3500 acres owned by the Society for the Protection of New Hampshire Forests.

Trout-n-Bacon Trail (USGS Stoddard quad)

The Trout-n-Bacon Trail provides access to secluded Trout Pond and views from Bacon Ledge. Follow NH 123 north for 1.7 mi. from its jct. with NH 9 to Mill Village. One trailhead is reached by following Shedd Hill Rd. (paved) north for 0.8 mi. to the trailhead, marked by an SPNHF sign (limited parking; do not block the woods road). The other is reached by following Old Antrim Rd. (gravel, also called Barrett Pond Rd.) 0.9 mi. east from Mill Village to a small parking area. Hiking the complete loop requires walking these two segments of road.

The trail leaves Old Antrim Rd. and follows a woods road. At 0.7 mi. a cross-country ski trail continues on the road, bypassing Bacon Ledge and Round Mtn., while the Trout-n-Bacon Trail leaves the road on the right and continues uphill, finally scrambling to the top of Bacon Ledge (1959 ft.) at 1.1 mi., where there are excellent views in all directions. (A short side path can be used to bypass the scramble up the ledge in adverse conditions.) Past Bacon Ledge the trail winds around on the ridge of Round Mtn. (1959 ft.), then descends, passing the jct. at 1.9 mi. where the cross-country ski trail rejoins from the left. The trail continues to descend to a clearing near a camp at 2.6 mi. The trail follows the right edge of the clearing uphill past the camp. In a short distance the continuation of the main trail turns left on another woods road, while a spur path continues down to beautiful Trout Pond on the original road. From the jct. below the camp, the main trail soon reaches another woods road jct., where it turns left and runs to Shedd Hill Rd. at 4.3 mi.

Distances from Old Antrim Rd. (1340')

   to Bacon Ledge (1959'): 1.1 mi., 600 ft., 50 min.

   to Trout Pond (1598'): 2.7 mi., 750 ft. (rev. 500 ft.), 1 hr. 45 min.

   to Shedd Hill Rd. (1540'): 4.3 mi. (6.9 km.), 1000 ft. (rev. 300 ft.), 2 hr. 40 min.

   to starting point by complete loop via Trout-n-Bacon Trail, Shedd Hill Rd., and Old Antrim Rd.: 6.0 mi. (9.6 km.), 1050 ft., 3 hr. 30 min.

DePierrefeu–Willard Pond Wildlife Sanctuary

This New Hampshire Audubon Society Reservation in the town of Antrim contains most of Willard Pond and Bald Mtn. (2037 ft.), which has two good outlook ledges. Several trails provide options for loop hikes over Bald Mtn. Refer to the USGS Stoddard quadrangle; a brochure with map may also available at the trailhead. Follow NH 123 north from Hancock village for 3.7 mi. or south from NH 9 for 3.3 mi., then turn east onto Willard Pond Rd.. and follow it for 1.6 mi., bearing left at two forks, to a parking area on the left. In addition to the trails described below, the Mill Pond Trail makes an 0.4 mi. loop around Hatch Mill Pond on the east side of Willard Pond Rd. near the parking area. The former trail up Goodhue Hill has been abandoned.

Tamposi Trail (USGS Stoddard quad)

This yellow-blazed trail makes a loop over Bald Mtn. that includes both of the fine viewpoints on the mountain. The upper part of the trail is mostly on private land. It leaves from the left side of the trailhead parking area and climbs through a rocky area, with occasional minor descents, to the loop jct. at 0.5 mi. The loop is described in the counterclockwise direction, taking the right (east) fork for the ascent. The east loop contours across the ledgy slope, then swings left and climbs to a fine outlook over Willard Pond and the mountains beyond at 0.8 mi. Here the trail turns left and climbs to a jct. with the red-blazed Bald Mountain Trail at 0.9 mi., where it turns left again. The two trails coincide, ascending to an excellent south outlook at 1.0 mi. On the ledges above the outlook the trails turn left into the woods and climb to a small clearing at the wooded, viewless summit at 1.2 mi. Here the Bald Mountain Trail ends and the west loop of the Tamposi Trail continues ahead for the descent. It soon bears left and descends steadily through spruces. It bears left again, passes a cleared view southeast, and winds down through selectively logged hardwood forest to the loop jct. at 1.8 mi. Turn right to return to the parking area.

Distances from parking area on Willard Pond Rd. (1160')

- *to* loop junction (1500'): 0.5 mi., 350 ft., 25 min.
- *to* Bald Mtn. summit (2037') via east loop: 1.2 mi., 900 ft., 1 hr. 5 min.
  for complete loop: 2.3 mi. (3.7 km.), 900 ft., 1 hr. 35 min.

Tudor Trail (USGS Stoddard quad)

This easy yellow-blazed trail runs along the shore of Willard Pond and provides access to the Bald Mountain Trail. It leaves Willard Pond Rd. on the left (sign), 140 yd. beyond the trailhead parking area. It runs along the west shore of the pond, passing through a small boulder field and crossing several small brooks. At 0.7 mi. the red-blazed Bald Mountain Trail diverges left. The Tudor

Trail bears right and continues through large white pines to Pine Point, where there is a fine view of the pond.

Distances from parking area on Willard Pond Rd. (1160')

   to   Bald Mountain Trail (1160'): 0.7 mi., 0 ft., 20 min.

   to   Pine Point (1160'): 1.1 mi., 0 ft., 35 min.

Bald Mountain Trail (USGS Stoddard quad)

This red-blazed trail ascends Bald Mtn. from the Tudor Trail on the shore of Willard Pond. It diverges left from the Tudor Trail 0.7 mi. from the parking area and ascends gradually at first, passing some interesting boulders, then rises more steeply. At 0.5 mi. the east loop of the yellow-blazed Tamposi Trail joins from the left, and the two trails coincide, climbing to a fine south outlook at 0.6 mi. On the ledges above the outlook the trails turn left into the woods and climb to a small clearing at the wooded, viewless summit at 0.8 mi. Here the Bald Mountain Trail ends and the west loop of the Tamposi Trail continues ahead for the descent.

Distance from Tudor Trail (1160')

   to   Bald Mtn. summit (2037'): 0.8 mi. (1.3 km.), 900 ft., 50 min.

Monadnock–Sunapee Greenway

The Monadnock–Sunapee Greenway, 49 mi. long, continues north from Mt. Monadnock to Sunapee Mtn. The SPNHF and AMC cooperatively built this trail, which runs mostly over hills and along ridges between these two major peaks in southwest New Hampshire. Volunteer maintenance and other support of this trail is coordinated by the Monadnock–Sunapee Greenway Trail Club, PO Box 164, Marlow, NH 03456. Because a large part of this trail is located on private property, users should be particularly aware of their status as guests and avoid thoughtless behavior that could jeopardize this privilege. Camping is permitted at designated sites only. Space constraints prevent its full and detailed coverage by this guide; what follows is a brief account of the entire trail and a more detailed account of two of its more important features (in addition to Mt. Monadnock and Sunapee Mtn.), Pitcher Mt. (2162 ft.) and Lovewell Mtn. (2470 ft.). The *Monadnock–Sunapee Greenway Guide*, with a GPS-surveyed, waterproof trail map, also includes additional details on several side trails in the Mt. Sunapee area; it is available from the MSGTC (address above).

Section 1. Monadnock to NH 101. From the summit of Mt. Monadnock, the Greenway descends on the Dublin Trail for 2.2 mi., then turns left (west) on Old Troy Rd. At 2.7 mi. the trail turns to the right off Old Troy Rd., following a woods road at first. It descends across a valley and climbs to Old Marlborough Rd, at 3.7 mi. It follows this road to the right (east), then at 4.0 mi. it turns left, passes around a swamp, and ascends to the top of a low ridge. Here it meets a well-used woods road and follows it to the right, swinging to the north and descending to meet NH 101 at 5.6 mi. just after passing a beaver pond (left).

Section 2. NH 101 to NH 9. The Greenway continues straight across NH 101 and ascends a woods road (sign, "Monadnock Wilderness Girl Scout Campsite"). It then ascends on woods roads across a power line clearing. It crosses a low, flat ridge and descends past the Splitoir Campsite on the left at 6.3 mi. It continues down to Howe Reservoir, crossing the outlet brook at Eliza Adams Gorge at the foot of the dam on a bridge at 6.9 mi. The Greenway continues to Brown Rd., follows it left for 100 yd., then at 7.3 mi. turns to the right onto a gravel road and continues past a private picnic area (left) and a millpond (right). It joins Seaver Rd. and follows it across Chesham Rd. at 7.9 mi., then continues northwest on Seaver Rd. past Chesham Pond almost to the foot of Silver Lake at 8.8 mi. Here, just after crossing the outlet brook from Silver Lake, it bears right at a fork, then turns right onto a gravel driveway, and finally diverges left into the woods on a woods road. This woods road runs past Childs Bog Dam at 9.4 mi. and continues to Nelson Rd. at 10.1 mi. The trail crosses this road and runs through the woods to Cabot Rd. at 11.2 mi., which it follows to the left. From here to Nelson village the trail follows well-maintained roads. At 12.2 mi. Cabot Rd. joins Tolman Pond Rd. (in the opposite direction, take the right fork), which continues to Harrisville Rd. at 12.6 mi. This road is followed to Nelson village. At 13.0 mi., just before reaching the Nelson Congregational Church, the trail makes a right turn onto Log Cabin Rd., which it follows past several houses, keeping straight ahead as it becomes a woods road that climbs across a height-of-land and descends to the outlet of a beaver pond, which it crosses on a bridge at 14.0 mi. The woods road climbs again over the sag between Felt Hill and Tolman Hill and descends to NH 9 at 15.4 mi.

Section 3. NH 9 to NH 123. After following NH 9 about 100 yd. to the right (east), the Greenway turns left onto Nye Rd. At 15.7 mi. it bears right onto an old woods road, then turns left onto another woods road at 15.9 mi. and follows it uphill across a power line clearing to the height-of-land at 16.9 mi. The woods road then descends, passing a trail on the right at 17.4 mi. that connects the Greenway to Daniel Upton Forest. The Greenway continues to descend, and at 18.4 mi. it passes a side path on the left that leads to Crider State Forest Shelter in 0.2 mi. The road improves and becomes Center Pond Rd., passing along the east shore of Center Pond. It then climbs away from the pond, and at 19.1 mi. the Greenway turns left onto a gated woods road and follows a succession of old roads and foot trails. The trail continues through the woods, crossing a private gravel road at 20.5 mi., then (relocated section) bears right onto another woods road, passes a gate, and then leaves the road and runs through the woods to NH 123 at the parking area for Pitcher Mtn. at 22.0 mi.

Section 4. NH 123 to NH 31. About 70 yd. from NH 123, the Greenway bears right at a fork where the blue-blazed steeper, more direct route to the summit of Pitcher Mtn. bears left. The Greenway climbs to the summit of Pitcher Mtn. at 22.4 mi., then descends on an old grassy road through blueberry barrens, and the direct blue-blazed summit trail enters on the left in about 70 yd. The Greenway now follows a succession of blazed paths and woods roads (follow with care) through woods and open areas that have not yet fully recovered from a 1941 forest fire. It crosses the open summit of Hubbard Hill (1896 ft.) at 25.0 mi. and descends past the side path (right) to Fox Brook Campsite at 25.5 mi. After crossing Fox Brook, it ascends to the summit of Jackson Hill (2057 ft.) at 26.3 mi., then descends north, then east, then north again, then east again. It crosses Barney Brook south of Ashuelot Pond on a snowmobile bridge at 28.3 mi., and at 28.7 mi. reaches Old King's Highway and follows it downhill to the left (north). At 29.3 mi. the Greenway passes an old church and graveyard in a rather desolate spot along this old deserted road with no houses nearby; this is regarded as the first church of the Seventh-Day Adventist denomination. At 29.7 mi. the Greenway bears right onto the paved Faxon Hill Rd., and at 30.0 mi. the trail leaves the paved road to follow a paved driveway on the right. The trail now climbs to the summit of Oak Hill (1959 ft.) at 30.8 mi., then descends past General Washington Lean-to at 32.2 mi. The trail soon reaches Symonds Lane and turns left, then turns right onto Faxon Hill Rd. and follows it to NH 31 at 32.5 mi.

Section 5. NH 31 to Washington-Bradford Road. The Greenway crosses NH 31 and bears right (east) through the public buildings of Washington village. At 33.1 mi. it takes a sharp left onto the Washington–Bradford road, passes Halfmoon Pond, then turns right at 34.4 mi. and ascends a rough old woods road to the height-of-land at 35.2 mi. Here it turns left and becomes a footpath, ascending Lovewell Mtn. (2470 ft.), passing viewpoints, and reaching the ledgy summit at 36.7 mi. The Greenway descends the long north ridge into a ravine at 38.0 mi., then makes a short climb over a lesser northern ridge and continues to the old Washington–Bradford road at 39.0 mi. This road is not passable for most cars at most times for the first half-mile or so south from this trail crossing.

Section 6. Washington–Bradford Road to Sunapee Mountain. *Note: This is the wildest section of the trail; except at the ends, there are only a few side approach routes, and they are fairly long. Therefore this trail section demands a degree of preparation and commitment far greater than the rest of the trail requires.*

The Greenway continues across the road, crosses Bog Brook (difficult at high water), and ascends on old woods roads into Pillsbury State Park, passing the jct. with the Ridge Link on the left in a saddle and reaching the summit of Kittredge Hill (2116 ft.) at 40.3 mi. It descends into a deep saddle, then crosses a flat hump and descends into a lesser saddle where the Bear Pond Trail enters on the left at 41.6 mi. The trail winds around two significant humps on the south ridge of Sunapee Mtn., passes a short side path left to Moose Lookout Campsite at 43.3 mi., then reaches the jct. where the Five Summers Trail enters on the left at 44.5 mi. The Greenway now climbs to Lucia's Lookout, a fine viewpoint toward Monadnock over the land crossed by the Greenway, at 44.7 mi. The Greenway then runs along the ledgy, lumpy ridge, passing several viewpoints, until it descends on the east side to reach the south end of Lake Solitude at 47.5 mi. It follows the west shore to the north end of the lake, where it meets the Andrew Brook Trail, which ascends from the east, at 47.8 mi. Here it also meets the Lake Solitude Trail from the summit of Sunapee Mtn., with which it coincides for the remainder of its length—and now becomes heavily used, in contrast to the light use received by many miles of the trail south of this point. At 47.9 mi. the Newbury Trail and a trail from the eastern side of the Mt. Sunapee ski area enter on the right. The trail climbs sharply, and at 48.0 mi. a side path leads left onto White Ledge, where there are fine views down to the lake and out to the east. At 48.6 mi. the trail comes out on the ski slopes, and in 30 yd. more the Goshen Trail enters on the left. The Greenway follows a service road and ski trails the rest of the way to the summit lodge at 48.8 mi.

Pitcher Mountain Trails (USGS Stoddard quad; MSGTC map)

This small mountain (2162 ft.) in the town of Stoddard has an open summit and a fire tower that offer an excellent view for little effort. Refer to the USGS Stoddard quadrangle. The parking lot is located on the northeast side of NH 123, 4.5 mi. north of its jct. with NH 9 and 3.1 mi. south of its jct. with NH 10. About 70 yd. above the parking area the trails divide; the left-hand path (with blue blazes) is the shorter, steeper trail, while the right-hand path (with white blazes) is the less steep Monadnock–Sunapee Greenway. The two trails rejoin about 70 yd. from the summit after the Greenway has already passed over it.

Distances from NH 123 (1870')

   to summit (2162') by either path: 0.4 mi. (0.7 km.), 300 ft., 20 min.

   to starting point via complete loop: 0.8 mi. (1.4 km.), 300 ft., 35 min.

Lovewell Mountain (USGS Lovewell quad; MSGTC map)

This mountain (2470 ft.), located in the town of Washington and crossed by the Monadnock–Sunapee Greenway, offers interesting views from a number of scattered ledges. Refer to the USGS Lovewell Mtn. quadrangle. From Washington village on NH 31, follow the gravel road that leads east from the village church and school for 0.5 mi., then turn sharp left and follow the old Washington-Bradford road past Halfmoon Pond; the best parking may be at the Halfmoon Pond boat launch at 1.4 mi. from NH 31. At 1.9 mi. turn right onto a rough woods road (limited parking). As this road is not passable for the vast majority of vehicles, the trail description begins here.

The road (part of the Monadnock–Sunapee Greenway) climbs to a level area at 0.9 mi., where ledges run down to the road past the stone wall that parallels it. Here the foot trail turns left through the stone wall and ascends through old pastures, and at 1.8 mi. enters a level section. At the end of this section, the trail turns left and ascends a steep, rough section, then continues on a fairly steep, rough, and ledgy pathway through mostly dark, mature coniferous woods. At 2.1 mi. a side path leads left 100 yd. to a piped spring, and in a short distance another side path leads right 60 yd. to a southeast outlook. The trail reaches the summit cairn at 2.3 mi.; a nearby overlook (sign) provides views to the northeast. It then descends north along a broad ridge, crosses a shallow sag and a minor hump. It then swings around to the west and descends into a ravine, where it crosses a small brook at 3.6 mi. and climbs to the crest of a lesser ridge. From there it descends, crossing several stone walls and passing the remains of old farms—a number of old cellar holes and foundations, and the remnants of an apple orchard. The trail continues to descend across several more stone walls and at 4.6 mi. reaches the old Bradford-Washington road at a point 1.9 mi. north of the jct. with the woods road where the description of this trail begins. This road is passable by cars only to a point about a half-mile south of this trail crossing.

Distances from junction of old Washington–Bradford Road and jeep road (1540')

> *to* summit of Lovewell Mtn. (2470'): 2.3 mi. (3.7 km.), 950 ft., 1 hr. 40 min.

> *to* crossing of old Washington–Bradford Road (1610'): 4.6 mi., 1200 ft. (rev. 1100 ft.), 2 hr. 55 min.

> *to* starting point via old Washington–Bradford Road: 6.5 mi. (10.5 km.), 1300 ft. (rev. 100 ft.), 3 hr. 55 min.

Pillsbury State Park

This 5500-acre park, located in the towns of Washington and Goshen, contains nine ponds and surrounding mountain ridges, including several miles of the Monadnock–Sunapee Greenway. A network of trails, mostly on logging roads, provides access to the Greenway and makes possible an extended loop hike to the fine viewpoint known as Lucia's Lookout. About 40 primitive campsites are available around the ponds. A day-use fee ($3 per person in 2004) is charged for admission to the park, which is open from early May through late October and gated at other times. The area is remote and hiking use is generally light. Due to the many wetlands, it is an excellent place for wildlife sightings.

The park entrance is on NH 31, 4.2 mi. north of the general store in Washington. The entrance fee should be paid at the office 0.2 mi. from the entrance; a park trail map is available. (The Monadnock–Sunapee Greenway Trail Club map also shows the area and some of the trails.) Trailhead parking is on a cul-de-sac by a picnic area on the shore of Mill Pond, 1.1 mi. from the entrance.

Five Summers Trail (MSGTC map)

This trail, blazed in blue, provides the most direct access to Lucia's Lookout. For most of its length it follows logging roads used as snowmobile trails— pleasant in the lower section, but often muddy and rough in the upper mile.

Walk up a gravel road that leads north from the cul-de-sac and swing right past Campsite #35. At 0.1 mi., just before an orange gate, the Balance Rock Trail diverges left. The Five Summers Trail continues on the road past the gate, descending gradually alongside Mill Pond and crossing the inlet brook on a bridge. At 0.5 mi. the Bear Pond Trail leaves on the right, while the Five Summers Trail takes the left fork and soon comes within sight of North Pond, passing a side path left to a campsite. At 1.1 mi. there is a viewpoint on the left over the pond. The trail continues at easy grades on the grassy road, passing a town boundary marker at 1.5 mi. It leaves the park at 1.9 mi., crosses a bridge, swings right in a logging yard, and at 2.2 mi. crosses another bridge and bears right at a fork (sign). After crossing another bridge the wide trail ascends through regenerating forest and becomes muddy and rough at times. At 3.0 mi. it swings right with a large beaver pond visible on the left. In another 0.1 mi. it bears left off the main road onto a footpath. The trail ascends gradually with some wet footing and meets the main road at 3.5 mi. It follows the road to the left for 20 yd., then turns right off it (sign) onto a footpath and ascends moderately to the Monadnock-Sunapee Greenway at 3.8 mi. For Lucia's Lookout, turn left (north) and climb steeply for 0.2 mile to a ledge with a view south. Here a side path descends 40 yd. right to a fine eastern outlook. For a view to the west, continue 90 yd. farther north on the main trail and take a short spur trail to the left.

Distance from parking area (1650')

   to Monadnock–Sunapee Greenway (2280'): 3.8 mi., 700 ft. (rev. 50 ft.), 2 hr. 15 min.

   to Lucia's Lookout (2490'): 4.0 mi. (6.5 km.), 900 ft., 2 hr. 25 min.

Bear Pond Trail (MSGTC map)

This trail follows a logging road/snowmobile trail from the Five Summers Trail up to the Monadnock–Sunapee Greenway, making possible a fairly long and remote loop hike. It diverges right (sign) from the Five Summers Trail 0.5 mi. from the parking area. At 0.1 mi. it passes close by a beaver swamp on the left. After crossing a bridge it ascends to a point near the shore of Bear Pond at 0.5 mi.; a good view of the pond is found 20 yd. to the right. The trail ascends moderately, crossing two bridges, then more steeply on an eroded section of road. At 0.9 mi. the grade eases, and in another 0.1 mi. the trail swings right at a fork and continues across a level area with muddy footing to meet the

Monadnock–Sunapee Greenway, 2.9 mi. south of the Greenway's jct. with the Five Summers Trail.

Distance from Five Summers Trail (1660')

> *to* Monadnock–Sunapee Greenway (2040'): 1.2 mi. (1.9 km.), 400 ft., 50 min.

Distance from parking area (1650')

> for loop to Lucia's Lookout (2490') via Five Summers Trail, Monadnock–Sunapee Greenway, and Bear Pond Trail: 8.8 mi. (14.2 km.), 1450 ft., 5 hr. 10 min.

Balance Rock Trail (Pillsbury State Park trail map)

This orange-blazed trail leads from the Five Summers Trail, 0.1 mi. from the parking area, to a viewpoint over North Pond and a large boulder perched on a ledge. It diverges left (sign) from the Five Summers Trail just before an orange gate. It follows a woods road for 70 yd., then bears left onto another woods road (sign). At 0.2 mi. it bears right off the road (sign) and follows a well-worn footpath. It ascends a southern shoulder of Bryant Mtn., dips to a col at 0.5 mi., then climbs steadily by switchbacks. It slabs across the east slope of the mountain and at 1.0 mi. reaches a ledge with a restricted but beautiful view of North Pond and the ridge to the east; Lovewell Mtn. can be seen to the southeast. The trail continues another 50 yd. to Balance Rock, where it ends. Beyond this point the former Clemac Trail has been abandoned.

Distance from Five Summers Trail (1700')

> *to* Balance Rock (2150'): 1.0 mi. (1.6 km.), 500 ft. (rev. 50 ft.), 45 min.

Other Pillsbury State Park Trails

Mad Road Trail. This trail leaves the south side of the park access road just before the cul-de-sac, crosses a footbridge, and runs at easy grades for about 1.0 mi. to a point near the shore of swampy Bacon Pond. It then swings southwest, climbs over a col on a ridge north of Jones Hill, and at about 3.0 mi. descends to NH 31, 1.8 mi. south of the park entrance.

Ridge Link. This trail diverges to the east from the Mad Road Trail near Bacon Pond and climbs about 0.5 mi. to the Monadnock–Sunapee Greenway in the col south of Kittredge Hill.

Narrows Trail. This trail leaves from a parking spot on the south side of the park access road, 0.4 mi. from NH 31, runs nearly level for 0.1 mi. to the shore of May Pond, then turns right and runs along the shore to the narrow strait between May Pond and Butterfield Pond at 0.2 mi.

Sunapee Mountain

Sunapee Mtn. (2726 ft.), the northern terminus of the Monadnock–Sunapee Greenway, is an irregular, massive, heavily wooded mountain located in the town of Newbury at the south end of Lake Sunapee. Lake Solitude near its summit is unique for its high elevation, remoteness, and beauty of setting. Nearby are cliffs that rise 300 ft. to White Ledge, where there is a fine view southeast over the wild country of the Merrimack-Connecticut watershed. Refer to the USGS Newport quadrangle. Mt. Sunapee State Park is on NH 103, 7 mi. east of Newport. There is a state-owned but now privately managed ski area on the north slope of the mountain. In addition to the trails described below, the mountain is easily climbed via the ski slopes (direct routes are about 1.5 mi. long); there is also a trail that leads from the eastern side of the ski area in about a mile to Lake Solitude, which can be used to make a loop trip to the summit and Lake Solitude from the ski area. A hikers' trail map is usually available at the ski area.

Lake Solitude Trail (USGS Newport quad; MSGTC map)

This very popular trail, which connects the summit of Sunapee Mtn. with beautiful Lake Solitude and the ledges that overlook it—ledges that are only slightly lower than the summit itself—is also the northern end of the Monadnock–Sunapee Greenway and a segment of Section 1 of the Sunapee–Ragged–Kearsarge Greenway. It is blazed in white and orange. From the summit of Sunapee Mtn., the trail descends on a gravel service road along the right edge of the ski slopes, with excellent views to the north, swinging right and passing under a chairlift. At 0.2 mi. the trail leaves the service road and ski trails and enters the woods on the right; just 30 yd. before this point the Goshen Trail, here a woods road, enters on the right. The Lake Solitude Trail follows a bumpy ridge through fine woods, and at 0.8 mi. a side path on the right leads 60 yd. across White Ledge to a fine viewpoint down to the lake and out to the east. The main trail descends sharply to Jack and June Junction at 0.9 mi. Here the Newbury Trail continues ahead, and the red-blazed trail from the eastern side of the ski area diverges left. The Lake Solitude Trail bears right and descends to its jct. with the Andrew Brook Trail at the north end of Lake Solitude.

Distance from summit of Sunapee Mtn. (2726')

   to Lake Solitude (2510'): 1.0 mi. (1.6 km.), 250 ft. (rev. 450 ft.), 40 min.

Andrew Brook Trail (USGS Newport quad; MSGTC map)

This trail ascends to beautiful Lake Solitude from the east and offers access to the summit of Sunapee Mtn. via the Lake Solitude Trail. Leave NH 103 0.8 mi. east of its jct. with NH 103A in Newbury, and follow Mountain Rd. 1.2 mi. to a woods road on the right just before Mountain Rd. crosses a bridge. There is limited parking here; do not block the woods road.

The trail follows the woods road for 0.5 mi., then bears right across Andrew Brook and follows it upstream. It recrosses the brook at 1.0 mi. and 1.4 mi., finally reaching Lake Solitude at a point where severe damage from illegal camping is evident. It follows the north shore of the pond and meets the Monadnock–Sunapee Greenway, which enters on the left (south) and follows the Lake Solitude Trail uphill toward the summit of Sunapee Mtn. Even if you do not intend to visit the summit, you should not miss the views from White Ledge, which is reached by following the Lake Solitude Trail uphill for 0.2 mi., then turning left across the ledges on a spur path to the outlook.

Distances from Mountain Rd. (1330')

   to Lake Solitude at the Lake Solitude Trail junction (2510'): 2.0 mi. (3.2 km.), 1200 ft., 1 hr. 35 min.

   to summit of Sunapee Mtn. (2726') via Lake Solitude Trail: 3.0 mi. (4.8 km.), 1650 ft. (rev. 250 ft.), 2 hr. 20 min.

Newbury Trail (USGS Newport quad; MSGTC map)

This orange-blazed trail ascends from Newbury village at the southern tip of Lake Sunapee to the Lake Solitude Trail at a point just above Lake Solitude. It is a segment of Section 1 of the Sunapee–Ragged–Kearsarge Greenway. It is probably best to park in Newbury village, but there is limited parking on the road just below the trailhead. Follow the road that leaves NH 103 directly opposite the information booth (sign: Newbury Hts.), then in less than 0.1 mi. take the second right (Lake View Ave.), which leads in a short distance to the path, which is marked by a sign on the right side of the road.

The trail climbs steadily and at 0.4 mi. passes the red-blazed path that leads to the right 0.2 mi. to Eagle's Nest, a ledgy outlook with a fine view across Lake Sunapee; in 80 yd. from the main trail the side path crosses an attractive ledgy brook. The main trail continues to climb at a moderate grade, then more steeply to a right turn onto a relocated section at 0.8 mi. It angles up across the slope, crosses a ledge with a restricted view, and descends slightly to a jct. with the yellow-blazed Rim Trail at 1.1 mi. (This trail ascends from a cul-de-sac at the end of a paved road, 1.4 mi. long, that leaves the east side of the main ski area access road 0.3 mi. from NH 103. The side road is sometimes gated, and hikers may have to walk all or part of it to reach the trail. The Rim Trail enters the woods at a sign, immediately crosses Johnson Brook, and ascends steadily with somewhat rough footing, at times in a streambed. Distance to Newbury Trail, 0.5 mi.; ascent 450 ft.) At the jct. the Newbury Trail turns sharp left and ascends steeply for 0.2 mi. to an outlook with a spectacular view north over Lake Sunapee. Here it turns right, climbs over several knolls, and turns right again onto the original route of the trail at 1.6 mi. It then follows a ridge to the South Peak of Sunapee Mtn. (2608') and continues along a bumpy ridgecrest with little change of elevation. At 2.6 mi. it meets the Lake Solitude Trail a short distance above the lake; the red-blazed trail from the eastern side of the ski area also enters here.

Distances from side road off NH 103 near Newbury village (1150')

   to Lake Solitude Trail (2580'): 2.6 mi. (4.2 km.), 1450 ft., 2 hr.

   to summit of Sunapee Mtn. (2726') via Lake Solitude Trail: 3.5 mi. (5.6 km.), 1850 ft. (rev. 250 ft.), 2 hr. 40 min.

Summit Trail (MSGTC map)

This trail, completed in 1998, provides an attractive, moderately graded route to the summit from the ski area parking lot. The upper part is a segment of Section 1 of the Sunapee–Ragged–Kearsarge Greenway. Ski trail development in the future may force relocations. Access the ski area by a road that leads 0.8 mi. south from a traffic circle on NH 103 on the southwest side of Sunapee Lake. Walk to the far right (west) side of the parking lot and follow a service road across a bridge to the South Peak Beginner Area. The road bears left in front of a chairlift, and in 200 yd. the trail, blazed in red, enters the woods on the right at the base of a ski slope (sign, "Hiking Trail to Summit"). It crosses a footbridge over a small brook, parallels the ski trail for 125 yd., then bears left and crosses it, re-entering the woods higher up the slope. It climbs moderately through hardwoods to a T-junction at 0.6 mi. Here the Summit Trail turns left and a link in the Sunapee–Ragged–Kearsarge Greenway (blazed in white) joins from the right. (This link provides an alternate access to the Summit Trail. From the intersection of NH 103 and NH 103B in Newbury, drive 1.1 mi. west on NH 103, turn left onto Brook Rd., and in another 1.2 mi. turn left onto Old Province Rd. The trailhead, signed "Province Trail," is 0.5 mi. up on the right, with parking for several cars. The trail ascends an old woods road for 80 yd., then turns right and runs nearly level, following a stone wall and the blue-blazed state park boundary, to the jct. Distance to Summit Trail, 0.4 mi.

From the jct., the Summit Trail descends slightly for 0.1 mi., then turns right onto an old woods road (bear left here on the descent.) It ascends moderately, traverses a plateau through a beautiful spruce grove, crosses a small brook, and resumes the ascent. After crossing several more small brooks, it turns sharp left at 1.6 mi. and ascends the west slope of the mountain by switchbacks through birch and hardwood forest, then conifers. It passes an outlook west at 2.3 mi., and in another 0.1 mi. it bears right where a side path leads 40 yd. left to another outlook. After a fairly steep climb it emerges on a grassy shelf on the south side of the summit lodge. Descending, walk 50 yd. south across the lawn from the front of the base lodge to a sign, "Hiking Trail," at the edge of the woods.

Distance from ski area parking lot (1270')

　　to summit of Sunapee Mtn. (2726'): 2.5 mi. (4.0 km), 1450 ft., 2 hr.

Goshen Trail (USGS Newport quad)

This trail, which follows an old woods road that was used to transport the materials to construct the summit lodge, provides an easy if unexciting route to the summit of Sunapee Mtn. from the west. It begins in the town of Goshen, which is notable as the birthplace of John Gunnison, an early explorer of the west whose name was given to a town, a river, and a national forest in Colorado. Follow NH 103 about a mile west from the complicated traffic circle at the ski area entrance, then take Brook Rd. (sign) south for 2.5 mi. to the point where the road makes a 90° turn to the west. There is some parking available here but very little beyond.

Follow the gravel road across a bridge; just after it starts to climb, the trail turns left onto a gated gravel road with signs forbidding the use of motorized vehicles. At 0.7 mi. the road enters a clearing and bears left, soon crossing a brook on a bridge and beginning to climb more seriously. At 1.4 mi. it passes to the right of a small gravel pit, and the old road becomes much rougher, climbing to reach the ski trail used by the Lake Solitude Trail at 2.4 mi., just after passing a large boulder. For the summit, turn left and follow the left edge of the ski trails; for Lake Solitude, turn right and enter the woods in 30 yd. On the descent, the entrance to the Goshen Trail is somewhat camouflaged, but once identified—it passes a beech tree with a light-blue blaze and a large boulder after 40 yd.—the trail is unmistakable.

Distance from Brook Rd. (1350')

   to   summit of Sunapee Mtn. (2726'): 2.6 mi. (4.1 km.), 1400 ft., 2 hr.

John Hay National Wildlife Refuge and SPNHF Hay Reservation

These two adjacent protected properties are on the southeast side of Lake Sunapee and are divided by NH 103A. The John Hay National Wildlife Refuge is on the west side of the road and encompasses 163 acres on the former estate of John Hay, who served as personal secretary to President Lincoln and as Secretary of State under Presidents McKinley and Theodore Roosevelt. Admission is charged to the grounds of the estate, known as The Fells. A 1.8 mi. loop hike along the grounds and around the John Hay II Forest Ecology Trail (including a stretch along the shore of Lake Sunapee) is described in the AMC's *Nature Walks in the New Hampshire Lakes Region*. The 673-acre Hay Reservation (no admission fee), managed by SPNHF, is on the east side of the road and includes scenic Sunset Hill (1841 ft.). The parking area for both properties (sign for The Fells historic site) is on the west side of NH 103A, 2.2 mi. north of its jct. with NH 103. Near the Fells visitor center is a kiosk with trail map.

Sunset Hill Trail (USGS Newport Quad)

This trail follows old woods roads from NH 103A, directly across from The Fells parking area, to open ledges near the summit of Sunset Hill, where there is a view over Lake Sunapee. From the trailhead on NH 103A (sign and kiosk), the trail, marked with yellow rectangles, climbs for 0.1 mi. to a T-junction, turns left, and runs at easy grades parallel to the highway. At 0.4 mi. it swings right and ascends to another T-junction at 0.7 mi. Here it turns right on an old woods road, then in 100 yd. turns left off it and climbs moderately to the broad, semi-open summit. Here a branch of the trail diverges left and descends about 0.5 mi. to a trailhead on Chalk Pond Rd., 0.4 mi. east of NH 103A. For the viewpoint, turn right at the summit and descend easily for 70 yd.

Distance from NH 103A (1273')

   to Sunset Hill summit (1841'): 1.2 mi. (1.9 km.), 550 ft., 55 min.

Saint-Gaudens National Historical Site

The estate where the noted sculptor Augustus Saint-Gaudens lived and worked from 1892 until his death in 1907 is now maintained by the National Park Service as a National Historical Site. It is located in the town of Cornish on NH 12A almost exactly halfway between Claremont and West Lebanon. In addition to the grounds of the estate itself, where there is an attractive 0.9-mi. loop walk that includes a path along the beautiful wooded ravine of Blow-Me-Up Brook, there is a forested area of about 80 acres called the Blow-Me-Down Natural Area. In this area an interesting loop walk of 2.3 mi. can be made. The route starts at the parking lot, runs 0.3 mi. across the estate grounds to the point where the Blow-Me-Down Trail enters the woods, then descends to a trail jct. where it follows the Sycamore Trail 0.1 mi. to the bank of Blow-Me-Down Brook opposite a stand of sycamore trees. Returning to the main trail, the route runs past Blow-Me-Down Pond to NH 12A at the Cornish Colony Historic Marker (another possible entrance point for the loop). The route then follows the trail back past the pond to the Return Trail, which it follows back to the main grounds of the estate.

Section 2

Cardigan and Kearsarge Region

See AMC Southern New Hampshire Map: Mount Cardigan.

SUGGESTED HIKES

Easy Hikes

Welton Falls [rt: 1.2 mi., 100 ft., 0:40]. This scenic waterfall and gorge is easy to reach from the end of Welton Falls Rd. via Old Dicey Road and the Manning Trail. It can also be approached from the Cardigan Lodge [rt: 2.4 mi., 300 ft., 1:20].

Mt. Kearsarge from the south [rt: 1.2 mi., 350 ft., 0:45]. The Warner Trail provides a short approach from Rollins State Park to this fine open summit.

Bog Mtn. [rt. 3.0 mi., 750 ft., 1:55]. This small peak offers several fine views on the approach along the Sunapee–Ragged–Kearsarge Greenway from Stearns Hill Rd.

Moderate Hikes

The Sugarloaves and Goose Pond [rt: 3.8 mi., 1200 ft., 2:30]. The Elwell Trail leads to views over Newfound Lake from Little and Big Sugarloaves, with a short side trip to Goose Pond.

Mt. Kearsarge from the north [lp: 2.7 mi., 1150 ft., 1:55]. A fine loop can be made from Winslow State Park via the Wilmot and Barlow Trails.

Pike's Peak [rt: 4.0 mi., 1300 ft., 2:40]. The Sutherland Trail and a side path lead to this excellent outlook on Plymouth Mtn.

Orange Mtn. [rt: 5.6 mi., 1300 ft., 3:25]. Good views arc found atop this southern spur of Mt. Cardigan; starting at Cardigan Lodge, use the Holt, Cathedral Forest, Vistamont, and Skyland Trails.

Mt. Cardigan. There are many possible routes up central New Hampshire's finest peak. The easiest approach is the West Ridge Trail from Cardigan State Park **[rt: 3.0 mi., 1250 ft., 2:10]**; this can be combined with the Clark and South Ridge Trails into a loop **[lp: 3.6 mi., 1300 ft., 2:25]**. From Cardigan Lodge on the east side, a popular and very scenic loop over Cardigan and Firescrew follows the Holt, Cathedral Forest, Clark, Mowglis, and Manning Trails **[lp: 5.6 mi., 1950 ft., 3:45]**. Orange Mtn. and the South Peak (via the Skyland and South Ridge Trails) can be added to make a longer loop with additional views **[lp: 7.9 mi., 2250 ft., 5:05]**.

LIST OF TRAILS

This section covers the northern part of the hill country of western New Hampshire, south of the White Mountains, where the main backbone of the mountains continues as a jumble of medium-sized mountains that generally do not group naturally into ranges. This area includes the highest and most impressive of these mountains, Mt. Cardigan (3155 ft.), which with its subsidiary peaks supports the most extensive and interesting trail system in the region. The AMC owns a 1,200-acre reservation here, which includes 50 miles of hiking and backcountry ski trails. For reservations at AMC's Cardigan Lodge (open year-round, full-service in summer), its adjoining campsites and tent platforms, or the rustic and secluded High Cabin near the Mt. Cardigan summit, see www.outdoors.org/lodging, or call AMC reservations at 603-466-2721.

Also included in this section of the guide is Mt. Kearsarge (2930 ft.), only about 200 ft. lower than Cardigan and almost equally impressive due to its comparative isolation from other mountains and its relatively great rise from base to summit. Ragged Mtn. (2286 ft.) and Bog Mtn. (1787 ft.), two interesting smaller mountains in the neighborhood of Kearsarge, are also crossed by the Sunapee–Ragged–Kearsarge Greenway. Plymouth Mtn. (2193 ft.), Cardigan's neighbor on the northeast side of Newfound Lake, and the SPNHF Cockermouth Forest on the north side of the lake, which includes Bald Knob (2050 ft.), also have trails that are described here.

Mount Cardigan

The outstanding peak of west central New Hampshire, Mt. Cardigan (3155 ft.) is located in Orange (near Canaan) and Alexandria (near Bristol). Excellent views are available from the steep-sided rock dome of "Old Baldy" itself, as well as from the South Peak (2864 ft.)—also noted for its blueberries in season —and from Firescrew (3064 ft.), the north peak, named for a spiral of fire and smoke that rose from it during the conflagration in 1855 that denuded the upper slopes of the mountain. Though relatively low, Cardigan provides a great variety of terrain, from low hardwood forests to the wind-swept summit. Its trails vary from gentle woods walks, to the West Ridge Trail (a traditional first "big mountain climb" for children), to the Holt Trail, with upper ledges that constitute one of the more difficult scrambles among the regular hiking trails in New England. From the east, you can make a fine circuit by ascending Cardigan by the Holt, Cathedral Forest, and Clark trails—or by taking the much more challenging Holt Trail all the way—and returning over Firescrew via the Mowglis and Manning trails.

In addition to Cardigan itself, there are excellent views from several of the smaller mountains on the two long ridges that run easterly toward Newfound Lake. On the northeast ridge, traversed by the Elwell Trail (although some sections are obscure) all the way from the edge of the lake to the north shoulder of Cardigan, Little Sugarloaf (1002 ft.), Sugarloaf (1370 ft.), and Bear Mtn. (1847 ft.) are easily accessible and offer excellent views. On the southeast ridge, traversed by the Skyland Trail, Church Mtn. (2270 ft.), Grafton Knob (2201 ft.), Crane Mtn. (2423 ft.), and Orange Mtn. (2684 ft., also sometimes called Gilman Mtn.) offer interesting outlooks.

Most of the mountain is contained in a state forest of more than 5000 acres. Adjacent to the park is the AMC's 1200-acre Cardigan Reservation, which occupies much of Shem Valley and portions of the east slopes of the mountain. The AMC Cardigan Lodge complex, mentioned at the beginning of this section, provides meals and lodging to the public during the summer season. Nearby Newfound Lake, with a major public beach at Wellington State Park, offers swimming, boating, and fishing. The usual approach is from Bristol, easily accessible from I-93. Turn left (west) from NH 3A onto West Shore Rd. at the stone church at the foot of Newfound Lake, continue straight ahead through the crossroads at 1.9 mi., bear right onto Fowler River Rd. at 3.1 mi., and turn left onto Brook Rd. at 6.3 mi. At 7.4 mi. from the church, turn right on Shem Valley Rd. (gravel), then bear right at 7.5 mi. at the red schoolhouse and continue to the lodge at 8.9 mi. There is an alternative route marked by small "AMC" arrow signs that is longer but may be better at some times; to follow this route, bear left onto North Rd. at 3.1 mi. from the stone church, turn right onto Washburn Rd. at 4.0 mi., then right again onto Mt. Cardigan Rd. at 4.2 mi., reaching the jct. of Brook Rd. (right, paved) and Shem Valley Rd. (straight ahead, gravel) at 7.9 mi. (the 7.4 mi. point on the other route). Shem Valley Rd. is plowed in winter, but must be driven with great care.

While many of the trails on Mt. Cardigan are heavily used and well beaten, others, noted in the individual descriptions, are lightly used, sparsely marked, and receive little maintenance. Such trails may be difficult to follow if not recently maintained, in the early part of the season when a footway is not clearly established, or in the fall when covered by leaves. Although these trails are not recommended for the inexperienced, they may be followed fairly readily by experienced hikers, although you should carry map and compass, keep track of your location on the map, and carefully follow whatever markings do exist. Mt. Cardigan is covered by the AMC Cardigan Map; the mountain itself and most of the trails are shown on the USGS Mt. Cardigan quadrangle, with lesser amounts of outlying areas on the Newfound Lake, Grafton, and Danbury quadrangles.

Volunteer maintenance efforts at Cardigan include those by the Cardigan Highlanders, whose address is PO Box 104, Enfield Center, NH 03749-0104. The AMC Cardigan Lodge Committee (c/o AMC, 5 Joy St., Boston, MA 02108) also sponsors several volunteer work weekends each year. The Cardigan region was hit hard by the January 1998 ice storm, and in some areas the loss of forest canopy has permitted a great proliferation of undergrowth. On trails in these areas the footway may be obscured by fast-growing vegetation during the summer months, particularly later in the season when shrubs and berry bushes reach their maximum growth. Hikers should be alert and be prepared at least to return to their starting point if a trail is obscure or impassable. It would be wise to check with Cardigan Lodge before attempting the less popular trails.

West Ridge Trail (map 2: D1–D2)

This is the main trail to Mt. Cardigan from the west, as well as the shortest and easiest route to the summit. From NH 118, 0.5 mi. north of Canaan, turn right at a large Cardigan State Park sign. Bear right 2.7 mi. from NH 118, shortly after crossing Orange Brook. At 3.4 mi. bear left to a parking area at 4.1 mi., where there are picnic tables and rest rooms. The former shelter called the Hermitage was removed in 1991.

The well-beaten trail, blazed in orange, starts at a sign in the parking area. At 0.5 mi. the South Ridge Trail diverges right at a sharp turn. The West Ridge Trail climbs moderately, crosses a small brook on a bridge, and climbs to a jct. with the Skyland Trail right. It then crosses Cliff's Bridge at 1.1 mi., and shortly beyond here a branch trail called the Ranger Cabin Trail (marked by a cairn) leads to the right 0.2 mi. to the South Ridge Trail. The West Ridge Trail—marked by cairns, paint on the rocks, and blaze boards—ascends the broad, open summit ledges and joins the Clark Trail just below the summit. Descending hikers should take note that this trail, and no other, is marked by cairns and blaze boards.

Distance from Cardigan State Park parking area (1930')

to Mt. Cardigan summit (3155'): 1.5 mi. (2.5 km.), 1250 ft., 1 hr. 20 min.

South Ridge Trail (map 2: D2)

This trail provides access to Mt. Cardigan, South Peak, and Rimrock, and also makes possible a scenic loop in combination with the West Ridge Trail. It is blazed in orange below Rimrock and white above. It diverges right from the West Ridge Trail 0.5 mi. from the state park parking area, crosses a brook and climbs, rather steeply at times, to Rimrock, where it crosses the Skyland Trail at 0.7 mi. (Descending, follow the left of two lines of cairns on the ledge below Rimrock.) The trail continues across marked ledges and passes the summit of South Peak at 1.0 mi., then turns left and descends to the jct. with the Hurricane Gap Trail on the right (the former portion of the Hurricane Gap Trail west of the South Ridge Trail has been closed to protect the extremely fragile area it used to cross). It then turns sharp right at a jct. (left is the Ranger Cabin Trail leading 0.2 mi. to the West Ridge Trail) and continues to the warden's cabin, where it ends at the Clark Trail.

Distance from West Ridge Trail (2250')

   to Clark Trail (2900'): 1.3 mi. (2.1 km.), 700 ft., 1 hr.

Distance from Cardigan State Park parking area (1930')

   to starting point by complete loop via West Ridge, Clark, and South Ridge trails: 3.6 mi. (5.8 km.), 1300 ft., 2 hr. 25 min.

Orange Cove Trail (map 2: A2)

This trail, which is really a dirt road (the old Groton–Orange highway) used as an access trail, provides a relatively short approach from the west to the Mowglis Trail, Crag Shelter, and the summit of Cardigan via the north ridge and Firescrew. Follow access directions above for the West Ridge Trail, but bear left onto New Colony Rd. 2.7 mi. from NH 118 immediately after crossing Orange Brook. Follow this road 1.3 mi. just past the end of the pavement and the state park boundary, and park on the right before the gate. The trail has no sign but is easy to follow. It climbs easily past a large beaver pond at 1.0 mi. to end at the Mowglis Trail in the col between Firescrew and Cataloochee Mtns. The Mowglis Trail continues straight ahead on the old road to Groton, or turns sharp right on a foot path to Firescrew and Mt. Cardigan.

Distance from end of paved road (1850')

   to Mowglis Trail (2310'): 1.6 mi. (2.5 km.), 450 ft., 1 hr.

Mowglis Trail (map 2: A3–C2)

This trail provides access to Cardigan and Firescrew from the north. From Hebron village on the north end of the lake, follow signs to Sculptured Rocks State Geological Site on the Cockermouth River, an interesting glacial gorge with potholes that is a popular picnic spot with a good swimming hole. Continue 1.0 mi. farther on Sculptured Rocks Rd. to a point just beyond the green bridge over Atwell Brook. The trail (no sign) follows the old Groton–Orange road, which forks left and follows Atwell Brook, ascending at a moderate grade. It may be possible to drive 1.4 mi. to a logging road fork, where the trail keeps right on the old road. The trail ascends past the state park boundary at 2.4 mi. to a jct. with the Orange Cove Trail at 3.5 mi. in the col between Cilley's Cave and Cataloochee Mtn. Here the Orange Cove Trail continues ahead on the old road, while the white-blazed Mowglis Trail turns left and climbs briefly to a jct. on the left with the Elwell Trail at 3.7 mi. Soon after this jct. an abandoned spur trail formerly led left 80 yd. to Cilley's Cave, a lonely, rocky retreat where it is said a hermit once lived.

The Mowglis Trail then ascends more steeply, and at 4.6 mi. passes Crag Shelter (an open shelter accommodating six with no reliable water source). It passes to the right of the shelter and climbs steeply to a ledgy area and a north outlook. There the trail turns sharp right and climbs to the summit of Firescrew at 5.1 mi., where it meets the Manning Trail. It then descends across wide ledges deeply marked by glacial action and passes a side trail left, marked by a sign painted on the rocks, that descends 0.2 mi. and 200 ft. to Grotto Cave and a smaller boulder cave. The main trail then ascends steeply to the summit of Mt. Cardigan.

Distances from Sculptured Rocks Rd. (800')

> *to* Elwell Trail (2450'): 3.7 mi., 1650 ft., 2 hr. 40 min.
>
> *to* Firescrew summit (3064'): 5.1 mi., 2300 ft., 3 hr. 40 min.
>
> *to* Mt. Cardigan summit (3155'): 5.7 mi. (9.2 km.), 2500 ft. (rev. 100 ft.), 4 hr. 5 min.

Elwell Trail (map 2: A5–B3)

The Elwell Trail (in theory at least) extends more than 10 mi. from Newfound Lake to the Mowglis Trail 2.0 mi. north of Mt. Cardigan. It is named in honor of Col. Alcott Farrar Elwell, who directed Camp Mowglis for fifty years and helped develop many of the trails in this region. It is marked with yellow blazes and Camp Mowglis signs. Recent logging has caused disruption and required some relocations, and the January 1998 ice storm added its severe destruction to the situation. The middle section of the trail (Bear Mtn. to Oregon Mtn.) should probably be regarded as a virtual bushwhack and attempted only by those with map and compass and the skills to use them. The upper (western) part of the trail, though brushed in 2004, should be attempted with caution and the willingness and ability to bushwhack, and cannot be recommended to inexperienced hikers.

The trail begins at a new parking area off the west side of West Shore Rd. about 100 yd. north of the entrance to Wellington State Park. It enters the woods at a kiosk, soon swings right, crosses a brook, and climbs easily. At 0.5 mi. it passes a spur trail that leads left 0.2 mi. to Goose Pond, then crosses the open summit of Little Sugarloaf at 0.8 mi., where there is a view over Newfound Lake. It continues along the ridge and finally climbs steeply to the summit of Sugarloaf at 1.7 mi., where there are more views over the lake. About 100 yd. past this summit the trail turns sharp left, descends steeply, then runs fairly level across the old Alexandria–Hebron turnpike.

It then climbs by steep switchbacks with rough footing, passing the jct. on the right with the Bear Mountain Trail at 2.8 mi., where the grade moderates. Soon it passes a good outlook over Newfound Lake and continues to climb, steeply at times, to the summit of Bear Mtn. (1847 ft.) at 3.3 mi., where there is a restricted view. The Elwell Trail continues along the ridge, swinging to the west, then descends and crosses under power lines, where the serious trail-finding problems begin. It enters recent logging, and passes a jct. on the right with the northern part of the Welton Falls Trail (which should be considered abandoned) at 4.6 mi. At 5.3 mi., where the southern part of the Welton Falls Trail (abandoned) formerly descended to the left, the Elwell Trail ascends gradually with occasional steep pitches past several scenic outlooks to a fork, where the right branch leads in a short distance to the summit of Oregon Mtn. (2239 ft.). At the top of a gravel log landing the trail turns sharp right (north) onto the Old Dicey Road and travels through a clear-cut marked by blazed two-by-fours until it reaches the jct. where the Carter Gibbs Trail (which may be difficult to follow, though it was brushed in 2004) continues straight ahead at 7.7 mi. Here the Elwell Trail turns left, crosses a brook, and climbs gradually to the summit of Mowglis Mtn. (2370 ft.) at 8.7 mi., where a tablet on the right honors Camp Mowglis. It descends, climbs over a knoll with a good view south, then descends again to the next col at 9.8 mi., where the Back 80 Trail diverges left for Cardigan Lodge. It then climbs fairly steeply to an abandoned spur trail leading left 130 yd. to Cilley's Cave and descends slightly to end at the Mowglis Trail.

Distances from West Shore Rd. (600')

> *to* Sugarloaf summit (1370'): 1.7 mi., 900 ft. (rev. 150 ft.), 1 hr. 20 min.
>
> *to* Bear Mtn. summit (1847'): 3.3 mi., 1750 ft. (rev. 350 ft.), 2 hr. 30 min.
>
> *to* Mowglis Mtn. summit (2370'): 8.7 mi., 3100 ft. (rev. 850 ft.), 5 hr. 55 min.
>
> *to* Mowglis Trail junction (2450'): 10.4 mi. (16.7 km.), 3550 ft. (rev. 350 ft.), 7 hr.

Bear Mountain Trail

This steep, rough trail provides an alternative route up the steep eastern side of Bear Mtn. from the old Alexandria–Hebron turnpike to the Elwell Trail 0.5 mi. south of the summit of Bear Mtn. The ledges are slippery when wet. To reach the trailhead, follow Bear Mtn. Rd., which leaves West Shore Rd. 2.0 mi. south of Hebron and 2.5 mi. north of Wellington State Park. After 0.3 mi., follow the gravel road to the left as the paved road swings right toward a housing development. Depending upon driving conditions, it may be advisable to park here and walk the remainder of the way. Follow the gravel road (the old Alexandria–Hebron turnpike) 0.7 mi. uphill to the trail (sign), which is on the right 0.2 mi. below the jct. of the road with the Elwell Trail in the saddle between Sugarloaf Mtn. and Bear Mtn. There is limited parking just above the trailhead; do not block the gated road on the left.

The trail (orange blazes) ascends through a logged area to a small stream, swings left, and immediately attacks the steep, rocky eastern slope of Bear Mtn., climbing steeply by longer, then shorter switchbacks. It reaches the Elwell Trail 0.5 mi. above its jct. with the old Alexandria–Hebron turnpike and 0.5 mi. below the main summit of Bear Mtn. The best outlook on Bear Mtn. is on the Elwell Trail 0.1 mi. to the right (north) of this jct.

Distance from old Alexandria–Hebron turnpike (900')

> *to* Elwell Trail (1600'): 0.5 mi. (0.7 km.), 700 ft., 35 min.

Carter Gibbs Trail (map 2: A4)

This trail was brushed in 2004 but, due to logging activity, maintenance has been sporadic, and it has been difficult to follow in the recent past. At the present time it should probably be attempted only by experienced route-finders. The trail leaves Sculptured Rocks Rd. at a small gravel turnout on the south side, 0.2 mi. east of the Sculptured Rocks parking area. It may be possible to drive the first 1.2 mi.

Leaving Sculptured Rocks Rd., it follows a gravel road for about 0.5 mi., then turns left where a right fork crosses Dane Brook on a snowmobile bridge. In another 0.3 mi. it bears right at a fork and follows an old logging road that gradually peters out. The trail then climbs more steeply to the height-of-land between Oregon Mtn. and Mowglis Mtn., where a side path (sign) leads right 0.2 mi. to an outlook on Carter's Knob. The main trail then descends sharply 0.3 mi. to the Elwell Trail at the upper terminus of the Old Dicey Road.

Distance from Sculptured Rocks Rd. (750')

   to Elwell Trail (1850'): 3.0 mi. (4.8 km.), 1400 ft. (rev. 300 ft.), 2 hr. 10 min.

Welton Falls Trail

This trail runs from Hobart Hill Rd., 0.8 mi. from the village square in Hebron to Welton Falls Rd. just north of the bridge over Fowler River, crossing the Elwell Trail on the ridgecrest. Although it was reportedly brushed out in 2004 and potentially would make possible a number of attractive loop trips involving sections of the Elwell Trail, this trail has been extremely difficult to follow by anyone not familiar with it for many years, and at present it should be considered abandoned by anyone not prepared to find their own way with map and compass.

Old Dicey Road (map 2: A4–B4)

Follow the first route described above for Cardigan Lodge but bear right 6.3 mi. from the stone church and follow Welton Falls Rd. for another 1.2 mi. Where the good road (Cream Hill Rd.) turns sharp right uphill, park on the left shoulder. Follow the unmaintained road, which is the Old Dicey Road, straight ahead across the bridge. At 0.3 mi. the Manning Trail diverges left on a cart track, while the Old Dicey Road continues to a clearing at 1.2 mi. Here the

Back 80 Loop continues straight ahead. Beyond this point the Old Dicey Road has been severely disrupted by damage from the January 1998 ice storm. It turns right and climbs up a gravel logging road to a landing at the top. Here the Elwell Trail enters on the right, and the trails turn left and run together through a clear-cut marked by blazed two-by-fours to the former jct. with the Carter Gibbs Trail.

Distance from Welton Falls Rd. (1000')

>   *to* junction with Carter Gibbs Trail (1850'): 2.1 mi. (3.4 km.), 850 ft., 1 hr. 30 min.

Back 80 Loop (map 2: B4–C4)

This short trail connects the Old Dicey Road with the Back 80 Trail and makes possible a circuit to Welton Falls from Cardigan Lodge. It follows an old road straight ahead from the clearing where the Old Dicey Road turns right, then bears left to cross two brooks within a short distance, and ascends across another brook and the 93Z Ski Trail to meet the Back 80 Trail at a cellar hole.

Distance from Old Dicey Road (1400')

>   *to* Back 80 Trail (1750'): 0.8 mi. (1.2 km.), 350 ft., 35 min.

Back 80 Trail (map 2: B3–D4)

This trail diverges right from the Holt Trail about 100 yd. west of Cardigan Lodge and follows an old logging road. At 0.3 mi. the Short Circuit Ski Trail diverges right, and at 0.4 mi. the Whitney Way Ski Trail diverges left. At 0.8 mi., where the Alleeway Ski Trail turns left, the Back 80 Trail turns sharp right and reaches a cellar hole. The trail to the right here is the Back 80 Loop to the Old Dicey Road; the Back 80 Trail turns left (follow the trail with care from here on). (*Note: A relocation, which is planned to be opened in the spring of 2005, will leave the existing route at this point and rejoin at the boundary line.*) It crosses the 93Z Ski Trail, then a brook at a scenic little waterfall. It turns sharp left at 1.2 mi. at the east corner of Back 80 Lot and runs along the northern border of the lot along the edge of a logged area. The trail goes around a flowage from a beaver dam, which may force a detour through the woods at 1.8 mi. It passes a jct. with the Duke's Link Ski Trail, then turns sharp right, crosses a brook, turns left, and follows the brook and the edge of another beaver pond to the back corner post (marked Draper-NHFS-AMC). The trail then ascends gradually across a brook to end at the Elwell Trail in the col between Mowglis Mtn. and Cilley's Cave. There is a good viewpoint on the Elwell Trail 0.4 mi. to the right (east) of this jct. For the summit of Mt. Cardigan, turn left on the Elwell Trail and ascend to the jct. with the Mowglis Trail on a section of trail that is usually relatively easy to follow.

Distance from Holt Trail (1400')

   to Elwell Trail (2000'): 2.4 mi. (3.9 km.), 600 ft., 1 hr. 30 min.

Manning Trail (map 2: C3–C5)

This trail was constructed by the AMC as a memorial to the three Manning brothers—Robert, Charles, and Francis—who were killed by a train during a blizzard in 1924 while hiking on a section of railroad near Glencliff that was once often used as a shortcut between Dartmouth Outing Club trails. The trail (yellow blazes, no sign) leaves the Old Dicey Road 0.3 mi. from Welton Falls Rd. (the second of two old roads that diverge left after crossing the bridge), and follows a cart path to the Fowler River, crosses on stones, and enters the Welton Falls Reservation (NHDP). It continues up the river to a deep, mossy ravine and the main falls. There are many attractive falls and rapids, as well as spectacular potholes, above and below the main falls, which are at 0.3 mi. From Welton Falls the trail climbs and descends two small ridges. Then at 0.5 mi. it turns right, crosses the river on rocks without a bridge (difficult at high water), and climbs along a bank above the stream. It swings right at 1.1 mi., ascends to a plateau, where it crosses the 93Z Ski Trail, and passes through a grove of spruces. It then descends through a picnic area to Cardigan Lodge. (To reach the Manning Trail to Welton Falls from the lodge, ascend through a picnic area to the road at the right of the fireplace.)

The Manning Trail continues past the lodge, coincides with the Holt Trail for 0.3 mi., then diverges right and passes the old Holt cellar hole. The Duke's Ski Trail leaves to the right, then the Manning Trail turns right at an arrow, crosses back over the Duke's Ski Trail, and climbs through the woods to the first ledges. It passes a small brook, then climbs again to a great open ledge with fine views. At the top of this ledge it turns left through scrubby woods, ascending steeply at times, then follows cairns and paint markings across flat ledges to the cairn where it ends at the Mowglis Trail, just below the summit of Firescrew. The summit of Mt. Cardigan is reached by turning left on the Mowglis Trail.

Distances from Old Dicey Road (1050')

> *to* Cardigan Lodge (1392'): 1.5 mi., 400 ft., 55 min.
> *to* Mowglis Trail near Firescrew summit (3060'): 4.0 mi. (6.4 km.), 2050 ft., 3 hr.

Distance from Cardigan Lodge (1392')

> *to* Mt. Cardigan summit (3155') via Manning Trail and Mowglis Trail: 3.0 mi. (4.8 km.), 1950 ft. (rev. 200 ft.), 2 hr. 30 min.

Holt Trail (map 2: D2–D4)

This is the shortest but far from the easiest route from Cardigan Lodge to the summit of Mt. Cardigan. The upper ledges are very steep, and the scramble up these ledges is much more difficult than on any other trail in this section and one of the most difficult in New England; it may be dangerous in wet or icy conditions. Allow extra time for this challenging and strenuous climb. The trail is named for the founder of Camp Mowglis, Elizabeth Ford Holt.

From Cardigan Lodge the Holt Trail follows a gravel road to a jct. with the Manning Trail, then a woods road almost to the Bailey Brook bridge. It crosses the bridge and continues to Grand Junction, where the Cathedral Forest Trail diverges left, providing an easier ascent of Mt. Cardigan via Cathedral Forest and the Clark Trail. The Alexandria Ski Trail also diverges left here, and shortly beyond the Alleeway Ski Trail diverges right. The Holt Trail continues along Bailey Brook to a point directly under the summit, climbs steeply on a rocky path through woods, then emerges on open ledges and makes a rapid, very steep ascent over marked ledges to the summit.

Distances from Cardigan Lodge (1392')

> *to* Grand Junction (1700'): 1.1 mi., 300 ft., 40 min.
> *to* Mt. Cardigan summit (3155'): 2.2 mi. (3.6 km.), 1750 ft., 2 hr.

Cathedral Forest Trail (map 2: D3)

This trail (also called the Holt–Clark Cutoff) diverges left from the Holt Trail at Grand Junction and ascends to the Clark Trail in the Cathedral Forest, providing the easiest route to the summit of Cardigan from the east. About 100 yd. above the jct. the Vistamont Trail branches left to Orange Mtn. Ascending in graded switchbacks, the trail joins the Clark Trail in a dense fir grove.

Distance from Holt Trail at Grand Junction (1700')

    to Clark Trail (2250'): 0.6 mi. (1.0 km.), 550 ft., 35 min.

Distance from Cardigan Lodge (1392')

    to Mt. Cardigan summit (3155') via Holt, Cathedral Forest, and Clark
trails: 2.6 mi. (4.2 km.), 1750 ft., 2 hr. 10 min.

Clark Trail (map 2: D2–E4)

This trail begins on the Woodland Trail 1.2 mi. from Cardigan Lodge, continuing straight ahead on an older road at a point where the Woodland Trail turns
sharp left on the logging road it has been following. It passes an old cellar hole,
enters the state reservation at a level grade in a beautiful forest, then climbs
steeply to cross the Vistamont Trail at 0.8 mi. The grade becomes easier, and
the Clark Trail reaches the Cathedral Forest, where the Cathedral Forest Trail
enters from the right at 1.1 mi. As the trail continues a moderate ascent, the
Alexandria Ski Trail enters right near P. J. Ledge, and 30 yd. farther the Hurricane Gap Trail leaves left for High Cabin and the South Ridge Trail at Hurricane Gap. The Clark Trail continues past a side trail left that leads to a spring
and High Cabin, then climbs on ledges and through scrub to the warden's cabin
at 1.8 mi., where it meets the South Ridge Trail. Turning right, it follows
marked ledges steeply to the summit.

Distance from the Woodland Trail (1600')

    to Mt. Cardigan summit (3155'): 2.0 mi. (3.2 km.), 1550 ft., 1 hr. 45 min.

Hurricane Gap Trail (map 2: D2–D3)

This trail connects the east side of the mountain to the South Ridge Trail in
Hurricane Gap, the pass between Cardigan and South Peak. The former western half passed through a fragile area—a wet depression with luxuriant
mosses, easily damaged by footsteps—and has been closed to all use. The trail
leaves the Clark Trail just above P. J. Ledge, passes an unsigned spur right to a
spring, then reaches the AMC High Cabin, where another spur trail leads right
60 yd. to the spring and 40 yd. farther to the Clark Trail. It then climbs to the
South Ridge Trail at the height-of-land at 0.4 mi.

Distance from Clark Trail (2600')

    to South Ridge Trail (2800'): 0.4 mi. (0.7 km.), 200 ft., 20 min.

Vistamont Trail (map 2: D3–E3)

The Vistamont Trail connects the Holt Trail with the Skyland Trail at Orange Mtn. (sometimes also called Gilman Mtn.). It leaves the Cathedral Forest Trail left about 100 yd. above Grand Junction and rises over a low ridge, where it crosses the Clark Trail at 0.6 mi. It drops to cross a branch of Clark Brook, then ascends by switchbacks up the east spur of Orange Mtn., climbing moderately on open ledges to the Skyland Trail 80 yd. southeast of the rocky summit, where there are fine views.

Distance from Cathedral Forest Trail (1750')

   to Skyland Trail (2650'): 1.6 mi. (2.6 km.), 1000 ft., 1 hr. 20 min.

Woodland Trail (map 2: D4–E4)

This trail runs from Cardigan Lodge to the Skyland Trail just northwest of the summit of Church Mtn., giving direct access from Cardigan Lodge to the interesting outlooks from the ledges along the Skyland Trail. It leaves the parking lot to the left of the pond, crosses the outlet brook on a bridge, and passes the east entrance of the Kimball Ski Trail. It continues through woods past the Brock Farm cellar hole and field, then turns right on a rough dirt logging road at 0.7 mi. At 1.2 mi., where the Clark Trail continues straight ahead on an older road, the Woodland Trail follows the more recent logging road as it turns sharp left and descends across a brook, then climbs to a large beaver pond at 2.1 mi. From here on the trail is harder to follow and great care must be used. It ascends along the inlet brook, crosses it, and doubles back along the edge of the pond, then climbs moderately past a corner post marked "Draper" in a boggy area near a large boulder. Finally it rises more steeply to end at the Skyland Trail on the northwest shoulder of Church Mtn.

Distance from Cardigan Lodge (1392')

   to Skyland Trail (2250'): 3.3 mi. (5.2 km.), 900 ft., 2 hr. 5 min.

Skyland Trail (map 2: D2–E3)

This trail runs from Alexandria Four Corners to the West Ridge Trail just below the former site of the Hermitage shelter. It follows the western and southern boundaries of Shem Valley, and in 4.5 mi. crosses five of the six peaks that extend south and southeast from Cardigan's summit. It is lightly marked for much of its distance and, particularly between Brown Mtn. and Orange Mtn., must be followed with great care. It is, however, a very scenic route.

The trail starts at Alexandria Four Corners, reached by following signs from the stone church at the foot of Newfound Lake to Alexandria village. Continue through the village on the main road, which turns sharp right, then left. Pass under the power lines and then, as the main road turns sharp left for Danbury, continue straight ahead for about 4.0 mi. to the crossroads (sign, "Rosie's Rd."). Best parking is here; do not block roads above.

The trail follows the road that runs right (north) from the corner and soon bears left at a fork. At 0.3 mi. it turns sharp left (arrow) on a short road to a clearing, and ascends moderately through woods to the edge of an open field and a dilapidated cabin in the woods. It climbs through woods again to an outlook near the wooded summit of Brown Mtn. (2270 ft.), then turns left and crosses the col to the east knob of Church Mtn. at 1.1 mi., where there is another outlook. It continues over the flat, wooded summit of Church Mtn. and past a jct. (right) at 1.3 mi. with the Woodland Trail coming up from Cardigan Lodge, then follows the ridge top over Grafton Knob to Crane Mtn. at 2.1 mi., with good views from several ledges near the summit. The Skyland Trail continues to Orange Mtn. at 3.3 mi., where the Vistamont Trail enters 80 yd. before the summit. There are excellent views from the summit ledges. The trail descends to a col, then climbs fairly steeply to Rimrock at 4.3 mi., where it crosses the South Ridge Trail. It descends along a ledge (follow the right of two lines of cairns), drops rather steeply, and soon enters the West Ridge Trail just below the Hermitage site.

Distances from Alexandria Four Corners (1800')

> *to* Orange Mtn. (2684'): 3.3 mi., 1400 ft. (rev. 500 ft.), 2 hr. 20 min.

> *to* South Ridge Trail at Rimrock (2900'): 4.4 mi., 1850 ft. (rev. 250 ft.), 3 hr. 10 min.

> *to* West Ridge Trail (2650'): 4.6 mi. (7.3 km.), 1850 ft. (rev. 250 ft.), 3 hr. 15 min.

> *to* Mt. Cardigan summit (3155') via South Ridge Trail and Clark Trail: 5.4 mi. (8.7 km.), 2150 ft. (rev. 50 ft.), 3 hr. 45 min.

Distance from Cardigan Lodge (1392')

> *to* Mt. Cardigan summit (3155') via Woodland Trail, Skyland Trail, South Ridge Trail, and Clark Trail: 7.4 mi. (11.9 km.), 2350 ft. (rev. 600 ft.), 4 hr. 55 min.

Ski Trails at Cardigan Lodge

The AMC maintains a number of ski trails in the woods around Cardigan Lodge, in addition to the hiking trails, many of which are also skiable. A map available at the lodge shows most of these trails and their ratings, which range from novice cross-country to expert alpine terrain on the ledges of Cardigan and Firescrew. Some of these trails were cut as alpine trails in the days before modern tows became common. Ski trails are not maintained for summer use, and hikers are requested not to use them.

Cockermouth Forest

This 1002-acre tract, owned by the Society for the Protection of New Hampshire Forests, is located on the west slopes of Mt. Crosby in the town of Groton. A network of recently opened trails provides access to several features, including Bald Knob (2050 ft.), a ledgy spur of Mt. Crosby, and secluded Little Pond. Where the trails utilize old woods roads they are easy to follow, though markings (yellow metal blazes) should be carefully noted at jcts. Other sections of trail may show little evidence of a footway but are well marked and fairly easy to follow for experienced hikers.

To reach the trailhead, follow North Shore Rd. west from NH 3A for 2.4 mi. to the village of Hebron at the north end of Newfound Lake. Continue ahead on Groton Rd., then bear right onto North Groton Rd. at 4.0 mi. and follow it to a sign for Cockermouth Forest and the John F. Woodhouse Trail on the right at 6.0 mi. from NH 3A. Drive 0.1 mi. down the woods road in front of the sign and park on the left before a gate; do not block the gate.

Bald Knob Trail (USGS Newfound Lake quad)

This trail provides access to fine views from the open ledges of Bald Knob. From the gate, follow the woods road across a bridge over a brook. In 100 yd. the trail passes through a clearing and bears left at a fork. At 0.4 mi. the lower end of the Little Pond Trail (sign) diverges left on another woods road, while the Bald Knob Trail bears right and descends slightly to cross a brook on a footbridge at 0.5 mi. The trail now rises moderately with stone walls lining both sides of the old road. The upper end of the Little Pond Trail (sign) diverges sharp left at 0.7 mi. The Bald Knob Trail continues climbing, crossing two small brooks, then levels and turns left onto another woods road at 1.0 mi. at a point where the road the trail has been following begins to descend. The trail climbs moderately with occasional wet footing, swinging to the southeast. At 1.6 mi. it turns left off the road and climbs to the ridgecrest on an obscure but well-blazed footway, then ascends steeply up the ridge to the north and ends at the open ledges of Bald Knob. Various outlooks provide views of New-found Lake, Mt. Cardigan, and the southern White Mountains.

Distances from gate (970')

> *to* upper junction with Little Pond Trail (1220'): 0.7 mi., 250 ft., 30 min.
>
> *to* Bald Knob (2050'): 1.9 mi. (3.1 km), 1100 ft., 1 hr. 30 min.

Little Pond Trail

This trail makes a loop from the Bald Knob Trail with spur trails leading to Lit-tle Pond and a ledge outlook. It diverges left (sign) from the Bald Knob Trail 0.4 mi. from the trailhead gate; avoid an unmarked trail that leaves sharp left. It ascends a woods road past a cascade, crosses a brook on an old wooden bridge at 0.2 mi. and follows the main road ahead (left) at a fork just beyond. At 0.5 mi. it turns left onto another woods road (arrow) and ascends gently to a T-intersection, marked with blazes but no signs, at 0.6 mi. Here the main trail turns sharp right while the Little Pond Spur diverges left.

Little Pond Spur. This trail leads to Little Pond, passing another spur trail to a ledge outlook. From the Little Pond Trail it follows a woods road 40 yds. to a clearing, turns left, then in another 70 yds. turns right and exits the clearing. It crosses a small brook and at 0.2 mi. turns right off the road onto a poorly defined but well-marked footway. At 0.3 mi., just beyond the crossing of a small brook, the Ledges Spur diverges right (sign). Here the Little Pond Spur turns left and ascends along a small ridge to the right of the pond's ledgy outlet brook. It enters a mossy spruce forest, crosses the brook near the outlet, and climbs over a knoll, ending at a ledge overlooking the pond and surrounding bog. Distance to Little Pond (1430'): 0.7 mi., 150 ft. (rev. 50 ft.), 25 min.

Ledges Spur. This path diverges right from the Little Pond Spur, 0.3 mi. from its jct. with the Little Pond Trail, and climbs 90 yds. alongside a brook to an interesting flume. It then turns left and climbs steeply, with several twists and turns, passing an overhanging ledge and ending at an open ledge with a good view west, including a glimpse of Little Pond. Distance to ledge (1500'): 0.2 mi., 200 ft., 10 min.

From the jct. with the Little Pond Spur, the Little Pond Trail turns sharp right and follows a woods road 100 yds. to a clearing, passing to the left of a cellar hole, and takes the left fork (sign for Bald Knob) at the far side of the opening. It crosses a small brook, swings right (southwest) and descends easily, crossing another brook at 0.8 mi. where an old rotting bridge is best avoided. It continues along the woods road with gentle ups and downs to its upper jct. with the Bald Knob Trail, 0.7 mi. from the trailhead gate.

Distances from lower junction with Bald Knob Trail (1100')

　to Little Pond Spur (1350'): 0.6 mi., 250 ft., 25 min.

　to upper junction with Bald Knob Trail (1220'): 1.2 mi. (1.9 km), 300 ft. (rev. 150 ft.), 45 min.

Plymouth Mountain

Plymouth Mtn. (2193 ft.) lies in Plymouth, northeast of Newfound Lake. The true summit is wooded, but nearby open ledges afford excellent views. Refer to the USGS Ashland quadrangle.

Plymouth Mountain Trail (USGS Ashland & Newfound Lake quads)

This trail, which has been in use for many years, is the easiest route to the summit of Plymouth Mtn. At the crossroads on NH 3A near the head of Newfound Lake, where North Shore Rd. to Hebron village runs west, go east on Pike Hill Rd. and bear left at 0.3 mi. and 0.8 mi. from NH 3A. At 1.3 mi. from NH 3A, just beyond a house on the left, park on the left side of the road (sign "TR-PK"). Continue up the road on foot a short distance to a point where the good road bears left as a private driveway. Continue straight ahead on the older, rougher road and in 0.1 mi. the trail leaves to the right on an old woods road (sign). It is marked by stenciled Camp Mowglis signs. It runs over a low ridge and descends to cross a brook (follow trail with care), follows another old road uphill, and turns sharp left where a branch trail enters right. (Descending, turn sharp right here where the branch trail, marked by a Mowglis sign, goes almost straight ahead.) The trail ascends to an outlook over Newfound Lake, becomes less steep, crosses a false summit, and climbs to the true summit (disc benchmark), where it meets the Sutherland Trail from Plymouth. From here an open ledge 30 yd. straight ahead (east) on the Sutherland Trail (for which the only sign at the summit reads "Outlook") provides fine views of Franconia Notch and the White Mtns., while a line of cairns leads right (southwest) 0.1 mi. to a partial outlook over Newfound Lake to Mt. Cardigan. The impressive outlook from the East

Cliff can be reached by following the Sutherland Trail for 0.2 mi. and then a side path (obscure) for another 0.2 mi. Hikers experienced in following obscure trails can reach the "Pike's Peak" outlook by taking the Sutherland Trail 0.4 mi. from the summit to a side path that leads right (sign) 100 yd. to the viewpoint.

Distances from parking spot on Pike Hill Rd. (1300')

  to Plymouth Mtn. summit (2193'): 1.6 mi. (2.6 km.), 900 ft., 1 hr. 15 min.

Sutherland Trail (USGS Ashland quad)

This newer trail from Plymouth on the north side of the mountain makes a longer but more satisfying ascent than the traditional route and provides access to a knob called locally "Pike's Peak," a ledge with an excellent view north and east. Between Pike's Peak and the summit the trail is obscure and requires care to follow (though there are plans to reblaze it in the near future), and the ledges in this section are very slippery when wet. There are also plans to relocate the trail to avoid the road walk on Scenic View Dr., with the trailhead possibly moved to a point on Hebron Rd.

From US 3/NH 25 at the south end of downtown Plymouth, take Warren St. for 0.2 mi. to a crossroads with four-way stop signs and "Dangerous Intersection" signs. Go through this intersection with a slight jog to the right onto Texas Hill Rd.; at 2.3 mi. pass the jct. with Hebron Rd., where there is a boulder in the triangular island between the converging roads. (The trailhead may be relocated to Hebron Rd.) At 2.6 mi. the trail begins on a gravel road to the right, signed Scenic View Dr; here there is also a sign for Plymouth Mtn. Park at a limited space on the shoulder opposite the gravel road, or at a pulloff about 0.1 mi. back toward Hebron Rd.

Follow the gravel road up a long grade past a house. At 0.3 mi. the road bears right and soon becomes a grassy logging road where a driveway leads right to a second house. The grass-grown road swings left around a rock outcrop and reaches the trailhead on the left at 0.6 mi. (small sign, blue blazes), just as the logging road starts to descend gradually. The trail, located on land protected by conservation easement, climbs moderately through hemlock woods, dips to cross an old logging road, and continues upward through more hemlocks interspersed with young hardwoods. At 1.1 mi. it turns sharp right where a side path leads left 40 yd. to an interesting rocky knob (no view). The trail climbs to a ridgecrest through hardwoods damaged by the 1998 ice storm; in many places it is overgrown with brambles in summer, but is well marked with blue blazes. It crosses a small brook at 1.5 mi., then continues climbing until it encounters a low rocky knob and runs along its margin to a trail jct. (faded signs) at 2.0 mi. The blue-blazed side path to the left runs 100 yd. to an excellent outlook north to the White Mtns. and east to Squam Lake and the Ossipee Range from "Pike's Peak."

Beyond this jct. the Sutherland Trail is marked with faded salmon blazes and is obscure in places. In 100 yd. it reaches the rough upper ledges of the mountain, which are slippery when wet. The trail crosses numerous small rocky knobs and great care must be taken to follow cairns and blazes as it winds over and between these ledges. At 2.2 mi., after a scramble up a sharp-edged ledge, an unsigned and very obscure side path leads 0.2 mi. left to a good viewpoint from the East Cliff. The main trail continues over more ledges, crossing two high rock knobs with views north and east just before reaching the wooded summit ledge (benchmark) and the Plymouth Mountain Trail at 2.4 mi. Descending, from the summit the Sutherland Trail heads east at a sign that reads "Outlook."

Distance from Texas Hill Rd. (830')

- *to* side path to Pike's Peak (2100'): 2.0 mi., 1300 ft., 1 hr. 40 min.
- *to* summit of Plymouth Mtn. (2193'): 2.4 mi. (3.8 km), 1400 ft., 1 hr. 55 min.

Sunapee–Ragged–Kearsarge Greenway

In the past few years the Sunapee–Ragged–Kearsarge Greenway, a loop trail about 75 mi. long that connects these three major mountains in western Merrimack County, has been under development. A route has been established but improvements are still being made—mostly rerouting off roads and onto woods trails. This greenway makes use of some previously existing trails and some new ones on Mt. Kearsarge, Sunapee Mtn., and Ragged Mtn. Information about this greenway (including a guidebook published in 2003) and about volunteer maintenance activities can be obtained from the Sunapee–Ragged–Kearsarge Greenway Coalition, PO Box 1684, New London, NH 03257-1684 or its website, www.srkg.com.

The following is a section-by-section overview of the SRK Greenway route, which is divided by the SRKGC into 14 sections running in a clockwise direction, starting and ending at Newbury village on NH 103 at the foot of Lake Sunapee.

Section 1. This trail traverses Sunapee Mtn. from Newbury village to Old Province Rd., using the Newbury Trail, Lake Solitude Trail, and the Summit Trail (all described in section 1 of this guide). [6.0 mi., 1850 ft. (rev. 1100 ft.)]

Section 2. This trail follows Old Province Rd., Brook Rd., and Harding Hill Rd., then becomes a footpath running generally northward through the woods for almost 4 mi., then follows Stagecoach Rd. and NH 103B to the Sunapee Town Hall. [7.0 mi., 600 ft. (rev. 1270 ft.)]

Section 3. This trail follows the road west from Sunapee Town Hall to Sunapee High School, then follows North Rd, which becomes progressively less well maintained, then ends with a short section down a power line to Baptist Pond Rd., which is followed to its intersection with Deer Hill Rd. [5.9 mi., 770 ft. (rev. 460 ft.)]

Section 4. This trail, called the Protectworth Trail, follows Deer Hill Rd. and a series of woods roads from the intersection of Deer Hill Rd. and Baptist Pond Rd. to NH 114 south of Springfield village. [4.2 mi., 500 ft. (rev. 630 ft.)]

Section 5. This trail, also called the Protectworth Trail for the first 5.4 mi. and the Great Brook Trail thereafter, ascends as a footpath from NH 114 south of Springfield village to a side path to a viewpoint from the ledges above Royal Arch Cave nearly at the summit of Royal Arch Hill. It continues down to Perley Rd. (gravel), follows that road north for a mile, then follows Old Poor Rd. to an overgrown former beaver pond known as Devil's Half Acre and, becoming the Great Brook Trail, descends to the jct. of Pleasant Street and Lake Shore Rd. at the northwest corner of Pleasant Lake in New London. [8.7 mi., 950 ft. (rev. 1750 ft.)]

Section 6. This trail begins at the jct. of Pleasant Street and Lake Shore Rd. at the northwest corner of Pleasant Lake in New London, follows the Wolf Tree Trail to the stone wall that marks the Wilmot–New London town line, then descends along the wall to a brook. Here it meets and follows the Webb Forest Interpretive Trail past a small glen with a waterfall up to a ridgecrest, from which it descends on the White Pine Trail, a series of logging roads, to NH 4A west of Wilmot village. [3.3 mi., 860 ft. (rev. 520 ft.)]

Section 7. This trail begins at NH 4A west of Wilmot village, follows the Kimpton Brook Trail to Stearns Rd., then traverses Bog Mtn. on the Bog Mountain Trail (described below) to Wilmot village. [4.6 mi., 800 ft. (rev. 1100 ft.)]

Section 8. This trail starts at Wilmot village and runs north, using North Wilmot Rd., then follows the Beaver Pond Trail and the Patterson Farm Trail through the woods mainly on old roads, and then follows Eagle Pond Rd. to US 4 and New Canada Rd. to the Ragged Mountain Trail trailhead. [4.1 mi., 600 ft. (rev. 480 ft.)]

Section 9. This trail, the Ragged Mountain Trail (described below, though in the opposite direction), traverses Ragged Mtn. from New Canada Rd. to Proctor Academy on NH 11 in Andover village. [6.5 mi., 1550 ft. (rev. 1900 ft.)]

Section 10. This trail runs from Proctor Academy on NH 11 in Andover village to the Winslow State Park parking area at the northern base of Mt. Kearsarge, using a series of roads with varying degrees of vehicular use. [6.0 mi., 1300 ft. (rev. 140 ft.)]

Section 11. This trail traverses Mt. Kearsarge from Winslow State Park to Kearsarge Valley Rd., using the Barlow Trail and the Lincoln Trail (both described below). [6.2 mi., 1150 ft. (rev. 2100 ft.).

Section 12. This trail runs from Kearsarge Valley Rd. to Wadleigh State Park in North Sutton, largely on roads (including a substantial portion on little-used woods roads). [4.0 mi., 290 ft. (rev. 200 ft.)]

Section 13. This trail runs from Wadleigh State Park in North Sutton to Chalk Pond Rd. in Newbury, mostly on paved or gravel roads. [5.4 mi., 950 ft. (rev. 580 ft.)]

Section 14. This trail begins on Chalk Pond Rd. and follows development roads to the north trailhead for the Fishersfield Trail, which circles around the east side of Bly Hill Rd. to a private gravel road. The greenway then follows a series of roads, ending with NH 103, to Newbury village. [4.5 mi., 670 ft. (rev. 840 ft.)]

Ragged Mountain

Ragged Mtn. (2286 ft.) is a sprawling ridge in the towns of Danbury and Andover with several summits of nearly equal elevation. The West Top, a ledge on the west knob of the East Peak, offers a sweeping view to the south and west. Old Top (2257 ft.), a spur of the eastern and highest summit, has a ledgy top with good views north. On the West Peak (2225 ft.) is the Ragged Mountain Ski Area, where there are views north. This mountain has had a number of trails in the past, but they usually lacked sufficient maintenance to make them attractive to the average hiker. It is now traversed from Andover on the southeast to Wilmot on the west by Section 9 of the Sunapee–Ragged–Kearsarge Greenway.

Ragged Mountain Trail (USGS Andover quad)

This trail, marked with white blazes and also in places with metal squares, uses a combination of logging and skid roads, previously existing hiking and cross-country ski trails, and newly cut segments of trail. Signs at both trailheads designate it as the Ragged Mountain Trail, but there are signs along the ridge with the original name for that portion, the Ridge Trail. Parts of this route pass through logged areas, where markings must be followed with care. Logging and other vagaries may cause future disruption and even relocation of some trail sections. All in all, this trail is rougher and more strenuous than the distance and elevation figures indicate.

The southeast trailhead (from which an out-and-back trip is more appealing) uses the parking area for the Farrell Field House of Proctor Academy, which is located on US 4 just west of the town center. Turn north onto Field House Lane and bear left into the parking lot. The trail (sign) starts on a gravel driveway at the far left corner of the parking lot, below the tennis courts. Additional parking may be found near the playing fields on the south side of US 4. The west trailhead is on New Canada Rd., which leaves the east side of US 4, 1.8 mi. north of its jct. with NH 11 in Andover. Drive 0.9 mi. up New Canada Rd. and park on the left; the trail (sign) starts on the right at a gated logging road.

From the field house parking lot, the trail ascends 70 yd. up the gravel driveway and turns right onto an old road (a cross-country ski trail) at a yellow blaze. In another 125 yd. it bears right as a path from the tennis courts joins from the left. At 0.3 mi. it turns left off the road onto a white-blazed footpath. The trail climbs moderately, crossing a stone wall, and at 0.7 mi. bears right onto an old road. In 0.1 mi. it turns left onto a skid road, and in 125 yd. turns left again onto another skid road at a cairn. The road rises at an easy grade, passing a private side path left at 1.1 mi. and crossing a deteriorating plank bridge at 1.5 mi. Another private path joins from the left, and the trail soon climbs to another old road, where it bears right; here a sign facing the opposite direction reads "Ski Trail." The trail then climbs up an eroded section into a logged area, going directly across a major logging road at 1.8 mi.; follow blazes carefully here as another skid road crosses the major road at an angle. The trail continues up a skid road, then leaves the logged area and climbs steeply on an older road for 0.3 mi. It then joins another recent skid road in a logged area (descending, take the right fork on the older road), soon re-enters the woods, skirts a large blowdown via a new path to the left, and continues up an older road. At 2.5 mi. a side path marked with metal disks diverges right (sign), leading 0.1 mi. to Balanced

Rock, a boulder perched atop a hogback ledge. Here the side path turns left and continues another 100 yd. to an open outcrop with a view south and east. The main trail climbs to a jct. at 2.7 mi. Here a spur path, the East Ridge Trail, diverges right, climbs over several ledgy knobs (including the mountain's highest summit, which is a wooded ledge a short distance to the right of the trail) and ends at open ledges on Old Top, where there are excellent views north. This lightly used path is intermittently marked with cairns and metal squares and must be followed with care. Distance to Old Top 0.4 mi. (100 ft., rev. 50 ft.).

From the jct. with the East Ridge Trail, the SRK Greenway turns left (west) on a section signed as the West Ridge Trail. In 0.1 mi. it passes a side path that leads 30 yd. left to a ledge with a view south. In another 40 yd. a private trail, signed "MT TR," comes in from the left. The SRK Greenway swings right and climbs to a ledge on the left with an extensive view south and west. In another 50 yd. it reaches its high point on the West Top, then descends, negotiating two very steep pitches with poor footing, to a col at 3.3 mi. It then rises moderately, crossing a red-blazed boundary several times, and swings right to the cleared area at the top of Ragged Mountain Ski Area at 3.8 mi. (In the reverse direction, the trail enters the woods to the right of the ski patrol building, crossing under a power line.) The trail now makes a horseshoe turn to the left behind a chairlift terminal and onto a grassy road that leads up toward a communications tower; at this turn, good views north may be found by descending a short distance right to the top of the ski trails. The trail skirts the left side of the fenced tower enclosure and descends, crossing and recrossing a recently cut ski trail. It drops down a steep pitch to the base of a cliff, meanders over a ledgy hump, then swings left and descends to a ferny glade surrounded by high ledges. Here the private Ash Trail continues down the ravine, while the SRK Greenway turns right to ascend a steep pitch to the crest of Buswell Ridge, a long southern spur. It descends along the ridge through spruce woods and over ledges, with occasional short ascents and limited views. At 4.8 mi. the trail turns right at a ledge with a partial view; for a good view of Mt. Kearsarge, descend the ledges 30 yd. to the left. In another 0.2 mi. the trail drops steeply to a logged area and crosses a slash-strewn skid road twice. It continues down the ridge to a sign at 5.3 mi., where it turns right (west) to descend off the ridge. In 0.2 mi. it enters a logged area and descends steadily on a wide skid road. (Ascending, bear right at two forks.) At 5.7 mi. the SRK Greenway bears left at a fork and in 40 yd. another skid road joins from the right. It continues down the road, with two brook crossings and a short bypass to the right between them, to a large logging yard at 6.3 mi. The trail crosses the yard to the far right corner, turns right on a gravel road, and continues to New Canada Rd.

Distances from parking lot at Proctor Academy (650')

> *to* East Ridge Trail (2170'): 2.7 mi., 1500 ft., 2 hr. 5 min.
>
> *to* Ragged Mountain Ski Area (2225'): 3.8 mi., 1850 ft. (rev. 300 ft.), 2 hr. 50 min.
>
> *to* New Canada Rd. (1010'): 6.5 mi. (10.5 km), 1900 ft. (rev. 1250 ft.), 4 hr. 10 min.

Bog Mountain Trail

This small mountain (1787 ft.) in the town of Wilmot, now traversed by the Sunapee–Ragged–Kearsarge Greenway, provides excellent views from several ledges, particularly south to Kearsarge from a ledge part of the way up on the west side. The Bog Mountain Trail and the Kimpton Brook Trail (which runs west from Stearns Rd. to NH 4A) comprise Section 7 of the Sunapee–Ragged– Kearsarge Greenway. Refer to the USGS New London quadrangle.

Bog Mountain Trail (USGS New London quad)

The ascent from the west is considerably shorter but the eastern approach has better parking. The east trailhead is at the Wilmot Town Library in Wilmot village, on North Wilmot Rd. just off NH 4A. For the west trailhead, take NH 4A west from Wilmot village for about 2.0 mi., passing along the south edge of extensive boggy areas on Kimpton Brook, which give the mountain its name and afford views across to it. Turn right on Stearns Rd. and follow it 0.4 mi. to the bridge over Kimpton Brook, where parking space may be available (take care not to block any road). Follow Stearns Rd. uphill for another 0.4 mi. (possible parking, though very limited, along this section of the road) until it becomes almost level at the top of the hill, where the Bog Mountain Trail begins on the right (sign) opposite the trailhead for the Kimpton Brook Trail (sign), the continuation of the Greenway southwest to NH 4A.

From Stearns Rd., the trail climbs moderately through beautiful woods, reaching a fine outlook ledge to the south at 0.7 mi. It continues to climb, winding around on or near the ridgecrest, until it scrambles up a broad open ledge with excellent views at 1.1 mi., which most people would consider the summit. The true summit is a ledge (no view) in the woods about 100 yd. to the east of the north end of this ledge, reached by a white-blazed path. From the north end of the summit ledge, the trail angles to the right into the woods and soon descends rather steeply with several turns through a grassy, ledgy oak forest. In this area the footway is indistinct in places (though well-blazed with the white trapezoids of the SRKG) and must be followed with care. At 1.9 mi. it turns right at a ledge with a view of Ragged Mtn. and Mt. Kearsarge and descends a very rocky section. At 2.1 mi. it turns left onto an old logging road and the grade eases. The trail bears right at a fork at 2.4 mi., ascends easily for 250 yds., then turns left off the road, passing through a stone wall. It descends for 0.1 mi. through a hemlock grove, then turns right and contours along the slope, crossing a skid road at 2.9 mi. In another 0.1 mi. it turns right and climbs alongside a stone wall, then swings left and meanders through more stone walls and a wet area to its eastern trailhead (sign, no parking) on the gravel Pinnacle Rd. at 3.3 mi. Turn left and follow the road, bearing left at a fork. At 3.6 mi. turn right on the paved North Wilmot Rd. and follow it 0.1 mi. to the parking area at the Wilmot Town Library on the right.

Distances from Stearns Rd. at the Kimpton Brook bridge (1030')

> *to* Bog Mountain Trail (1200'): 0.4 mi., 150 ft., 15 min.
>
> *to* summit of Bog Mtn. (1787'): 1.5 mi. (2.4 km.), 750 ft., 1 hr. 10 min.
>
> *to* Wilmot Town Library (900'): 3.7 mi. (6.0 km), 900 ft. (rev. 1050 ft.), 2 hr. 20 min.

Mount Kearsarge

Mt. Kearsarge (2930 ft.) is a high, very prominent isolated mountain located in Warner, Wilmot, Andover, and Salisbury. It has a bare summit, topped by a fire tower, with magnificent views in all directions. Mt. Kearsarge probably was discovered shortly after the Pilgrims landed. On a seventeenth-century map (Gardner's) it appears as "Carasarga," but since Carrigain's map of 1816 "Kearsarge" has remained the accepted spelling. Refer to the USGS Andover quadrangle for the summit and most of the upper part of the mountain, and to the Warner, Bradford, and New London quadrangles for the lower slopes.

Wilmot (Northside) Trail (USGS Andover quad)

From NH 11 between Wilmot Flat and Elkins, take Kearsarge Valley Rd. south, then follow signs to Winslow State Park and the site of the old Winslow House (caretaker's cabin, picnic area, water, and parking; there is a substantial admission fee in season). The trail starts from the parking area to the left of a service garage, at the same point as the Barlow Trail. It is well beaten and marked with red paint. It crosses under power lines and climbs moderately to the foot of Halfway Rock, where it climbs more steeply. It then angles to the left, climbing moderately again past an outlook to the north, then turns south and ascends over increasingly bare ledges, marked with orange paint. It meets the new Barlow Trail about 100 yd. below the summit.

Distance from parking area, Winslow State Park (1820')

    to Mt. Kearsarge summit (2930'): 1.1 mi. (1.8 km.), 1100 ft., 1 hr. 5 min.

Barlow Trail (USGS Andover quad)

This trail was cut and opened in 1998 and named in memory of Peter Barlow. It is a segment of Section 11 of the Sunapee–Ragged–Kearsarge Greenway. It is a very scenic trail that provides a gentler alternative to the steeper and rockier Wilmot Trail. It is particularly enjoyable for the descent of the mountain.

The trail leaves the parking area at the same place as the Wilmot Trail, crosses under the power line, and descends slightly for the first 0.1 mi. It angles around toward the east side of the mountain, climbing at easy to moderate grades, and at 0.7 mi. it bears left at a rock outcrop where there is an arrow placed for the benefit of descending hikers. More ledges are encountered—but not views, yet. At 1.2 mi. a side path leads right 25 yd. to an excellent northern outlook ranging from Cardigan through the White Mtns. to the Ossipee Range. Soon there is the first restricted view from the trail itself, and more extensive views are reached at short intervals. The trail turns sharp right on an open ledge and climbs to its top, reaching the end of the mountain's east shoulder at 1.4 mi. (For the descending hiker approaching this point, it appears for a short distance that one is about to step off the edge of the mountain—an exciting prospect.) The Barlow Trail passes a small pond in a swampy area (right) and dips down on the south side of the ridge to pass around a sharp canyon-like formation on the ridgecrest, then wanders back across to the north side of the ridge to join the Wilmot Trail (sign) on the open ledges 100 yd. below the summit.

Distance from parking area, Winslow State Park (1820')

    to Mt. Kearsarge summit (2930'): 1.6 mi. (2.6 km.), 1150 ft., 1 hr. 25 min.

Warner (Southside) Trail (USGS Andover quad)

Leave NH 103 in Warner and follow signs to the gate at Rollins State Park. There is a substantial admission fee in season, and the gate is often closed on weekdays before Memorial Day and after Labor Day. There is a picnic area with tables, fireplaces, and water. The road then mainly follows the route of the old carriage road along the crest of Mission Ridge and ends at a parking area 3.7 mi. above the toll gate. There are toilets, picnic tables, and fireplaces here, but no water. From there the trail follows the old carriage road, now badly eroded, to a ledge with a fine view. The trail then swings left and rises to the foot of the summit ledges and, blazed in silver across the ledges, continues to the summit and fire tower.

Distance from parking area, Rollins State Park (2600')

   to Mt. Kearsarge summit (2930'): 0.6 mi. (1.0 km.), 350 ft., 30 min.

Lincoln Trail (USGS Andover, Warner, and Bradford quads)

This interesting and varied trail runs from Kearsarge Valley Rd. along a meandering route up the western ridge of Black Mtn. to the summit of Mt. Kearsarge via the parking area at Rollins State Park. It is lightly used, particularly compared with the other shorter, more popular trails from Winslow and Rollins state parks and provides a much wilder, rougher experience than those heavily-trodden trails. It is a segment of Section 11 of the Sunapee–Ragged–Kearsarge Greenway and is well marked with white blazes. The trail begins on Kearsarge Valley Rd. at a turnout 0.4 mi. south of the golf course entrance and 0.4 mi. north of North Rd. It is signed initially as the "Link Trail," because the original route of the Lincoln Trail started at Kearsarge Regional High School off North Rd.—what was once a link to the main trail has become the official trail.

   The trail leaves the parking area and ascends gradually through a mixed forest 0.5 mi. to a wide woods road, where it turns left uphill (signs) and coincides with a snowmobile trail. It follows the road straight through a large clearing (where there is a snowmobile trail map to the right), and at 1.5 mi. turns left onto an older woods road (trail sign) uphill in company with the snowmobile route. At 2.0 mi. a short spur leaves left to Baker's Ledge (no view), and the Lincoln Trail soon turns right onto a footpath where the snowmobile route continues straight toward Wilmot. The trail zigzags to a grassy knoll where there are views of Lovewell Mtn. to the west and Mt. Cardigan to the north, then continues on alternately ascending and level grades across the western shoulder of

Black Mtn., a subsidiary peak on the southern flank of Mt. Kearsarge. After a moderate ascent through an attractive birch grove, the trail reaches the western end of the upper parking area in Rollins State Park and turns left uphill. From here, at a sign, the summit of Mt. Kearsarge may be reached in either 0.4 mi. via the steep and rocky Lincoln Trail (left) or in 0.5 mi. by the heavily used and more gradual Rollins Trail (right). On the descent, the Lincoln Trail leaves the Rollins Trail at a flat ledge 0.1 mi. below the summit. It is unsigned and unblazed at this point so as not to attract inexperienced hikers to the short steep, rocky section, which may be hazardous in wet or icy conditions.

Distances from Kearsarge Valley Rd. (850')

> *to* Baker's Ledge spur (1650'): 2.0 mi., 800 ft., 1 hr. 25 min.

> *to* Rollins State Park parking area (2600'): 4.2 mi., 1750 ft., 3 hr.

> *to* Mt. Kearsarge summit (2930'): 4.6 mi. (6.4 km.), 2100 ft., 3 hr. 20 min.

Section 3

The Merrimack Valley

To Lincoln

To Conway

Squam Lake

25 West Ossipee

Newfound Lake

MT. CARDIGAN

Meredith

16

MAINE

Lebanon

4

Alexandria

104

93

Laconia

Lake Winnipesaukee

11

89

MT. KEARSARGE

4

Rochester

VERMONT

Concord

4 202 9

BEAR BROOK SP

PAWTUCKAWAY SP

Portsmouth

9

202

Manchester

101

95

293

Keene

101

93

PISGAH SP

MT. MONADNOCK

124

Jaffrey

3

Nashua

**3.
THE MERRIMACK
VALLEY**

M A S S A C H U S E T T S

SUGGESTED HIKES

Easy Hikes

North Uncanoonuc Mtn. [rt: 1.2 mi., 700 ft., 0:55]. This mountain's semi-open summit allows for views.

   The Pulpit, short walk [lp: 1.5 mi., 200 ft., 0:50]. This short walk via the Kennard, Granite, Ravine, and Kennard Trails features an interesting glacial rock formation.

   Hall Mtn. Ledges [rt: 2.0 mi., 200 ft., 1:05] Hall Mountain Trail visits an interesting outlook ledge.

   Oak Hill Vista Loop [lp: 2.2 mi., 400 ft., 1:20]. This loop, via Ovenbird Trail, Luti Loop, Win's Way (to the Vista and back), and Luti Loop, traverses an interesting hillside and visits a good outlook to Mt. Kearsarge. One can also take the more challenging Murray Loop instead of the upper Ovenbird Trail, which adds 0.2 mi. This hike can be extended by using one of several available longer loop routes to the Vista.

Moderate Hikes

The Pulpit, long walk **[lp: 2.7 mi., 300 ft., 1:30].** This loop hike, via the Kennard, Tufts, Ravine, and Kennard Trails, follows a rocky, cascading stream as well as visits an interesting rock formation.

   Catamount Hill [lp: 3.6 mi., 500 ft., 2:05]. This loop, via One Mile Road, the Catamount Hill and Cascade Trails, and One Mile Road, visits a ledge with a good view and a brook in a small, but interesting hemlock ravine. This trip can easily be extended to any length desired by attaching other loops, or it can be reduced by omitting either the ledge or the ravine.

   Hall Mtn. Loop [lp: 5.0 mi., 200 ft., 2:35]. The Hall Mountain Trail, with return via Podunk Rd., offers a ledgy outlook and runs through a typical variety of Bear Brook State Park terrain.

LIST OF TRAILS

The Merrimack River divides the southern part of New Hampshire nearly in half. For more than two centuries it has been the central artery of the state, providing a route for transportation and travel and a supply of water power that helped establish the state's three largest cities: Manchester, Nashua, and Concord. The Merrimack was once said to "turn more spindles than any other river in the world"—a reference to the massive textile industry that spawned the mills in Manchester and Nashua as well as in the Massachusetts cities of Haverhill, Lawrence, and Lowell. Manchester, a sleepy village with less than a thousand residents in 1830, was the largest town in the state with a population of nearly 14,000 in 1850 and had grown to almost 57,000 by 1900. The extent of the river-powered industry is most noticeable to the casual visitor in the almost unbroken line of old brick mill buildings—now preserved as a historical landmark—that borders the river across from the Everett Turnpike in Manchester below Amoskeag Falls. The falls themselves (now the site of a fishways educational center), along with the rapids below them, remain an impressive sight despite having been dammed for well over a century.

Though there are no high mountains in the Merrimack Valley, there are a number of interesting hills and other features, as well as a myriad of historical sites along the river itself. The State of New Hampshire is engaged in a long-term project to construct a trail, called the New Hampshire Heritage Trail, along the Merrimack Valley from the Massachusetts border to—eventually—the Canadian border via Franconia Notch and the Connecticut River valley. This is a tremendously complex and difficult project due to the large amount of development along the river corridor, but many sections of trail already exist and offer a variety of walks both in flood-plain and riverbank natural areas and in urban areas with a wealth of history. The major hiking area covered in this section is 9300-acre Bear Brook State Park several miles east of the river, roughly between Concord and Manchester. Trails are also described on the Uncanoonuc Mtns. in Goffstown, the Pulpit in Bedford, Hooksett Pinnacle in Hooksett, and Oak Hill in Loudon and Concord.

In addition, short walks with an emphasis on ecology and conservation are available at the state headquarters of the New Hampshire Audubon Society and the Society for the Protection of New Hampshire Forests, both located in Concord. The Audubon Society headquarters, located on Silk Farm Rd., is easily reached by following signs from I-89 at Exit 2; the principal trail is a loop that descends to the shore of Turkey Pond. The SPNHF headquarters is on Portsmouth St., reached from I-93 at Exit 16 either by following East Side

Drive uphill to the right and then turning right on Portsmouth St. (sign, "Conservation Center") or by turning right onto Eastman St. then sharp left onto Portsmouth St. at a small park. The main building, which incorporates a number of advanced energy-conservation measures, is situated on top of a bluff overlooking the river, while the trails lie on the flood plain at the foot of the bluff; loop hikes of 1.5 mi. or more are possible.

Uncanoonuc Mountains

These two nearly symmetrical and almost perfectly paired rounded hills in the town of Goffstown are visible from many points in the Merrimack Valley. Refer to the USGS Pinardville quadrangle. The North Mtn. (1324 ft.) is wooded but offers some views from the summit area, and can be reached fairly easily by an unofficial but well-beaten trail. The South Mtn. (1315 ft.) supports what is probably the finest forest of communications towers in New Hampshire (even though the former fire tower has been removed), giving it a distinctively bristly appearance even from a considerable distance. There is a paved road to the unattractively overdeveloped summit, and the actual high point is now within a fenced-off area. A hiker who nonetheless finds this mountain irresistibly attractive and wishes to ascend on foot would probably do best to seek out the grade of the former incline railway, which once carried fashionable tourists to the summit. From NH 114 0.6 mi. east of its jct. with NH 13, take Wallace Rd., immediately passing Goffstown High School, then turn right onto Mountain Base Rd. at 1.5 mi. and follow it 1.0 mi. to its end at the small town beach on Uncanoonuc Lake. The old railroad grade can be found easily just behind the beach, climbing rather steeply to the summit in about 0.6 mi. and 650 ft.

North Mountain Trail (USGS Pinardville quad)

To reach the trail to the North Mtn., start from NH 114 in Goffstown, just east of the jct. with NH 13, and follow Mountain Rd. south, bearing left at 0.9 mi. The trailhead is on the right at 1.4 mi., nearly opposite a small parking area that has been created by blocking a woods road with large rocks. The trail is marked with white blazes, circles, and painted can tops. It climbs the bank above the road and soon passes through a stone wall and in front of a small cave. It climbs steeply through a fine hemlock forest, then moderates, passes an outlook, and approaches the summit, passing a side path, which leads down to a view of Manchester.

Distance from Mountain Rd. (625')

   to summit of North Mtn. (1324'): 0.6 mi. (1.0 km.), 700 ft., 40 min.

The Pulpit

This interesting rock formation is the central feature of a reservation owned by the town of Bedford. It is a remnant of New Hampshire's glacial history, a ledge with a large pothole. Such potholes are formed in torrential streams, where the actual carving of the pothole is done mainly by the rocks and gravel swirled around by raging waters. The tiny stream that now trickles into the pothole—it is not even the main branch of Pulpit Brook—is obviously insufficient to create such a formation. But during the melting of the last continental glacier, a large lake formed in the basin to the north of the Pulpit, its natural outlet to the northeast (the present-day Piscataquog River) dammed by the ice on its north edge. For a period of perhaps a few years Pulpit Brook served as the outlet to this lake, and during that period its unusual features were formed by the torrent that passed through its valley.

The trailhead is at a parking area on New Boston Rd. a few yards east of the Bedford–New Boston town line. From I-293 in Manchester, take NH 101 west to the traffic lights where it turns sharp left at its jct. with NH 114. Follow NH 114 straight ahead for 0.7 mi. to the next set of traffic lights, turn left here onto New Boston Rd., and follow this road for 5.7 mi. to the trailhead on the left. The trailhead can also be reached from NH 101 in Amherst at the Horace Greeley Birthplace historical marker. Follow Horace Greeley Rd. for 1.2 mi., then bear left on Chestnut Hill Rd. At 4.2 mi. the road passes the New Boston Air Force Station and makes a sweeping turn to the right. The trailhead is on the right at 5.1 mi.

There is a small network of trails that provides walks in the range of about 1.5 mi. to 3 mi. The short walk (1.5 mi., 200 ft., 50 min.) follows the Kennard Trail to the Pulpit, then makes a loop down through the gorge and pothole area via the Granite Trail and the upper part of the Ravine Trail (because the Granite Trail has generally better footing, it is recommended to descend the Granite Trail and ascend the Ravine Trail). The longer loops use either the Tufts Trail or the Campbell Trail to approach the south end of the Ravine Trail, then follow the Ravine Trail back up the brook to the Pulpit. (While the Granite Trail is easier than the corresponding part of the Ravine Trail, it misses the best views of the pothole. However, it is possible to follow the Ravine Trail into the pothole area, then backtrack and climb out of the gorge on the Granite Trail.) Obviously it is equally possible to descend on the Ravine Trail and return by the Campbell Trail or Tufts Trail, but most hikers will probably find the footing on the Ravine Trail easier in the ascending direction. The trails end at an old mill dam and pond, where it is interesting to reflect on how the relatively massive dam was constructed with only human and animal muscle power. A trip from the parking area to the mill dam and back, using the Ravine Trail one way and the Tufts Trail or Campbell Trail·the other, is about 2.7 mi., 300 ft., 1 hr. 30 min. It should be noted that there are many old woods roads and beaten paths in the area, so trail markings (mostly painted wooden squares or diamonds) should be followed carefully. Trails are described in the direction indicated by the recommended routes.

Caution: While this is an excellent trip for small children, they must be closely supervised in the vicinity of the potentially dangerous Pulpit ledges.

The Kennard Trail (white markers) leaves the trailhead parking area, crosses a swamp on an extensive boardwalk, then continues through woods with several minor ups and downs. At 0.4 mi. a spur path (sign) leads right about 35 yd. to an outlook over a small marsh. At 0.5 mi. it passes an intersection where the Campbell Trail leaves left and the Blue Trail (a connecting path 0.1 mi. long with blue markers to the head of the Pulpit gorge) leaves right. At 0.6 mi. an old road enters left, and in another 30 yd. Pulpit Brook is crossed on a bridge. Just beyond the bridge the Granite Trail leaves on the left. In quick succession the Kennard Trail runs along the right edge of the Pulpit ledges, passes the jct. on the right with the Blue Trail, crosses the head of the gorge (railing), and ends at the jct. with the Ravine Trail and Tufts Trail at 0.7 mi.

The Tufts Trail (white markers) is the easy route on the west side of Pulpit Brook. It begins at a jct. with the Kennard Trail and Ravine Trail near the Pulpit, and mostly descends at an easy grade, crossing a tributary brook at 0.4 mi. It reaches brook level just before the point where it joins the combined Campbell Trail and Ravine Trail at 0.6 mi., at the bridge where these two trails cross to the west side of Pulpit Brook.

The Campbell Trail (red markers, also green markers for the first 0.4 mi.) is the easy route on the east side of Pulpit Brook. It leaves the Kennard Trail on the left (east) opposite the Blue Trail jct., 0.5 mi. from the trailhead. It soon makes a sharp right turn and reaches an old road at 0.1 mi. (To the right, the muddy old road (green markers) leads back to the Kennard Trail in about 100 yd.) The Campbell Trail follows the road to the left for 10 yd., then turns right, off the road, and becomes a foot trail climbing easily for a short distance then descending gradually. At 0.3 mi. the Scouting Way (purple markers) leaves on the left for nearby Pulpit Rd.; this trail is primarily an access route for Pulpit Rd. residents. At 0.4 mi. the Campbell Trail crosses a stone wall and soon turns sharp right (sign. "To Ravine Trail") where the green markers continue straight ahead (this trail runs to open fields off Pulpit Rd.). It descends into a small valley and crosses a tributary brook at 0.7 mi., then reaches its jct. with the Ravine Trail in another 25 yd. {The trail sign, "To Campbell Trail," is located at the tributary crossing, easy to see from the jct. but easy to miss from the Ravine Trail, especially in the southbound direction.) The Campbell Trail and Ravine Trail continue together, crossing a bridge in another 50 yd. where the Tufts Trail joins on the far side, and ending at the mill dam at 0.8 mi.

The Ravine Trail (orange markers) has rough, occasionally muddy footing but provides the best views of the brook and gorge. It begins at the old mill dam and, together with the Campbell Trail, passes the jct. with the Tufts Trail on the left in 100 yd., and immediately crosses Pulpit Brook on a bridge. In another 50 yd. the Campbell Trail leaves on the right, and the Ravine Trail continues along the brook. It passes a ledge eroded into a natural overhanging shelter, climbs away from the brook briefly, passes a small waterfall, then crosses the brook three times on bridges. The Granite Trail diverges to the right at 0.6 mi., between the second and third bridges. After the third bridge, the trail passes under an overhanging rock then soon makes a sharp left turn away from the brook. At this point it is possible, depending on water levels, to continue ahead to views into the pothole and perhaps into the pothole itself. The Ravine Trail climbs steeply out of the gorge, with slippery footing and a number of alternate beaten paths (the "official" path is not well defined here), to the jct. with the Tufts Trail and Kennard Trail at 0.7 mi.

The Granite Trail (yellow markers) leaves the Kennard Trail on the left 0.6 mi. from the trailhead, just after the bridge over Pulpit Brook. It quickly passes a right branch that leads to the Pulpit ledges, crosses a tributary brook, passes another unmarked path on the right that leads to the Pulpit ledges, crosses another tributary, and winds its way down into the gorge, ending at the Ravine Trail between its upper two bridges at 0.1 mi.

Hooksett Pinnacle

This small but steep-sided hill (485 ft.) in the town of Hooksett rises abruptly from the edge of the Merrimack River. It also overlooks picturesque Pinnacle Pond on its west side, a pond that borders on I-93, making the hill and pond a familiar and attractive landmark from the interstate just north of the Hooksett toll plaza. The interesting summit monolith is composed of a tough, erosion-resistant quartzite that has enabled it to survive the leveling current of the Merrimack River; the land on both sides of it, now essentially a terrace about 100 ft. above the current river level, was once evidently part of the river's bed and then its flood plain. The summit offers some interesting views of the river and nearby hills, particularly to the northeast; tree growth has thankfully screened out the former undesirably intimate views of the toll plaza area on the interstate, though the highway sounds are still intrusive. Thoreau, in *A Week on the Concord and Merrimack Rivers*, praises the view of the river that this little peak provided at a time when the river itself was the interstate, and the sounds made by the main means of transportation in the valley could not compete with the roar of nearby Hooksett Falls. He comments that the Pinnacle affords "a scene of rare beauty and completeness, which the traveler should take pains to behold." An imaginative modern visitor might be able to reconstruct the bucolic scene that Thoreau enjoyed from its ledges. Refer to the USGS Manchester North quadrangle.

To climb the hill, go west on Pine St. from NH 3A a short distance north of the traffic lights at the jct. where the main bridge crosses the Merrimack, connecting the two halves of Hooksett village. After 0.1 mi. on Pine St., turn left on Ardon Drive and continue 0.2 mi. to a paved turnaround at the end of the road, where a newer road descends on the right. (Since this is a residential area, visitors should be scrupulous about not disturbing the residents; cars can be carefully parked in the turnaround without interfering with traffic or privacy.) Several beaten paths climb a few yards up the bank above the turnaround to a woods road. Follow the woods road to the right as it climbs up the west flank of the hill to the crest of the south ridge, where it swings north to the summit.

Distance from Ardon Drive turnaround (310')

   to summit of Hooksett Pinnacle (485'): 0.3 mi. (0.5 km.), 200 ft., 15 min.

Bear Brook State Park

This 9300-acre park lies mostly in Allenstown, with smaller portions in the towns of Deerfield, Hooksett, and Candia. In this area of generally rolling terrain there are only a few significant hills—including Hall Mtn. (941 ft.), Bear Hill (835 ft.), and Catamount Hill (721 ft.)—but there are many interesting streams, ponds, and wetlands, and extensive and varied stands of fine forest. There is a wide-ranging system of multi-use trails, most of which are woods walks with few summits or long-distance views. The park's trail maps, are available at the park's tollbooth and information offices or online at www.nhstateparks.org. The park is also covered by four USGS quadrangles that meet almost in the center of the park, a short distance to the northwest of Bear Hill: Suncook (northwest), Gossville (northeast), Manchester North (southwest), and Candia (southeast). The main entrance of the park is reached by taking NH 28 north from US 3 in Suncook or south from US 4 at the Epsom traffic circle, then taking Bear Brook Rd. and following signs to the park's tollbooth just west of the main developed recreation facilities near Catamount Pond.

Black Hall Road

This gravel road runs north from the State Park Rd. to the northern park boundary at River Rd. in Epsom. (The entire road is called River Rd. on the USGS map.) It is an attractive walk or bike ride with varied terrain and easy grades.

The road (no sign) begins at an orange gate 0.2 mi. west of the tollbooth, passes through a pine forest, then descends to cross Catamount Brook on a bridge. This marshy waterway carries the outflow from Catamount Pond to the east on its way to the Suncook River, which lies a short distance west of this point. The road then ascends gradually, passes several unmarked old woods roads, crosses beneath a power line in a semi-open area, and ends at an orange gate at the blue-blazed park boundary and a Snowmobile Route #15 sign.

Distance from State Park Rd. (330')

  to River Rd. (320'): 1.0 mi. (1.6 km.), 30 min.

One Mile Road

This scenic road, one mile in length, connects several of the most popular trails in the northwest corner of the park and allows for numerous possible loop hikes. In winter it is heavily used as a snowmobile trail. It is marked with yellow blazes and is easy to follow.

The road leaves the State Park Rd. just west of the tollbooth and heads southeast through an attractive red pine grove. At 0.2 mi. the road swings left (east) and passes a woods road (right) that is a winter snowmobile access route. Shortly, a trail on the left leads 0.1 mi. to the Bear Brook Trail at the Bear Brook bridge, 0.3 mi. south of the Catamount Pond recreation area. Just a few feet beyond, the Catamount Hill Trail leaves on the right for Catamount Hill and the Cascade Trail. At 0.5 mi. the yellow-blazed, unsigned Shortcut Trail crosses, ascending to the right 0.3 mi. to the Catamount Hill Trail and Cascade Trail, and descending to the left 0.1 mi. to the Bear Brook Trail. One Mile Road crosses a tributary of Bear Brook, then almost immediately passes an unsigned yellow-blazed trail (left) which leads in 25 yd. to the Bear Brook Trail 0.5 mi. east of the Bear Brook bridge. The road enters another red pine grove, passes the jct. with the Sentinel Pine Trail on the right at Snowmobile Sign #2, then merges with the Bear Brook Trail coming in from the left, and ends at a turnaround that is 0.1 mi. west of the Lane Trail and Cascade Trail by way of the Bear Brook Trail.

Distances from State Park Rd. (330')

- *to* Catamount Hill Trail (340'): 0.3 mi., 10 min.
- *to* Shortcut Trail (350'): 0.5 mi., 15 min.
- *to* Sentinel Pine Trail (330'): 0.9 mi., 25 min.
- *to* Bear Brook Trail (330'): 1.0 mi. (1.6 km.), 30 min.
- *to* Lane Trail and Cascade Trail (330') via Bear Brook Trail: 1.1 mi. (1.8 km.), 35 min.

Catamount Hill Trail

This trail ascends from One Mile Road to the summit of Catamount Hill (721 ft.), the third highest point in Bear Brook State Park. A section of the trail that once formed a loop near the western park entrance was abandoned due to logging activity on private land; the present trail, which is completely on park land, heads south, then east to the western end of the Cascade Trail. There are several interesting views from semi-open ledges near the summit.

The trail leaves One Mile Road, 0.3 mi. east of the tollbooth on State Park Rd. and 0.4 mi. south of the Catamount Pond recreation area by the Bear Brook Trail and Connector Trail. It ascends, passing almost immediately the abandoned section (right). The trail swings left, angles up the slope and passes an east view just beyond some boulder caves. At 0.5 mi. it reaches an excellent northwest outlook toward Mt. Kearsarge and Concord from a small ridge. After a short descent, the Summit Loop Trail is reached. This 0.4-mi. loop leads across semi-open ledges to several attractive southern outlooks surrounding the clearing at the summit of Catamount Hill. A blue-blazed trail and a beaten path, not officially maintained and not described in this guide, continue from the summit.

The main trail descends off the ridge and swings left (north-northeast) along the blue-blazed park boundary markers. At 0.9 mi. the Shortcut Trail descends to the left on an old road through a pine forest 0.3 mi. to One Mile Road, then continues briefly as a yellow-blazed trail to Bear Brook Trail, 0.5 mi. from the Catamount Pond recreation area.

From here, the Catamount Trail coincides with the Cascade Trail and descends in an easterly direction, crossing a tributary of Bear Brook on stepping-stones. After a brief ascent on scattered ledges, it reaches a lookout ledge on the left with partial views toward Fort Mtn. and Nottingham Mtn. The two trails descend 0.2 mi. to the Sentinel Pine Trail, then continue through a hemlock grove to a log bridge over Catamount Brook, where the Cascade Trail continues east toward the Carr Ridge Trail, Bear Brook Trail, and Lane Trail.

Distances from One Mile Road (350')

- *to* Summit Loop Trail (650'): 0.6 mi., 300 ft., 25 min.
- *to* Catamount Hill (721') via Summit Loop Trail: 0.8 mi., 400 ft., 35 min.
- *to* Shortcut Trail and Cascade Trail (500'): 0.9 mi., 350 ft. (rev. 150 ft.), 40 min.
- *to* Catamount Brook (450'): 1.6 mi. (2.6 km.), 400 ft. (rev. 50 ft.), 1 hr.

Cascade Trail

This scenic trail connects the Bear Brook Trail with several paths in the northwest corner of the park, allowing numerous circuits. It is named for the small cascades on Catamount Brook, located in a beautiful hemlock grove near the trail's eastern terminus. The western 0.7 mi. of this trail coincides with the Catamount Hill Trail and provides easy access to the summit of Catamount Hill.

The trail leaves the Bear Brook Trail next to the terminus of the Lane Trail, 0.3 mi. from the tollbooth and a short distance east of the east end of One Mile Road. It ascends onto a narrow ridge in a generally south–southwest direction through a mixed pine forest, following Catamount Brook to the right. At 0.1 mi. the Carr Ridge Trail leaves left toward Hayes Marsh, and the Cascade Trail enters a hemlock grove along the brook. At 0.4 mi. the Cascade Trail swings right (west), crosses Catamount Brook on a log bridge, and coincides with the Catamount Hill Trail from here on.

The two trails cross the Sentinel Pine Trail at 0.5 mi., ascend on scattered ledges through a mixed oak forest, and reach the height-of-land, with a partially obscured outlook (right) toward Fort Mtn. and Nottingham Mtn. at 0.7 mi. The trails descend to cross Bear Brook on stepping-stones, then ascend briefly to the Shortcut Trail, which enters on the right (see the description of the Shortcut Trail under the Catamount Hill Trail). From here, the Catamount Hill Trail continues alone to the Summit Loop Trail and Catamount Hill.

Distances from Bear Brook Trail (350')

- *to* Catamount Brook and Catamount Hill Trail (450'): 0.4 mi., 100 ft., 15 min.

- *to* Sentinel Pine Trail (450'): 0.5 mi., 100 ft., 20 min.

- *to* Shortcut Trail (500'): 1.1 mi. (1.8 km.), 150 ft., 40 min.

- *to* Catamount Hill (721') via Catamount Hill Trail and Summit Loop Trail: 1.6 mi. (2.6 km.), 400 ft., 1 hr.

Bear Brook Trail

This scenic trail follows Bear Brook upstream from the point where it enters Catamount Pond at the recreation area to the Podunk Rd. bridge, just north of the park winter office and Campground Rd. It is marked with yellow blazes and is easy to follow, with the exception of a small recently logged area near Podunk Rd.

The trail leaves the swimming and picnic area and crosses the yellow-blazed footbridge over Bear Brook inlet at the south end of Catamount Pond. The route then crosses Deerfield Rd., winds south through the picnic area (watch for sparse blazes), and passes around the baseball diamond to the footbridge across Bear Brook. At 0.3 mi. the Catamount Trail heads straight uphill, and the Bear Brook Trail turns left up an embankment and parallels the south bank of Bear Brook upstream (left) and One Mile Road (right).

At 0.6 mi. the trail enters as the left branch of a fork, where the unsigned Shortcut Trail ascends right 0.3 mi. to the Cascade Trail and Catamount Hill Trail northeast of Catamount Hill. At 1.0 mi. the Sentinel Pine Trail diverges uphill to the right. The Bear Brook Trail merges left onto One Mile Road, then continues straight ahead onto an old road at a chain-link gate. After crossing Catamount Brook, the trail turns left onto a footpath at a three-way intersection, where the Cascade Trail leaves uphill on the right and the Lane Trail continues straight on the old road.

The Bear Brook Trail then turns right (east) along the south bank of Beaver Brook and passes a beaver dam (left) and then a bridge that crosses the brook to an old road (left). It enters an attractive hemlock forest, then emerges into a recently logged area where much of the trail has been disrupted. If the trail is lost in this area, continue in a generally easterly direction parallel to the brook until Podunk Rd. is reached. The trail itself passes a small bluff overlooking a marshy area, then swings alongside a logging road (Little Bear Trail). At 2.5 mi., a short yellow-blazed trail leaves right and runs 0.1 mi. to a parking area directly across from the park winter office and Campground Rd. The main trail swings left, then right, along the brook and reaches the Podunk Rd. bridge, just north of the park winter office and south of Deerfield Rd.

Distances from Catamount Pond Beach (300')

> *to* Catamount Trail (300'): 0.3 mi., 10 min.
>
> *to* Shortcut Trail (300'): 0.6 mi., 20 min.
>
> *to* Sentinel Pine Trail (300'): 1.0 mi., 30 min.
>
> *to* Lane Trail and Cascade Trail (320'): 1.1 mi., 35 min.
>
> *to* Little Bear Trail (350'): 2.5 mi., 1 hr. 15 min.
>
> *to* Podunk Rd. (350'): 2.6 mi. (4.2 km.), 1 hr. 20 min.

Lost Trail

This old road heads southwest from the Hayes Farm Trail and Lowland Trail to Dodge Rd., the unofficial western entrance to the park, then turns east to end at the Ferret Trail south of Bear Hill Pond. It forms two sides of a 5.6-mi. triangular snowmobile loop that is normally entered from Dodge Rd. Though less popular for hiking than the more central trails, it offers solitude and several scenic areas, particularly near the Old Reservoir in the southwestern corner of the park. It passes in and out of the park several times, and with a few exceptions is easy to follow.

The road leaves the western terminus of the Hayes Farm Trail and the northern terminus of the Lowland Trail (Snowmobile Sign A) and ascends gradually onto a small ridge, leaving the state park at the blue-blazed boundary. It passes several frog ponds, re-enters the park where an old woods road leaves left, descends for 0.1 mi., and then turns left onto a dirt road (in the reverse direction, turn right here onto an orange-blazed road). In another 0.1 mi. the trail crosses a tributary of Boat Meadow Brook on a bridge, then turns left onto another dirt road (in the reverse direction turn right, following orange blazes and snowmobile markers). In another 0.2 mi., the small parking area at the Dodge Rd. trailhead is reached. To reach this point by automobile, leave NH 28 0.7 mi. south of the main park access road; take a left onto unsigned but paved River Rd., which parallels NH 28 for 0.8 mi.; then turn left onto Dodge Rd. (sign). In 0.4 mi. the road becomes rough dirt and may be impassable for automobiles beyond this point. In another 0.4 mi. it reaches the trailhead at a fork (no sign).

The Lost Trail continues by turning sharp left at the fork and following the dirt road in an east–southeast direction. It passes an old gated woods road (right), crosses the tributary of Boat Meadow Brook, and re-enters the state park (blue-blazed boundary). After passing a large open gravel pit and field (right), the route passes several unmarked roads, leaves and re-enters the park, and passes a swampy area (right). At 1.0 mi. from Dodge Rd. it reaches the western end of the Old Reservoir (right) in an attractive hemlock and pine grove next to a small clearing where illegal camping has occurred. The road swings left, follows the northern shore of the reservoir, then crosses a bridge over an inlet brook at its eastern end next to a beaver lodge (right). Shortly the route passes alongside Boat Meadow Brook in a marshy area (right), bears left at a fork, passes by several swampy sections, and reaches the southern terminus of the Lowland Trail (left) at Snowmobile Sign C.

The Lost Trail continues straight here, crosses a tributary brook and then Boat Meadow Brook, passes through several wet and swampy areas, and ends at the Ferret Trail (Snowmobile Sign #12), 0.4 mi. south of Bear Hill Pond.

Distances from Hayes Farm Trail and Lowland Trail, northern terminus (500')

   to Dodge Rd. trailhead (350'): 1.5 mi., 0 ft. (rev. 150 ft.), 45 min.

   to Old Reservoir campground (450'): 2.5 mi., 100 ft., 1 hr. 20 min.

   to Lowland Trail, southern terminus (500'): 3.8 mi., 150 ft., 1 hr. 55 min.

   to Ferret Trail (550'): 4.2 mi. (6.8 km.), 200 ft., 2 hr. 10 min.

Lowland Trail

This old road is used primarily as a snowmobile trail in winter and is part of a 5.6-mi. triangular loop originating from Dodge Rd. at the southwestern end of the park. It connects the Hayes Farm Trail south of Hayes Marsh with the Lost

Trail near Bear Hill Pond, thus linking the trails in the center of the park with those in the southern part. The grades are gentle and the road is easy to follow.

The trail begins at Snowmobile Sign A, at the jct. of the Lost Trail (north terminus) with the Hayes Farm Trail, 1.0 mi. from Podunk Rd. and 1.5 mi. from Dodge Rd. It heads in a generally southeast direction, bypasses several wet sections, crosses a stream, and at 0.7 mi. reaches an unmarked road (left) at Snowmobile Sign B which leads 0.3 mi. to the Hedgehog Ledge Trail, 0.5 mi. south of Podunk Rd.

The Lowland Trail ascends gradually by a switchback, enters a pine grove, passes a small frog pond (left), descends through several wet areas, and ends at the Lost Trail (south terminus) at Snowmobile Sign C, 0.5 mi. west of the Ferret Trail and 1.3 mi. east of the Old Reservoir.

Distance from Hayes Farm Trail and Lost Trail, north terminus (350')

   to Lost Trail, south terminus (500'): 1.8 mi. (2.9 km.), 150 ft., 1 hr.

Sentinel Pine Trail

This trail connects the Bear Brook Trail at a point 1.0 mi. east of the Catamount Pond recreation area with the Hayes Farm Trail a short distance north of Hayes Marsh. It passes though attractive pine forests and by a small upland marsh.

It leaves the Bear Brook Trail at Snowmobile Sign #2 and ascends gradually on an old road through red pines, then white pines, in a southerly direction. At 0.3 mi., the road crosses the Cascade Trail and descends gradually to Catamount Brook, which it crosses on a small bridge. It enters a mixed oak forest and ascends a small ridge angling left (east), with an attractive small marsh to the right. At 1.2 mi. it reaches height-of-land, descends into a white pine forest, swings left, and crosses the yellow-blazed Carr Ridge Trail at 1.3 mi. After a brief descent, it ends at the Hayes Farm Trail (Snowmobile Sign #3), 0.5 mi. west of Hayes Field and Podunk Rd.

Distances from Bear Brook Trail (300')

   to Cascade Trail (450'): 0.3 mi., 150 ft., 15 min.

   to height-of-land (500'): 1.2 mi., 200 ft., 40 min.

   to Carr Ridge Trail (500'): 1.3 mi., 200 ft., 45 min.

   to Hayes Farm Trail (500'): 1.4 mi. (2.3 km.), 200 ft., 50 min.

Carr Ridge Trail

Carr Ridge is a minor subsidiary ridge extending northwest from Hayes Marsh to the ravine of Catamount Brook just east of Catamount Hill. The trail traverses this ridge through a wide variety of forests with interesting vistas of several natural features. It links the Lane Trail 0.3 mi. west of Podunk Rd. near Hayes Marsh to the Cascade Trail, thus providing access to Catamount Hill and the Catamount Pond recreation area in the northwest corner of the park. It is well marked with yellow blazes.

Leaving the Lane Trail, the Carr Ridge Trail heads west, skirting the northern end of Hayes Marsh in a pine forest. It swings right (northwest) and ascends Carr Ridge, crossing the Hayes Farm Trail at 0.3 mi. and the Sentinel Pine Trail at 0.4 mi. It becomes level on the ridge at 0.6 mi. in a mixed oak forest, then descends with minor ups and downs through small stands of white pine. It passes several large glacial erratic boulders in a gully, then ascends briefly and swings right onto a small ridge before descending into a pine and hemlock forest, where it meets the Cascade Trail at a point overlooking Catamount Brook.

Distances from Lane Trail (500')

   to Sentinel Pine Trail (500'): 0.4 mi., 10 min.

   to Cascade Trail (400'): 1.4 mi. (2.3 km.), 0 ft. (rev. 100 ft.), 45 min.

Hayes Farm Trail

This scenic woods road connects Podunk Rd. with the Lost Trail and Lowland Trail just southwest of Hayes Marsh, a beautiful open wetland through which Catamount Brook passes on its way to Bear Brook and the Suncook River. The trail skirts open meadows and the western edge of the marsh with its fine views, attracting mountain bikers in summer and snowmobilers and cross-country skiers in the winter. The grades are gentle and the trail is easy to follow.

The trail leaves Podunk Rd. (Snowmobile Sign #6), 0.5 mi. south of the park winter office on Campground Rd., and ascends gradually, passing the Little Bear Trail (which has cross-country ski trail markers) almost immediately. The Hayes Farm Trail passes an unmarked road (left) that leads to the east end of an open meadow, and the Lane Trail leaves on the right at 0.4 mi. at Snowmobile Sign #5 and runs to Bear Brook Trail and the northwest region of the park. The Hayes Farm Trail ascends into a pine grove and reaches the

Sentinel Pine Trail, which enters on the right at Snowmobile Sign #3. The Hayes Farm Trail now swings left (south) and descends gradually, passing the unsigned yellow-blazed Carr Ridge Trail at 0.7 mi., and reaches the west end of Hayes Marsh along an aqueduct wall over Catamount Brook at 0.8 mi. The view overlooking this wide watery expanse is one of the finest in the park. The old road continues generally south into a pine grove (Snowmobile Sign #4), passes a small frog pond (left), and ends at the northern terminus of the Lost Trail and the Lowland Trail (Snowmobile Sign A).

Distances from Podunk Rd. (510')

    to Sentinel Pine Trail (500'): 0.5 mi., 15 min.

    to Lost Trail and Lowland Trail (500'): 1.1 mi. (1.8 km.), 35 min.

Lane Trail

This attractive woods road leads from Hayes Field at Podunk Rd. west over a small ridge to the Bear Brook Trail and Cascade Trail, 1.1 mi. east of the Catamount Pond recreation area. Although the trail follows a woods road for its entire length, it is poorly signed and should be followed with care.

The trail follows an unmarked road that leaves Podunk Rd. 0.8 mi. south of Campground Rd. and the park winter office and follows the northern edge of Hayes Field. Almost immediately it passes the Little Bear Trail (right), an unmarked cross-country ski trail. At 0.2 mi., it leaves the field at its northwest corner and enters a pine forest. The trail passes the Carr Ridge Trail (left) at 0.3 mi., then ascends gradually to a beautiful open field, which it traverses on the southwest side. After crossing the Hayes Farm Trail at 0.5 mi., the trail re-enters the woods, ascends gradually to the height-of-land, then descends past several unmarked trails (use care to identify the proper route). The trail makes a wide swing to the right, then turns left at the bottom of the hill in a fine pine and hemlock forest and ends at the Bear Brook Trail and Cascade Trail. Continue straight on the Bear Brook Trail for the Catamount Pond recreation area.

Distances from Podunk Rd. at Hayes Field (500')

    to Hayes Farm Trail (500'): 0.5 mi., 15 min.

    to Bear Brook Trail and Cascade Trail (320'): 1.5 mi. (2.4 km.), 0 ft. (rev. 200 ft.), 45 min.

Bear Hill Trail

Bear Hill (835 ft.) is the second highest hill in the park and is the site of a former fire tower located in a pine and oak forest; at present there are no views. The trail leads from Podunk Rd. over Bear Hill and down to the Ferret Trail, just south of Podunk Rd. It is poorly marked in the section east of the top of Bear Hill but is not difficult to follow.

From Podunk Rd., just east of the trailhead for the Hedgehog Ledge Trail, the Bear Hill Trail ascends gradually on an old road marked with yellow blazes, which runs in a generally southeast direction through a pine and beech forest. It passes through several hemlock groves, through which Podunk Rd. may be seen to the left. At 0.8 mi. the trail meets another old road that ascends from the left from Podunk Rd. The trail turns to the right onto this road and ascends 0.2 mi. to the fire tower remains at the summit of Bear Hill.

To continue on the trail, backtrack a short distance, then make a sharp right (which is a left for one ascending toward the summit) onto an old road at a double blaze, and descend gradually to the Ferret Trail, an unsigned road. From here it is 0.2 mi. south (right) to the eastern terminus of the Hedgehog Ledge Trail and 0.2 mi. north (left) to Podunk Rd.

Distances from Podunk Rd. (600')

   to Bear Hill (835'): 1.0 mi., 250 ft., 40 min.

   to Ferret Trail (700'): 1.3 mi. (2.1 km.), 250 ft. (rev. 150 ft.), 45 min.

Hedgehog Ledge Trail

The Hedgehog Ledges are an interesting series of rock outcroppings and erratic boulders that extend down the southern slope of Bear Hill. The Hedgehog Ledge Trail leads from Podunk Rd. past these ledges to the Ferret Trail south of Podunk Rd. It also provides access to the Lowland Trail and the Hayes Marsh region by a short woods road shown on the map in this guide but not on the park map.

The trail leaves Podunk Rd. at a small parking area 1.3 mi. south of Deerfield Rd., and descends south on an old woods road past stone walls in a small clearing (left) to a jct. at 0.5 mi. Here the short woods road that is not shown on the park map continues 0.3 mi. straight ahead to the Lowland Trail at Snowmobile Sign #B, while the Hedgehog Ledge Trail turns left (signs). Soon the trail ascends along the south slope of Bear Hill past large boulders and along the base of multiple rock outcrops in an oak forest. At 1.1 mi., the trail emerges onto a small ridge in a mixed pine and oak forest, then passes blue boundary blazes and a semi-open marsh (right) before ending at the Ferret Trail, 0.4 mi. south of Podunk Rd.

Distances from Podunk Rd. (600')

   to Lowland Trail (550') via old road: 0.8 mi. (1.3 km.), 25 min.

   to Ferret Trail (700'): 1.3 mi. (2.1 km.), 150 ft., 45 min.

Bobcat Trail

This attractive trail connects Podunk Rd. opposite Hayes Field with the Broken Boulder Trail, 0.2 mi. south of the Smith Pond Shelter. It follows an old road that runs east with gentle grades, for much of its length through a mixed pine forest.

It leaves Podunk Rd. at a chain-link gate opposite Hayes Field (Cross-Country Ski Sign #9), 0.8 mi. south of Campground Rd. and the park winter office. It passes through an attractive pine plantation and reaches the Salt Lick Trail (left) at 0.1 mi. and the Chipmunk Trail on the right at Cross-Country Ski Sign #14 at 0.3 mi. At 0.9 mi. the trail swings sharp left off the old road to bypass a short swampy section, then zigzags back to rejoin the road, which it follows past a swampy area to end at the Broken Boulder Trail (Cross-Country Ski Sign #7).

Distance from Podunk Rd. (500')

   to Broken Boulder Trail (500'): 1.5 mi. (2.4 km.), 45 min.

Little Bear Trail

Due to recent logging operations, the northern section of this trail has been temporarily obliterated. It now leaves Hayes Field and follows a circuitous course north to the park winter office by either the Bear Brook Trail (which has also recently been disrupted) or a new logging road. It should be followed with care, and is best hiked in a south-to-north direction due to poor signage and blazing at its northern end.

The trail leaves the gravel road in Hayes Field on a cross-country ski trail approximately 60 yd. west of Podunk Rd., and heads north through a pine forest. The trail swings left, crosses the Hayes Farm Trail at 0.3 mi., and continues straight past a green gate onto an old road. Almost immediately, the route turns right onto a trail (sign) and bears left at a fork. The trail descends gradually, zigzagging through a section with blowdowns (use care in skirting around this area) until the route merges right onto a logging road (arrow) in a recently logged area. The route follows the logging road in an easterly direction through a clearing and begins to parallel the Bear Brook Trail (left). From here, the Bear Brook Trail may be followed 0.1 mi. to Podunk Rd. at the bridge over Bear Brook, or the yellow-blazed cross-country ski trail may be followed to the right uphill 0.1 mi. to a parking area directly across from the park winter office at the intersection of Podunk Rd. and Campground Rd. Allow extra time due to the obstacles and the logging disruption mentioned.

Distances from Hayes Field (500')

> *to* logging road (450'): 1.0 mi., 30 min.

> *to* Podunk Rd. and park winter office (400'): 1.4 mi. (2.3 km.), 40 min.

Salt Lick Trail

This attractive walk leads from the Pitch Pine Trail, 0.3 mi. east of the park winter office, to the Bobcat Trail, 0.1 mi. east of Podunk Rd. and 0.2 mi. west of the Chipmunk Trail. It heads generally south by wide zigzags, occasionally touching the east edge of Podunk Rd. along the way. Due to recent logging activity, it is probably best to approach this trail directly from Campground Rd.

The Salt Lick Trail leaves the Pitch Pine Trail on a cross-country ski trail next to a quarry entrance (Cross-Country Ski Sign #2) and crosses Campground Rd. almost immediately, then descends into a pine forest and turns sharp right onto an old road that ascends gradually to Podunk Rd. opposite a cross-country ski trail entrance. The trail now turns sharp left onto another old road, continues south making several sharp turns, passes a marshy area (left), and ends at the Bobcat Trail next to a beautiful red pine grove.

Distances from Pitch Pine Trail near Campground Rd. (450')

> *to* Podunk Rd. opposite cross-country ski trail (500'): 0.5 mi., 15 min.

> *to* Bobcat Trail (500'): 1.3 mi. (2.1 km.), 40 min.

Pitch Pine Trail

This trail runs east from the park winter office on Podunk Rd. through the Archery Range to the Broken Boulder Trail at its northern terminus. It then swings south, crosses Campground Rd., and ends at the Broken Boulder Trail, just north of Smith Pond. Due to recent logging activity near its beginning and the potential danger for hikers within the archery range during shooting season, the trail can be recommended only from the northern terminus of the Broken Boulder Trail toward Smith Pond.

The recommended part of the trail (westbound) leaves the Broken Boulder Trail just north of Smith Pond (Cross-Country Ski Sign #6) and follows an old road north 0.4 mi. to Campground Rd. (Cross-Country Ski Sign #5). It crosses the road diagonally right, passes a recent skidder road shortly thereafter, then swings left (west) and descends gradually along the side of a small ridge to the Broken Boulder Trail at its northern terminus.

Distances from Broken Boulder Trail near Smith Pond (500')

> *to* Campground Rd. (450'): 0.4 mi., 0 ft. (rev. 50 ft.), 10 min.
>
> *to* northern terminus of Broken Boulder Trail (400'): 0.8 mi. (1.3 km.), 0 ft. (rev. 50 ft.), 25 min.

Chipmunk Trail

This trail parallels Podunk Rd. from the Bobcat Trail to the Broken Boulder Trail near its southern terminus. Due to recent and extensive logging activity, it cannot be recommended south of Spruce Pond Rd. The northern half, however, is scenic with several interesting natural and historic features.

The trail leaves the Bobcat Trail (Cross-Country Ski Sign #14) and heads in a southeast direction through a pine forest. At 0.2 mi., it passes a stone wall and a Forest Demonstration Area (left), crosses a small stream, enters a hardwood forest, and passes the nineteenth-century Leavitt Family burial ground (right) as the trail ascends gradually. The route zigzags through a hemlock grove, reaches a small height-of-land, and descends gradually to Spruce Pond Rd. (Cross-Country Ski Sign #13), just 0.1 mi. east of Podunk Rd. From here the Chipmunk Trail has been virtually obliterated by logging activity. To reach the Broken Boulder Trail, turn right (southwest) onto Spruce Pond Rd., then left (southeast) onto Podunk Rd., and walk 1.0 mi. to the old road and trail sign on the left.

Distances from Bobcat Trail (550')

> *to* Leavitt Family burial ground (550'): 0.4 mi., 10 min.
>
> *to* Spruce Pond Rd. (600'): 1.0 mi. (1.6 km.), 50 ft., 35 min.
>
> *to* Broken Boulder Trail (500') via Spruce Pond Rd. and Podunk Rd.: 2.1 mi. (3.4 km.), 50 ft. (rev. 100 ft.), 1 hr. 5 min.

Broken Boulder Trail

This scenic trail follows old roads from the Pitch Pine Trail just east of the archery range, crosses Campground Rd., then continues south past Smith Pond Shelter and Spruce Pond Rd., ending at Podunk Rd. midway between Spruce Pond Rd. and the gated eastern entrance off Currier Rd. It passes through fine pine and hemlock forests, passing by Smith Pond, Broken Boulder itself (located on Spruce Pond Rd.), and the ruins of an old mill on Bear Brook. With its strategic location, bisecting the eastern half of the park, it makes many loop hikes possible.

The trail leaves the Pitch Pine Trail and descends gradually, crossing a small stream on a bridge, then ascends to cross Campground Rd. at 0.3 mi. It continues south on an old road (Cross-Country Ski Sign #4) with views through the trees toward Smith Pond (right) until it reaches the southeast terminus of the Pitch Pine Trail (left, Cross-Country Ski Sign #6) at 0.6 mi. In a short distance, an unmarked road leaves right and runs 0.1 mi. to the Smith Pond Shelter with its beautiful views of Smith Pond and the surrounding marshlands.

At 1.0 mi. the Bobcat Trail leaves right (Cross-Country Ski Sign #7) for Podunk Rd. at Hayes Field. The Broken Boulder Trail enters a fine pine and hemlock forest, crosses a small bridge, and at 1.4 mi. turns left (east) onto Spruce Pond Rd. (Cross-Country Ski Sign #10). In a short distance, Broken Boulder (a large erratic split by frost action) is passed, and the trail turns right (south) off of Spruce Pond Rd. onto an old road (Cross-Country Ski Sign #11) and re-enters the woods. The road passes through a wet and swampy section, crosses several small streams, then ascends gradually by the remains of an old mill on Bear Brook (left). The trail climbs a small embankment, merges left onto a logging road in a recently logged area, and continues straight through a large clearing past the Chipmunk Trail (right) at 2.3 mi. just before reaching Podunk Rd. at granite boulder barriers.

Distances from Pitch Pine Trail (400')

   to   southern terminus of Pitch Pine Trail (500'): 0.6 mi., 100 ft., 20 min.

   to   Spruce Pond Rd. (500'): 1.4 mi., 100 ft., 45 min.

   to   Podunk Rd. (600'): 2.4 mi. (3.9 km.), 200 ft., 1 hr. 20 min.

Hall Mountain Trail

This varied trail swings through the southeast corner of the park, crossing over Hall Mtn. (941 ft.), an ill-defined ridge with several semi-open viewpoints.

Though Hall Mtn's summit is the highest point in the park, there are no trails leading directly to it. Hall Mountain Trail runs in a clockwise direction from Podunk Rd., 0.1 mi. west of the gated entrance off Currier Rd. It climbs south, then west, over Hall Mtn., then descends to a beaver bog and continues north to Podunk Rd., 1.4 mi. west of the trail's origin. Extra time should be allowed on the less well-defined sections of the trail.

It leaves Podunk Rd. nearly opposite the Lynx Trail (Snowmobile Sign #18) —directly opposite the Lynx Trail there is a short path to a pleasant outlook— and descends gradually on an old road (Snowmobile Sign #17) in a southerly direction past several stone walls. It enters a fork as the right branch (no sign); in the opposite direction, bear left at the fork. It ascends gradually past a recently logged area (right) on the northern slope of Hall Mtn. After passing a large old elm (right), the grade eases as the road passes a stone wall, descends, swings sharp right (west), and ascends to its high point on Hall Mtn. It passes about 0.1 mi. north of the true summit, descends through a sag, and emerges on a semi-open ridge at 1.0 mi., where there are several viewpoints to the south from attractive quartz ledges on the left, partly covered with oaks, pines, and blueberry bushes.

The trail continues along the ridge briefly, then descends on a path marked by Snowmobile Sign #16 (left), leaves the park and shortly re-enters it (blue boundary blazes) in a hemlock grove. The route passes a beaver bog near a beaver lodge and dam (right) in a wet area, turns sharp right (north) onto a boardwalk, and follows an old road through a beech forest.

At 2.8 mi. the trail turns right onto the Ferret Trail (Snowmobile Sign #15) and coincides with it for 0.1 mi. through a recently logged area. At a double blaze (right) marked by orange ribbons, the route leaves the Ferret Trail and runs downhill on a circuitous and faded pathway (often difficult to follow). As an alternative, inexperienced hikers may prefer to follow Bear Hill Rd. north through the 4-H Camp to Podunk Rd. During the summer season, however, the park management requests that hikers use the Hall Mountain Trail to Podunk Rd. if possible.

After 0.9 mi. of zigzag descent (watch carefully for yellow blazes and orange ribbons), a stone wall is passed (left) and the trail merges with an old grassy road that leads directly to Podunk Rd., 0.1 mi. east of Bear Hill Rd. and 0.4 mi. west of the Broken Boulder Trail.

Distances from Podunk Rd. at Snowmobile Sign #17 (750')

   to Hall Mtn. (941'): 1.0 mi., 200 ft., 35 min.

to Ferret Trail and Bear Hill Rd. (750'): 2.8 mi., 200 ft. (rev. 200 ft.), 1 hr. 30 min.

to Podunk Rd. (700'): 3.7 mi. (6.0 km.), 200 ft. (rev. 50 ft.), 1 hr. 55 min.

Ferret Trail

This trail loops in a clockwise direction around Bear Hill Pond in the southeastern corner of the park, passing through oak forests and hemlock groves and near open marshes. Bear Hill Pond is extremely attractive, particularly along its western and northern shores. Park management requests that during the summer season hikers should not use Bear Hill Rd. through the 4-H Camp; this section may be bypassed on the Hall Mountain Trail (see trail description), which begins on Podunk Rd. 0.1 mi. east of Bear Hill Rd.

The Ferret Trail begins at the automobile turnaround on Podunk Rd. where the Bear Hill Rd. (Snowmobile Sign #9) leaves to the south through an orange gate. The route ascends along this road 0.3 mi. to the 4-H Camp and its cabins, then turns left onto a gravel driveway by Channell Hall (left). It swings right, then left, and follows the dirt road past the camp's cabins (right) overlooking the pond. The trail passes a silo (right), cuts left across a field, and enters a grassy road (Snowmobile Sign #14) just before the Hall Mountain Trail (the preferred summer route) comes in on the left from Podunk Rd.

The Ferret Trail merges with the Hall Mountain Trail and continues straight ahead through a recently logged area until it reaches a jct. (Snowmobile Sign #15) at 0.8 mi., where the Hall Mountain Trail turns left toward Hall Mtn. From there the route continues on the grassy road (Snowmobile Route 15S) through an oak forest and is easier to follow.

One mile later, after passing the park boundary blazes and an old stone wall, the road reaches a T intersection (Snowmobile Sign #13) at an old grassy road lined with stone walls. The trail turns right (northwest) here, passes more park boundary markers, and descends gradually. It passes another grassy road (left) at 2.5 mi., where Snowmobile Route 15S leaves the trail, and in another 0.2 mi. reaches a jct. (Snowmobile Sign #12) where the unsigned Lost Trail continues straight ahead toward the Lowland Trail, Hayes Marsh, and points west.

The Ferret Trail turns sharp right (northwest) here onto an old road in a pine and hemlock grove and ascends gradually. It crosses several streams on small bridges, the largest being the outlet brook flowing from Bear Hill Pond. After attaining a small height-of-land, the road descends through an attractive section with marshlands to the left and Bear Hill Pond to the right. The road crosses a small culverted inlet stream, and at 3.7 mi. reaches the yellow-blazed Hedgehog Ledge Trail (left). In less than 0.1 mi. an unmarked road (right) leads in 200 yd. to a beautiful view of Bear Hill Pond from a rocky promontory on its northwest shore. The main route crosses another culverted stream, ascends gradually, and in 0.1 mi. reaches an unsigned and unblazed road (left), which is the Bear Hill Trail. The Ferret Trail ascends a short distance over a small oak ridge and descends to Podunk Rd. at Snowmobile Sign #8, 0.1 mi. west of the trail's origin.

Distances from Podunk Rd. at Snowmobile Sign #9 (700')

> *to* Hall Mountain Trail (750'): 0.8 mi., 50 ft., 25 min.
>
> *to* Lost Trail (550'): 2.7 mi., 50 ft. (rev. 200 ft.), 1 hr. 20 min.
>
> *to* Hedgehog Ledge Trail (700'): 3.7 mi., 200 ft., 1 hr. 55 min.
>
> *to* northwest shore of Bear Hill Pond (650') via short spur: 3.9 mi., 2 hr.
>
> *to* Bear Hill Trail (700'): 3.9 mi., 2 hr.
>
> *to* Podunk Rd. at Snowmobile Sign #8 (700'): 4.1 mi. (6.6 km.), 2 hr. 5 min.

Lynx Trail

This trail follows old roads over rolling terrain, connecting the southern end of Beaver Pond with Podunk Rd. near its gated southeast entrance off Currier Rd. It leaves the Beaver Pond Trail at a three-way intersection (Snowmobile Sign #19) 0.9 mi. south of the campground store, and ascends gradually south on an old road through several logged clearings. At 0.4 mi. the trail turns sharp right (signs) onto an overgrown old road. (The road straight ahead continues as a snowmobile route 0.2 mi. to Currier Rd.)

The trail turns sharp right, then left, and soon reaches a height-of-land. It descends into a mixed hemlock forest, passing a rocky outcropping (right) and a marshy wetland area (right). It passes through a corduroy section in a wet area and ascends gradually past two stone walls to Podunk Rd. at Snowmobile Sign #18, 0.1 mi. west of the gated entrance to Currier Rd. and diagonally across from the Hall Mountain Trail at Snowmobile Sign #17 under a set of utility lines.

Distance from Beaver Pond Trail (500')

> *to* Podunk Rd. at Hall Mountain Trail (750'): 1.3 mi. (2.1 km.), 250 ft., 45 min.

Beaver Pond Trail

This easily followed, scenic loop may be used to explore the interesting and varied terrain and ecology of Spruce Pond and Beaver Pond, and also as an access to the Hall Mtn. region from Beaver Pond Campground. The easiest parking access during the warmer months is in the vicinity of the campground store near the end of Campground Rd.; there is limited parking at Beaver Pond Beach and at the southern end of the campground, where the trail begins. In winter it is necessary to walk the 2.9 mi. on Campground Rd. (also used as a snowmobile trail) from the park winter office, on Podunk Rd. just south of Deerfield Rd. To reach the trailhead, walk south from the campground store on a paved road past campsite #64 onto an old road marked with Snowmobile Sign #20. At 0.2 mi. from the store, the road bears right (arrow and yellow blazes) where there is limited parking on the left.

The trail heads south on an old road between Spruce Pond (right) and Beaver Pond (left). The route bears left at a fork, then passes a side path to Spruce Pond (right) in a beautiful oak, birch, and hemlock grove. It shortly passes a side path to Beaver Pond (left) and at 0.6 mi. crosses a scenic board-walk and bridge (dedicated to the Indiana Fire Crew 1995), and continues through a marsh of cattails, leatherleaf, and maples. The trail passes a log bench (left), swings left (east), crosses a boardwalk through a swampy area, and at 0.9 mi. reaches a three-way intersection where the Lynx Trail (Snowmobile Sign #19) leaves right toward the Hall Mountain Trail.

The trail now makes a left turn, then a right turn onto a path along the south shore of Beaver Pond. It follows the southern and then the eastern shoreline of the pond until it reaches a hemlock grove, where it turns sharp right, crosses an outlet stream on a small bridge, then swings left along a small cove. The trail passes through a marshy area and swings away from the pond again, until it turns left onto an old road along the north shore of the pond at 1.7 mi. The trail crosses the Beaver Pond Beach toward a campground road at a steel barrier; from here it is 0.3 mi. back to the campground store on the paved road.

Distances from campground store (500')

 to Spruce Pond (500'): 0.4 mi., 10 min.

 to Lynx Trail (500'): 0.9 mi., 25 min.

 to Beaver Pond Beach (490'): 1.7 mi., 50 min.

 to campground store (500') via complete loop: 2.0 mi. (3.2 km.), 1 hr.

Oak Hill

Oak Hill (990 ft.) is a long ridge running east and west, located in Loudon and Concord. On the wooded summit is a high fire tower that affords expansive views stretching from Monadnock to Mt. Washington in clear weather, and there are several other viewpoints with less sweeping views (but views unobstructed by the several communications towers in the vicinity of the fire tower). Oak Hill stands in the middle of a fairly large (for this part of the state) area that is almost completely undeveloped (except as stated at the summit), covered with beautiful woods where only the ever-present stone walls and a few cellar holes remind the visitor that Oak Hill was once almost entirely open pasture and farm land. Today deer and coyotes are common residents. The easiest access is by the road to the summit and fire tower; this road is normally closed to public vehicular travel but open to pedestrians and bicyclists. The City of Concord owns a large area on the western slopes—abandoned farmland taken over for unpaid taxes—and manages it as a conservation and public recreation area administered by the Concord Conservation Trust. A network of trails has been established in this area. Refer to the USGS Penacook and Loudon quadrangles.

Oak Hill Summit Road (USGS Penacook and Loudon quads)

This road, usually closed to automobiles, provides an easy and very popular hike to the fire tower and its views. From I-93 at the end of the Exit 16 eastern off-ramp, go almost straight up a short, steep hill on Shawmut St., then bear left at 0.7 mi. as Shawmut St. becomes Oak Hill Rd. at the jct. with Appleton St. Pass Turtletown Pond and continue up the road, with an occasional glimpse up to the white quartzite south ledge. The summit road (gated) is on the left, 4.0 mi. from the Exit 16 off-ramp, just before the height-of-land on Oak Hill Rd. There is a hanging sign for the fire tower here, giving a mileage exactly double the actual distance. Parking is severely restricted; park carefully along the roadside, avoiding posted No Parking areas—particularly the entrance to the road itself.

Easy to moderate ascents alternate with long level sections, and at 0.6 mi. the road comes to a fork where a woods road diverges to the right headed north toward Loudon's School St., used as a snowmobile route to Canterbury. On the main road at this fork a large cellar hole is located on the right, opposite an old former millpond that has reverted to a swamp. At a small rise about 100 yd.

before this fork is reached, a beaten path diverges to the left (for an ascending hiker) uphill from the road through an opening in the stone wall that lines the road; this path winds through the woods with minor ups and downs for 0.4 mi. to the white quartzite south ledge mentioned above, where there is a fine view out over Concord to the hills and mountains of southwestern New Hampshire, including Monadnock. The road continues to alternate moderate ascents and flat sections until it reaches the summit and fire tower.

Distance from Oak Hill Rd. (568')

   to summit of Oak Hill (990'): 1.3 mi. (2.0 km.), 450 ft., 50 min.

Oak Hill Trails

This network of trails on the western part of Oak Hill, maintained by the Concord Conservation Trust, passes two outlooks and traverses interesting woods, and is connected to the summit and fire tower by a recently constructed trail. Walks of low to moderate strenuousness of virtually any length can be selected, with loop hikes including a visit to the summit running in the range of 4 to 6 mi. Trails are marked by yellow plastic strips nailed to trees. There are presently three trailheads: two are on Shaker Rd., reached from the end of the eastern off-ramp of I-93's Exit 16 by turning left on Mountain Rd., then bearing right on Shaker Rd. in 0.3 mi. The south trailhead is 2.3 mi. from the Exit 16 off-ramp, and the north trailhead is 0.5 mi. beyond. Neither trailhead is obvious, but with a little searching both can be found fairly readily. Distances to various points are generally shorter from the north trailhead, but if the Vista is included, the south trailhead generally provides shorter distances. The third trailhead is on Oak Hill Rd., 2.0 mi. from I-93 Exit 16—see directions above for Oak Hill Summit Road; this trailhead (small sign) is on the left (north) at the top of the first hill beyond (east of) Turtletown Pond. Trail maps are sometimes available at the Shaker Rd. trailheads in boxes a short distance from the road, but they can also be downloaded and printed from the official Concord website, www.onconcord.com (choose "Maps" from first menu, then "Hiking Trails" from list of maps; the Oak Hill map is currently #12.). Some trail names have been altered since the last edition of this guide, and some names on signs differ slightly from those on the map.

    The *Tower Trail* leaves the north Shaker Rd. trailhead and climbs past jcts. on the right with the Lower Trail at 0.2 mi. and the Ledges Trail (sign: Ledges Pass) 25 yd. beyond. At 0.4 mi. the trail swings right uphill where an overgrown woods road continues straight ahead, and at 0.5 mi. the Upper Trail enters on the right. The Tower Trail continues to climb easily across the side of a knoll, then descends into a shady sag where it crosses a small brook. It then climbs again, passing at 0.8 mi. the jct. on the left with the Dancing Bear Trail to Swope Slope outlook and reaching an intersection where the Krupa Loop leaves on the right and the Dancing Bear Trail enters on the left, providing a short direct path 0.1 to Swope Slope outlook. At 0.9 mi. the Tower Trail crosses the Krupa Loop, from this point, according to the map, it is called the Way-to-Go Trail. It swings to the right (southeast) from its former location, crosses a small ridge and descends gently to reach a power line corridor at the stone wall that marks the Concord–Loudon boundary, where Ron's Way joins on the right, at 1.5 mi. The power line corridor is followed to the summit and tower at 1.9 mi.

The *Dancing Bear Trail* diverges left from the Tower Trail 0.8 mi. from the north Shaker Rd. trailhead and runs 0.4 mi. to Swope Slope, a cleared area with views to the north. Here the Krupa Loop continues ahead, while the Dancing Bear Trail climbs to meet the Tower Trail opposite the other end of the Krupa Loop at 0.5 mi.

The *Krupa Loop* begins at the Swope Slope outlook and climbs to cross the Tower Trail at 0.2 mi. At 0.6 mi. Ron's Way leaves left to connect with the Tower Trail at the power line corridor. The Krupa Loop swings through a rocky area to end at the four-way jct. with the Tower Trail and the Dancing Bear Trail, 1.1 mi. from the north trailhead.

Ron's Way leaves the Krupa Loop 0.4 mi. south of the latter trail's crossing of the Tower Trail and mostly ascends gradually to meet the Tower Trail (Way-to-Go Trail) at the stone wall at the edge of the power line corridor.

The *Lower Trail* leaves the Tower Trail 0.2 mi. from the north Shaker Rd. trailhead and runs south, climbing gently over a low ridge and then passing the jct. with the Upper Trail on the left at 0.2 mi., and ends at the Vista Trail at 0.3 mi., 0.2 from the south Shaker Rd. trailhead.

The *Upper Trail* begins on the Lower Trail and climbs steadily, crossing the Ledges Trail at 0.1 mi. It passes the jct. on the right with Terry's Turn (a link to the trails from the Oak Hill Rd. trailhead) at 0.4 mi., continues to rise slightly, then descends to the Tower Trail at 0.5 mi.

The *Vista Trail* leaves the south Shaker Rd. trailhead, passes jcts. with the Lower Trail on the left at 0.2 mi. and the Ledges Trail on the left at 0.3 mi., and climbs to a rocky knob with a fine view toward Mt. Kearsarge at 0.5 mi. It then descends to rejoin the Ledges Trail at 0.6 mi.

The *Ledges Trail* leaves the Vista Trail 0.3 mi. from the south Shaker Rd. trailhead, and at 0.1 mi. the Vista Trail rejoins on the right. At 0.2 mi. the Ledges Trail crosses Upper Trail, and at 0.4 mi. it ends on the Tower Trail 25 yd. above the jct. with the Lower Trail.

The *Ovenbird Trail* (Ovenbird Scuttle on signs) is the middle trail of the three that ascend from the Oak Hill Rd. trailhead. It crosses a field and enters the woods, then passes jcts. with the Luti Loop on the left at 0.1 mi. and the Murray Loop on the right at 0.3 mi. It climbs steadily, its upper section in a small curving ravine, to the jct. at 0.7 mi. where the Luti Loop and Murray Loop rejoin.

The *Murray Loop* (Murray Bluff Trail on signs) is the easternmost of the three trails that ascend from the Oak Hill Rd. trailhead. Its upper section is the steepest and roughest trail segment on Oak Hill. It diverges to the right from the Ovenbird Trail at 0.3 mi. and climbs, steadily at first and then rather steeply, up a rough slope to a plateau. Terry's Turn, a link that runs 0.1 mi. to the Upper Trail and connects the Oak Hill Rd. trails to the Shaker Rd. trails (including the trail to Oak Hill's summit), leaves on the right at 0.5 mi., and the Murray Loop continues to a jct. with the Ovenbird Trail and Luti Loop at 0.6 mi.

The *Luti Loop* is the westernmost of the three trails that ascend from the Oak Hill Rd. trailhead; it is the longest of the three but provides the shortest route to the Vista from the Oak Hill Rd. trailhead. Its signs insist that it is not a loop—technically speaking, it is merely part of a loop. It diverges left from the Ovenbird Trail 0.1 mi. from the trailhead and meanders through the woods to a jct. on the left at 0.8 mi. with Win's Way, a link path that runs 0.2 mi. to the Vista Trail at the Vista. The Luti Loop then swings to the right and climbs to the jct. with the Ovenbird Trail and Murray Trail at 1.0 mi.

Section 4

The Lakes Region

SUGGESTED HIKES

Easy Hikes

West Rattlesnake [rt: 1.8 mi, 450 ft., 1:05]. The very popular Old Bridle Path provides an easy climb to ledges with beautiful views over Squam Lake. A good alternative to this often crowded route is the Pasture Trail **[rt: 1.2 mi, 600 ft., 0:55]**.

Piper Mtn. [rt: 1.8 mi., 350 ft., 1:05]. The White Trail and Old Piper Trail provide easy access to the open north summit of Piper.

Belknap Mtn. Of the several trail routes to this fire tower peak, one of the nicest is to ascend by the Red Trail and descend by the Blue Trail **[lp: 1.9 mi., 700 ft., 1:20]**. A longer but very attractive route is the East Gilford Trail **[rt: 4.2 mi., 1300 ft., 2:45]**.

Moderate Hikes

Mt. Major [lp: 3.9 mi., 1150 ft., 2:30]. A large area of open rock with wide views over Lake Winnispesaukee makes this one of the most popular hikes in southern New Hampshire. For a loop, ascend via the Mount Major Trail and descend via the Belknap Range and Brook Trails.

Bald Knob [rt: 2.2 mi., 1100 ft., 1:40]. This open rock knob on the side of the Ossipee Range affords a sweeping view over Lake Winnipesaukee after an often steep and rough climb.

Red Hill [rt: 3.4 mi, 1350 ft., 2:20]. The Red Hill Trail follows an old jeep road to a tower with wide views of the Lakes Region.

Mt. Percival & Mt. Morgan [lp: 5.4 mi., 1550 ft., 3:30]. This loop hike via the Mount Morgan Trail, Morgan–Percival Connector, Mount Percival Trail, Crawford-Ridgepole Trail, and Mount Morgan Trail offers exceptional views for the effort required.

Doublehead Mtn. Ledge [rt: 4.4 mi., 1400 ft., 2:55]. A ledge on the Doublehead Trail 0.1 mi. below the mostly wooded summit is one of the best viewpoints on the Squam Range.

Green Mtn. [lp: 4.3 mi., 1450 ft., 2:55]. The views from the fire tower atop this peak are outstanding. This loop from the south follows the Dearborn Trail, Libby Road Trail, Libby Rd. and Hobbs Rd.

Mts. Klem and Mack [lp: 5.0 mi., 1050 ft., 3:00]. This loop on the Round Pond Woods Road, Mount Klem Loop, and Belknap Range Trail takes in two summits with views and beautiful Round Pond.

Strenuous Hikes

Mt. Shaw [rt: 7.6 mi., 2400 ft., 5:00]. The Mount Shaw Trail leads to the highest peak in the Ossipee Range, where there are sweeping views north and east. A spur trail leads to Black Snout, a knob with views west and south over Lake Winnipesaukee.

Circuit of Eastern Belknap Range [lp: 11.3 mi., 3400 ft., 7:20]. This challenging loop trip from the Mt. Major trailhead leads over eight small peaks (including Major, Klem, Mack, Anna, and Straightback) with numerous views. It follows the Mount Major Trail, Belknap Range Trail, Quarry Trail (via its eastern link), Mount Klem Loop, and Belknap Range Trail again (east from Mt. Mack), with descent on the Brook Trail.

LIST OF TRAILS

South of the White Mtns. and east of the natural central dividing line formed by the Merrimack River and its northern extension, the Pemigewasset River, the terrain consists of a multitude of medium and small mountains and hills, many with interesting views. But the dominating feature is the fine collection of lakes and ponds generously scattered among the hills, including Lake Winnipesaukee, New Hampshire's largest lake, and numerous smaller lakes, of which Squam Lake is the most prominent. For the purposes of this book the Lakes Region is restricted to the area east of the Pemigewasset River, though in tourist publications the Lakes Region includes some areas to the west, notably Newfound Lake. The unifying theme of the hills and mountains covered in this section is that views usually include a significant lake, most often either Winnipesaukee or Squam. The mountains with trails described here include Green Mtn. in Effingham south of Ossipee Lake, the Squam Range and the Rattlesnakes north of Squam Lake, Red Hill between Squam Lake and Lake Winnipesaukee, the Ossipee Range east of Lake Winnipesaukee, the Belknap Range and Mt. Major west of Lake Winnipesaukee, and Devils Den Mtn. in New Durham and Copple Crown Mtn. in Brookfield south of Lake Winnipesaukee.

Green Mountain

Green Mtn. (1884 ft.) is an isolated small mountain in the town of Effingham. The state owns 15 acres on the summit, where there is a 61-ft. fire tower. The views are excellent and extensive in all directions—the White Mtns., particularly the Sandwich Range over Ossipee Lake, are seen from an unusual and interesting perspective—but the high tower must be climbed to obtain any significant views. Refer to the USGS Freedom quadrangle. In addition to the fire warden's trail on the north side of the mountain, now called the High Watch Trail, there are also two trails on the south side, the Dearborn Trail and Libby Road Trail that make a loop hike possible. Much of the north side of the mountain is in the SPNHF High Watch Preserve. For information concerning conservation efforts on Green Mtn., contact the Green Mtn. Conservation Group, PO Box 95, South Effingham, NH 03882.

High Watch Trail (USGS Freedom quad)

From the western jct. of NH 25 and NH 153 (northbound) near Effingham Falls, go south on Green Mtn. Rd. for 1.2 mi., then turn left on a gravel road (sign: "Green Mt. Fire Tower") and follow it for 0.2 mi. to a T intersection with a paved road, High Watch Rd. Turn left here and follow High Watch Rd. At 1.2 mi., just past the Lakeview Neurorehabilitation Center, the road becomes rough gravel and continues another 0.2 mi. to a crossroads in the woods (sign: "Green Mt. Fire Tower"). Park here. This trail is shown accurately on the USGS Freedom quadrangle.

The High Watch Trail follows the road to the right (south), passing a High Watch Preserve sign. The old woods road that the trail uses is moderately steep and severely eroded in places. It runs toward the fence of the Lakeview Center's parking area and then climbs across a service road that runs to a fenced-in building on the left at 0.4 mi. Soon it bears left at a fork where the road to the right is becoming overgrown. At 0.9 mi. the grade becomes easy for a while, then climbs more steeply again until it swings to the left and becomes progressively less steep until it reaches the summit and its fire tower.

Distance from crossroads on High Watch Rd. (740')

   to summit of Green Mtn. (1884'): 1.4 mi. (2.2 km.), 1150 ft., 1 hr. 15 min.

Dearborn Trail (USGS Freedom quad)

This trail, blazed in white, ascends Green Mtn. from the southeast. It is not shown on the USGS Freedom quadrangle, though its approximate route up the ridge northeast of Salmon Brook is easily identified. It is probably the most attractive trail on Green Mtn. due to the light use it has received and the ledgy, wooded terrain it passes through, but because of the light use the footway is not well established and the blazes must be followed with care. In one section the destruction of trees caused by the January 1998 ice storm may cause this part of the trail to become somewhat overgrown by low vegetation in midsummer, making it even more necessary to follow the markings with care. To make a loop hike, it is recommended that you ascend by this trail and descend by the Libby Road Trail.

The trailhead for the Dearborn Trail is on Hobbs Rd. From NH 153 on the north edge of Effingham village, at a jct. where there is a historical marker for the First Normal School in New Hampshire, follow Hobbs Rd. for 1.3 mi.; the last 0.2 mi. is rough and has not been plowed in winter. The trailhead is in a small field on the right at the height-of-land opposite a house. There is a trail sign at the back edge of the field. To reach the trailhead for the Libby Road Trail from this trailhead, follow Hobbs Rd. (not passable for most cars) west to the jct. with Old Pound Rd. (passable for cars) at 0.4 mi., then bear right on Libby Rd. (no sign, not passable for most cars) to a woods road with a green gate on the right at 1.0 mi.

From the trailhead, the Dearborn Trail follows an old woods road uphill, on private land at first. It passes a property boundary line at 0.7 mi., where it narrows to a footpath, and then climbs steadily through a section of large pines, which permit glimpses across the valley. At 0.9 mi. there is a split boulder to the right of the trail that looks as if it had been sliced into three pieces with a knife. At 1.1 mi. the trail reaches a shoulder where it runs level for a short distance, then swings right and climbs moderately past a yellow-blazed property boundary and continues to ascend below a rocky ridgecrest to the left of the trail. It becomes less steep and winds through woods with ledges, crosses the blue-blazed state land boundary, and reaches the summit.

Distances from Hobbs Rd. (550')

>   *to* summit of Green Mtn. (1884'): 1.4 mi. (2.3 km.), 1350 ft., 1 hr. 25 min.

>   *to* starting point by complete loop via Libby Road Trail, Libby Rd., and Hobbs Rd.: 4.3 mi. (6.9 km.), 1450 ft., 2 hr. 55 min.

Libby Road Trail (USGS Freedom quad)

This trail is a woods road currently used by the fire warden to ascend the mountain in an ATV. It has some loose rock footing and is not a particularly attractive trail, but it is easy to follow and makes possible a loop hike in combination with the Dearborn Trail. It is accurately shown on the USGS Freedom quadrangle. From NH 153 in Center Effingham opposite the Baptist church, take Town House Rd. west for 1.8 mi., then turn right on Libby Rd. (sign: "Green Mt. Fire Tower") and follow it for 0.5 mi. to a woods road with a green gate on the left (sign: "Green Mt. Fire Tower"). Libby Rd. is rough but passable to this point in most cars. To reach the trailhead for the Dearborn Trail from this trailhead, follow Libby Rd. (not passable for most cars) east to the jct. with Old Pound Rd. (passable for cars) at 0.7 mi., then bear left on Hobbs Rd. (no sign; not passable for most cars) to a small field on the left at 1.0 mi.

The trail follows the woods road past the gate, passing a cabin (left) at 0.2 mi. and reaching a small brook at 0.7 mi. At 0.9 mi. the trail swings to the right away from the brook and climbs to a hairpin turn to the right at 1.6 mi. (avoid an eroded woods road that diverges left here and rejoins the main road higher up). From here the trail climbs past the fire warden's cabin to the summit and tower. To find this trail from the summit, descend to the front of the fire warden's cabin; the woods road can be seen clearly from there.

Distance from Libby Rd. (720')

    to summit of Green Mtn. (1884'): 1.8 mi. (2.9 km.), 1150 ft., 1 hr. 30 min.

The Squam Range and the Rattlesnakes

The Squam Range begins at Sandwich Notch across from Mt. Israel and runs roughly southwest toward Holderness. This area is almost entirely private property, open to day hikers by the gracious permission of the landowners, but camping is not permitted. Its peaks, from northeast to southwest, are an unnamed knob (2218 ft.), Mt. Doublehead (2158 ft.), Mt. Squam (2223 ft.), Mt. Percival (2212 ft.), a knob sometimes called the Sawtooth (2260 ft.) that is the actual high point of the range, Mt. Morgan (2220 ft.), Mt. Webster (2076 ft.), Mt. Livermore (1500 ft.), and Cotton Mtn. (1270 ft.). The Crawford-Ridgepole Trail crosses over or near all of these summits except for Cotton Mtn. (although it does go to the lower southeast summit of Cotton Mtn.), and several trails ascend the ridge from NH 113; curiously, the Sawtooth, the high point of the range, is bypassed by the trail. By far the most popular hike on the range, often fairly crowded, is the loop over Mts. Morgan and Percival, which offer superb views south over the lake and hill country and north to the higher mountains; the rest of the range is lightly visited and the trails, including the Crawford-Ridgepole Trail, often require some care to follow, though the rewards of pleasant walks to several excellent viewpoints are great.

The Rattlesnakes—West Rattlesnake (1260 ft.) and East Rattlesnake (1289 ft.)—are a pair of hills that rise just across the highway from Mt. Morgan and Mt. Percival and offer excellent lake views for little effort. West Rattlesnake has fine views to the south and west from its southwest cliff. East Rattlesnake has a more limited but still excellent view over Squam Lake. Five Finger Point, which lies southeast of the Rattlesnakes and has a perimeter trail connected to the Rattlesnakes' trail network, offers attractive lakeside walking on undeveloped rocky shores.

The area containing these trails is shown on the USGS Squam Mtns. and Holderness quadrangles, though the Crawford-Ridgepole Trail up to the southeast summit of Cotton Mtn. is not shown, and the Old Highway is shown but not titled. The Squam Lakes Association (SLA), which maintains most of the trails on the Squam Range, publishes Bradford Washburn's detailed map of the

Squam Range (scale 1:15,000) and a trail guide to the paths they maintain, both of which can be ordered from the SLA, PO Box 204, Holderness, NH 03245 (603-968-7336), www.squamlakes.org. The Washburn map, although offering much greater detail than any other map, also covers the Rattlesnakes but omits the southwestern end of the Squam Range. However, the SLA trail guide has a waterproof map that, while not nearly as detailed as the Washburn map, covers the southwest end of the Squam Range (and also Red Hill) to an extent that will probably be adequate for the great majority of hikers. The AMC Crawford Notch–Sandwich Range map (map #3 in the *AMC White Mountain Guide*) also covers most of the Squam Range (and also the Rattlesnakes), but omits approximately the same part of the Squam Range as the Washburn map.

Crawford-Ridgepole Trail (SLA trail map)

This trail follows the backbone of the Squam Range from Sandwich Notch Rd. to the south knob of Cotton Mtn. The trail starts on the Sandwich Notch Rd. 3.7 mi. from NH 113 in Center Sandwich and 0.5 mi. beyond Falls (Sandwich town park parking area) and 2.0 mi. south of the power line along the Beebe River. There is parking space for one or two cars at the trailhead; other spaces may be found a short distance east along the road. Except for the very popular segment between Mt. Percival and Mt. Morgan, the trail is used infrequently, despite fine views in the Squam–Doublehead section.

From the road (sign) the trail ascends steeply, with one difficult ledge scramble; you may need to remove your pack and climb up a cleft in the rock (use caution). Higher up the grade eases and the trail passes southeast of the summit of an unnamed wooded peak (2218 ft.), and continues along the ridge across a saddle to Doublehead Mtn. (2158 ft.), where there is a good view north just before the summit of East Doublehead. At 1.9 mi., 100 yd. beyond the summit of East Doublehead, the trail bears right and descends where the Doublehead Trail diverges left to NH 113. There is a very fine viewpoint, well worth the side trip, on the Doublehead Trail 0.1 mi. from this jct. After passing over West Doublehead, where there is a limited outlook to the north, the Crawford-Ridgepole Trail continues along the ridge, much of the way over ledges, which are slippery when wet. It climbs steeply out of a muddy saddle, with one fairly difficult ledge scramble, passes an excellent south outlook, then crosses an open ledge with fine views to the north. It crosses the east summit of Mt.

Squam (2223 ft.), where there is a restricted view, at 3.0 mi. The trail continues along the ridge, passing over the west summit of Mt. Squam and descending through a notch, then climbing to the Mount Percival Trail and Mt. Percival's excellent views at 4.4 mi. Continuing along the ridge, it passes just west of the actual high point of the range (sometimes called the Sawtooth, it can be reached by a short but thick bushwhack and has a good view), and continues to a jct. with the Mount Morgan Trail at 5.2 mi. Here the Mount Morgan Trail leads to the right 90 yd. to a fork; the left branch (almost straight ahead) leads another 50 yd. to a cliff-top viewpoint, while the right branch leads 50 yd. to the true summit of Mt. Morgan, where there is an interesting view north.

From this jct. the Crawford-Ridgepole Trail and the Mount Morgan Trail coincide, descending a set of steps. Shortly a spur path branches right, ascends a ladder, and climbs about 100 yd. through a boulder cave to the cliff-top viewpoint. The main trail descends to a jct. at 5.6 mi. where the Mount Morgan Trail continues its descent to NH 113, while the Crawford-Ridgepole Trail turns right for Mt. Webster. It continues south across a saddle, then climbs at easy grades with occasional minor descents, keeping to the west side of the ridgecrest. At 7.2 mi. a spur path leads left 50 yd. to the wooded summit of Mt. Webster, and at 7.5 mi. an unmarked spur leads left a few steps to the beautiful east outlook.

The trail descends to the jct. with the Old Mountain Road at 9.6 mi., then climbs to the summit of Mt. Livermore (view) at 10.0 mi. Coinciding with the Prescott Trail, it descends west from Mt. Livermore along a stone wall, then turns left on an old carriage road and descends by switchbacks. At 10.3 mi. the Prescott Trail branches left; the Crawford-Ridgepole Trail crosses two tiny streams near a low pass, then climbs through a rocky area in a beautiful hemlock grove to the southeast summit of Cotton Mtn. at the jct. with the Cotton Mountain Trail. A short distance down this trail, a spur path leads left to a viewpoint over Squam Lake. Here the Crawford-Ridgepole Trail ends, since the Science Center of New Hampshire has closed the former connector to its trails, because it requires an admission fee for use of its trails. From the spur of Cotton Mtn., descent can be made by following the Cotton Mountain Trail down to NH 113 near the Old Highway trailhead.

Distances from Sandwich Notch Rd. (1220')

   to East Doublehead summit (2158'): 1.9 mi., 1150 ft. (rev. 200 ft.), 1 hr. 30 min.

to Mt. Squam, east summit (2223'): 3.0 mi., 1450 ft. (rev. 250 ft.), 2 hr. 15 min.

to Mt. Percival summit (2212'): 4.4 mi., 1700 ft. (rev. 250 ft.), 3 hr. 5 min.

to upper junction with Mount Morgan Trail (2200'): 5.2 mi., 1800 ft. (rev. 100 ft.), 3 hr. 30 min.

to Mt. Livermore summit (1500'): 10.0 mi., 2300 ft. (rev. 1200 ft.), 6 hr. 10 min.

to spur of Cotton Mtn. (1210'): 11.3 mi. (18.1 km.), 2600 ft. (rev. 600 ft.), 6 hr. 55 min.

Doublehead Trail (SLA trail map)

This trail provides access to a ledge high on Doublehead Mtn. that provides one of the finest views in the Squam Range. It begins on NH 113 at an SLA sign for "Old Highway" 3.5 mi. southwest of Center Sandwich, following a gravel road (part of the old Holderness–Center Sandwich highway) that diverges right (west) at an angle past an old cemetery and a residence. Vehicles should be parked nearby on NH 113, with care taken not to block any roads.

Continue on foot on the old highway, avoiding a new gated logging road on the right at 0.6 mi. The trail proper (sign, yellow blazes begin) leaves the old highway on the right 0.9 mi. from NH 113, across from a large clearing, and follows a recent skid road. At 1.2 mi. it bears right onto an older logging road and soon swings right, crossing a small brook. At 1.5 mi. the trail turns left onto a skidder road and enters an overgrown logged area where the footway is poorly defined and blazes must be followed with care. In another 100 yd. the trail turns sharp right (arrow) across a small brook, follows another skidder road, and joins a small brook. At the top of a steep pitch it turns sharp left and soon crosses a stone wall, where it re-enters mature woods. It crosses a skid road at 1.9 mi. and ascends steeply up the valley of a small brook, then swings right and climbs to a ledge at 2.2 mi. with excellent views to the south. It then turns left off the ledge and climbs to the Crawford-Ridgepole Trail 80 yd. west of the summit of East Doublehead.

Distance from NH 113 (720')

to Crawford-Ridgepole Trail (2120'): 2.3 mi. (3.7 km.), 1450 ft. (rev. 50 ft.), 1 hr. 50 min.

Mount Percival Trail (SLA trail map)

This trail provides access to the fine views and interesting boulder caves on Mt. Percival, and in combination with the Mount Morgan and Crawford-Ridgepole trails and Morgan–Percival Connector offers one of the most popular and scenic loop hikes on the southern fringe of the White Mtns. It begins on the north side of NH 113, 0.3 mi. northeast of the Mt. Morgan/Rattlesnake parking area. Parking is available at the end of a short gravel road.

The trail follows an old logging road past a chained gate and ascends at an easy grade. At 0.2 mi. the Morgan-Percival Connector diverges left for the Mount Morgan Trail. The Mount Percival Trail passes through a clearing, and at 0.4 mi. it turns left onto a relocated section, then loops back to rejoin the original route at 0.6 mi. At 0.9 mi., after a slight descent, it crosses a brook and climbs moderately. At 1.5 mi. it turns right (northeast) and traverses the south slope of Mt. Percival for 0.1 mi. The trail then swings left and climbs steeply to a fork at 1.9 mi. Here the main trail turns right, struggles up a steep, rough ledgy section, crosses a cliff top with a fine view of Squam Lake, and continues over ledges to join the Crawford-Ridgepole Trail at the summit. From the fork an alternate route diverges left and ascends a very strenuous and difficult route through a boulder cave (not recommended in wet weather), then continues up ledges to the summit.

Distances from NH 113 (800')

  to Mt. Percival summit (2212'): 2.0 mi. (3.2 km), 1450 ft., 1 hr. 45 min.

Mount Morgan Trail (SLA trail map)

This trail leaves the west side of NH 113, 5.5 mi. northeast of its jct. with US 3 in Holderness and 6.3 mi. southwest of its jct. with NH 109 in Center Sandwich. From the small parking area, the trail follows a logging road, turning left off it almost immediately. At 0.1 mi. the Morgan–Percival Connector diverges right, leading 0.5 mi. to the Mount Percival Trail. The trail climbs west at a moderate grade, then swings right and traverses to the north. At 1.4 mi. it swings left to begin the steeper ascent of the southeast slope of the mountain. At 1.7 mi. the Crawford-Ridgepole Trail enters left from Mt. Webster, and the two trails coincide, passing a spur path that branches left, ascends a ladder, and climbs about 100 yd. through a boulder cave to the cliff-top viewpoint. After climbing a set of steps, the trails soon reach a jct. where the Crawford–Ridgepole Trail diverges right for Mt. Percival. Here the Mount Morgan Trail leads left to the cliff-top viewpoint; partway along, a short spur leaves it on the right and runs to the true summit.

Distance from NH 113 (800')

> *to* Mt. Morgan summit (2220'): 2.1 mi. (3.4 km.), 1450 ft., 1 hr. 45 min.

Morgan–Percival Connector (SLA trail map)

This trail links the lower ends of the Mount Morgan and Mount Percival trails, making possible an excellent loop hike without a road walk on NH 113. It diverges right from the Mount Morgan Trail 0.1 mi. from NH 113 and descends easily to cross a small brook. It passes through a stone wall and ascends gradually, crosses a brook on a footbridge at 0.4 mi., passes through another stone wall, and bears right to meet the Mount Percival Trail, 0.2 mi. from NH 113.

Distance from Mount Morgan Trail (820')

> *to* Mount Percival Trail (850'): 0.5 mi. (0.8 km.), 50 ft., 15 min.

Distance from Mt. Morgan parking area (800')

> for loop over Mts. Percival and Morgan via Mount Morgan Trail, Morgan–Percival Connector, Mount Percival Trail, Crawford-Ridgepole Trail, and Mount Morgan Trail: 5.4 mi. (8.7 km.), 1550 ft., 3 hr. 30 min.

Old Highway (SLA trail map)

This trail, used for access to the lower ends of the Prescott Trail and Old Mountain Road, continues straight where NH 113 turns right 1.3 mi. northeast of Holderness and 0.2 mi. beyond a gravel pit (the trailhead for the Cotton Mountain Trail) where parking is available on the shoulder of NH 113. A century ago, the old road followed by this trail was part of the main highway between Holderness and Center Sandwich. It leaves NH 113 at the same point as a paved driveway. It climbs at moderate, then easy grades through an area with many stone walls. At 0.8 mi. it turns left onto a newer road. The Prescott Trail diverges left (north) at the height-of-land at 0.9 mi., 100 yd. beyond the Prescott Cemetery, and after a short descent the Old Mountain Road diverges left at an acute angle at 1.1 mi. and runs near the edge of a large field. The Old Highway continues past a field with a view east and a sugarhouse to a locked gate (no parking here) at the edge of Burleigh Farm Rd., a paved road that runs to NH 113.

Distances from NH 113 (585')

> *to* Prescott Trail (900'): 0.9 mi., 300 ft., 35 min.
>
> *to* Burleigh Farm Rd. (750'): 1.4 mi. (2.2 km.), 300 ft. (rev. 150 ft.), 50 ﬆﬆﬆﬆ.

Prescott Trail (SLA trail map)

This trail to Mt. Livermore (1500 ft.) turns left off the Old Highway at the height-of-land 0.9 mi. from NH 113, 100 yd. beyond the Prescott Cemetery. It follows a logging road for 0.2 mi., turns sharp left off it and ascends gradually, then turns right uphill at 0.3 mi. The trail now climbs by switchbacks over a low ridge and descends gradually to the Crawford-Ridgepole Trail, which enters left at 1.0 mi. From this point the two trails ascend together via switchbacks. Just below the summit they turn sharp right and ascend steeply to the summit, where there is a view over Squam Lake.

Descending, the Crawford-Ridgepole Trail heading south and the Prescott Trail leave the summit together, turn sharp right (west) and descend along an old stone wall, then turn left onto an old bridle trail. After 0.4 mi. the Crawford-Ridgepole Trail leaves on the right.

Distances from Old Highway Trail (900')

> *to* Crawford-Ridgepole Trail (1200'): 1.0 mi., 350 ft. (rev 50 ft.), 40 min.
>
> *to* summit of Mt. Livermore (1500'): 1.4 mi. (2.2 km.), 650 ft., 1 hr.

Distance from NH 113 (585')

> for loop over Mt. Livermore (1500') via Old Highway, Prescott Trail, Crawford-Ridgepole Trail, Old Mountain Road, and Old Highway: 4.5 mi. (7.2 km.), 1050 ft., 2 hr. 45 min.

Old Mountain Road (SLA trail map)

This trail leaves sharp left from the Old Highway Trail 1.1 mi. from its western end at NH 113. It ascends on an old road to the left of the field; at the top of the field there is a view of Red Hill. The trail continues climbing at a moderate grade to the Crawford-Ridgepole Trail at the low point between Mt. Livermore and Mt. Webster. The old road continues on from here descending to the north, but this section is not an official trail.

Distance from Old Highway (800')

   to Crawford-Ridgepole Trail (1300'): 0.7 mi. (1.1 km.), 500 ft., 35 min.

Cotton Mountain Trail *(SLA trail map)*

This trail provides access to a ledge with a fine view located on a south spur of Cotton Mtn. and connects with the south end of the Crawford-Ridgepole Trail. It has been recently reconstructed by the SLA. The trail (sign) starts at a pull-off on the west side of NH 113, 1.1 mi. north of its jct. with US 3 in Holderness. It follows a dirt road through a brushy gravel pit, curving right at 0.2 mi. into an open area, then left (cairns) to an SLA signpost, where the road bears left again and ends in 15 yd. at the top of the bank. Here the trail turns right into the woods (sign) and ascends, crossing an old road in 60 yd. It climbs rather steeply up the east slope of the mountain, circling around to the south side to reach the summit of the spur and the jct. with the Crawford-Ridgepole Trail. A few yards before the jct. a spur leads 20 yd. right to a ledge with a view over Squam Lake.

Distance from NH 113 (590')

   to summit of south spur of Cotton Mtn. (1210'): 0.7 mi. (1.1 km), 600 ft., 40 min.

Rattlesnake Paths *(SLA trail map)*

Old Bridle Path. This is the easiest route to the West Rattlesnake outlooks. A very short and easy route to an excellent viewpoint, it receives very heavy use. It leaves the southeast side of NH 113, 5.5 mi. northeast of its jct. with US 3 in Holderness and 6.3 mi. southwest of its jct. with NH 109 in Center Sandwich, and about 70 yd. southwest of the entrance to the Mount Morgan Trail (where there is a small parking area). It follows an old cart road 0.9 mi. with a 450-ft. ascent (40 min.) to the cliffs near the summit. Descending, this trail begins slightly northwest of the summit cliffs.

   Ramsey Trail. This is a much steeper route to West Rattlesnake. It leaves Pinehurst Rd. 0.7 mi. from NH 113 and 90 yd. east of the entrance to Rocky-wold and Deephaven camps, along with the Undercut Trail (sign), which has another entrance almost opposite the camp entrance. There is no parking at the trailhead; cars should be parked off the road before the gate 0.2 mi. east on Pinehurst Rd. In 0.1 mi. there is a crossroads, where the Ramsey Trail takes a sharp right and climbs steeply 600 ft. in 0.4 mi. to a point just north of the summit cliffs, joining the Old Bridle Path. Left at the crossroads is the alternate route 0.1 mi. to Pinehurst Rd.; the *Undercut Trail* continues straight ahead from the crossroads and runs 0.9 mi. (follow markings very carefully) to NH 113 0.1 mi. west of the Old Bridle Path parking area.

Pasture Trail. This trail leads to West Rattlesnake from Pinehurst Rd. 0.9 mi. from NH 113. Park in the small area to the right before the first gate just past the jct. with Bacon Rd. The trailhead (sign) is on the left 100 yd. past the gate. Start on a road to the left, then after 25 yd. turn right onto a footpath past Pinehurst Farm buildings. At 0.2 mi. the East Rattlesnake and Five Finger Point trails diverge right, and in 15 yd. the Pasture Trail bears left where the Col Trail continues straight ahead. The cliffs are reached at 0.6 mi. from the gate after a moderate ascent of 600 ft. Descending, the Pasture Trail leaves the east side of the lower (southern) of the two levels of ledge atop the cliffs.

Col Trail. This trail continues straight where the Pasture Trail bears left 0.2 mi. from the gate on Pinehurst Rd. It ascends moderately for 350 ft. in 0.3 mi. and joins the Ridge Trail, follows it right for 30 yd., then turns left, passes over the height-of-land, and descends (follow with care) about 250 ft. to the edge of a beaver swamp. It enters an old road and turns left, then bears right and reaches a woods road 0.7 mi. from the Ridge Trail jct. The trailhead on NH 113 is reached in another 0.2 mi. at a point 0.3 mi. east of the Holderness–Sandwich town line. To start from NH 113, park near the highway and continue on foot on the woods road, continuing straight ahead (yellow blazes) at a fork where the better road bears right.

Ridge Trail. This trail connects West and East Rattlesnake. It begins just northeast of the cliffs of West Rattlesnake and descends gradually 250 ft. to a saddle at 0.4 mi., where the Col Trail comes in from the right and just beyond leaves again to the left. The Ridge Trail ascends, and the East Rattlesnake Trail enters right at 0.8 mi. The Ridge Trail reaches the outlook ledge at 0.9 mi. and continues to the summit, where it meets the Butterworth Trail at 1.0 mi. with a total ascent from the saddle of 300 ft.

East Rattlesnake Trail. This trail branches right from the Pasture Trail 0.2 mi. from the gate. In 25 yd. the Five Finger Point Trail continues straight ahead. The East Rattlesnake Trail turns left and ascends steadily 500 ft. in 0.4 mi. to the Ridge Trail, 0.1 mi. west of the East Rattlesnake outlook. The Five Finger Point Trail runs on a slight downgrade for 0.7 mi. to a loop path 1.3 mi.

long that circles around the edge of Five Finger Point, with several interesting viewpoints and attractive small beaches where swimming is permitted (no lifeguards).

Butterworth Trail. This trail leads to East Rattlesnake from Metcalf Rd., which leaves NH 113 0.7 mi. east of the Holderness–Sandwich town line. The trail leaves Metcalf Rd. on the right 0.5 mi. from NH 113 (no parking at trailhead; parking is available on the right 100 yd. beyond the trailhead) and climbs moderately 700 ft. in 0.7 mi. to the summit. The East Rattlesnake viewpoint is 0.1 mi. farther via the Ridge Trail.

Red Hill

Red Hill (2030 ft.) and its ledgy northern spur, Eagle Cliff (1410 ft.), rise between Squam Lake and Lake Winnipesaukee. The summit of Red Hill (which has a fire tower) offers excellent views in all directions for very modest effort; Eagle Cliff offers interesting but much less extensive views and a somewhat more challenging trail to ascend. Refer to the SLA trail map or the USGS Center Sandwich and Center Harbor quads.

Red Hill Trail (SLA trail map)

This trail follows an old jeep road and provides a fairly easy route to the fire tower on Red Hill, where there are fine views from the tower and some good outlooks from the summit ledges. In Center Harbor at the jct. of NH 25 and NH 25B, go northwest on Bean Rd. for 1.4 mi., turn right (east) and follow Sibley Rd. (sign for fire lookout) for 1.1 mi., then turn left and continue 0.1 mi. to a new parking area on the right with a Lakes Region Conservation Trust kiosk (sign for fire lookout). The trail ascends on an eroded road, and at 0.1 mi. makes a right turn onto an older road, ascending steadily and crossing a brook on a bridge. At 0.3 mi. another old road joins from the right (bear right here on the descent). At 0.4 mi. the trail crosses the newer road and swings left around a cellar hole, entering the old fire warden's road for a moderate, winding ascent to the summit. At 1.0 mi. there is a piped spring left. The Eagle Cliff Trail enters on the left just before the fire tower and fire warden's cabin on the summit of Red Hill.

Distance from parking area (680')

   to   Red Hill summit (2030'): 1.7 mi. (2.7 km.), 1350 ft., 1 hr. 30 min.

Eagle Cliff Trail (SLA trail map)

This trail ascends Red Hill via Eagle Cliff, providing fine views. However, the part of this path that ascends to the best viewpoints is steep and rocky, much more difficult than the Red Hill Trail (though the upper part of this trail is fairly similar in difficulty), and may be hazardous in wet or icy conditions. A bypass path—recommended in adverse conditions, particularly for the descent—has been cut to avoid the most difficult and dangerous section. The Teedie Trail is also available as an alternative descent route in hazardous conditions. From the jct. of NH 25 and NH 25B in Center Harbor, follow Bean Rd. for 5.2 mi. to a turnout at the edge of Squam Lake, about 0.4 mi. north of the Moultonborough–Sandwich town line. The trail (sign) leaves the highway on the opposite side, 200 yd. south of the turnout.

The trail begins by crossing a ditch in a thicket, then climbs through an overgrown field and enters more mature woods, ascending on a well-beaten path. At 0.5 mi. a newly-cut bypass trail leaves on the right; it is about 0.1 mi. longer than the main trail, which becomes steep and rough with several rocky scrambles as it gets well up on the ledge. The bypass trail rejoins the main trail just below the main viewpoint on Eagle Cliff at 0.6 mi. From the upper ledge, the trail enters the woods and climbs over two knolls, then descends sharply to a small pass at 1.0 mi., where the Teedie Trail enters right.

Teedie Trail. This path descends by switchbacks in 0.7 mi. to a gravel driveway next to a private tennis court on Bean Rd. at the Moultonborough–Sandwich town line, about 0.4 mi. south of the beginning of the Eagle Cliff Trail. It is much less scenic than the Eagle Cliff Trail and, though it may not be well cleared and may take some care to follow, it should be considered as a way of avoiding the descent over the Eagle Cliff ledges in adverse conditions. The trailhead (no parking here) is marked by a sign at the back edge of a small field, where the trail enters the woods.

Eagle Cliff Trail. This trail crosses another knoll and ascends steadily through a mixture of young growth in cutover areas and mature woods, and about a quarter mile below the summit it enters an area burned over by a fire set by an arsonist in April 1990. It finally levels out and meets the Red Hill Trail just below the summit of Red Hill. Descending, it diverges right from the Red Hill Trail (jeep road) just below the fire warden's cabin (sign).

Distances from Bean Rd. (580')

   to Eagle Cliff viewpoint (1270'): 0.6 mi., 700 ft., 40 min.

to Red Hill fire tower (2030'): 2.7 mi. (4.3 km.), 1650 ft. (rev. 200 ft.), 2 hr. 10 min.

Ossipee Mountains

These mountains, located just northeast of Lake Winnipesaukee, occupy a nearly circular tract about 9 mi. in diameter. They are the result of an unusual geological formation called a ring dike, where magma wells up into a circular fracture in the earth's crust. The range shelters beautiful Dan Hole Pond on its southeast edge, and harbors areas of old-growth forest and a great diversity of vegetation, including several rare species.

Mt. Shaw (2990 ft.), the highest of the Ossipees, affords excellent views north toward the White Mtns. and other mountains to the east from its partly-cleared summit; it is most easily ascended by a trail from NH 171. A southern shoulder called Black Snout (2803 ft.) offers excellent views to the south and west, particularly over Lake Winnipesaukee. (This is not the Black Snout shown on USGS maps, which is at the north end of the range.) Bald Knob (1801 ft.) is a rocky promontory that also offers excellent views across Lake Winnipesaukee to the mountains beyond. Farther north along the main ridge-crest are two other outlooks accessible by trail: a viewpoint on the south slope of Faraway Mtn. (2782 ft.), and one at the summit of Mt. Roberts (2582 ft.), which offers views north to the White Mtns. Other viewpoints are found on the knoll above Bald Knob unofficially called Turtleback Mtn. (2203 ft.), and on Oak Ridge (also an unofficial name), a southern spur of the range.

Hiking opportunities on the Ossipees were greatly expanded with the purchase of the 5400-acre Castle in the Clouds property by the Lakes Region Conservation Trust (LRCT) in December 2003. The parcel, now called the Castle in the Clouds Conservation Area, encompasses most of the south slopes of the range, including all of the summits listed above. In the summer of 2004 the LRCT blazed about 20 mi. of carriage roads and bridle paths built in the late 1800s and early 1900s when the area was a private estate, owned first by Benjamin Shaw, for whom Mt. Shaw was named, and later by eccentric millionaire Thomas Plant. These are now available as hiking trails for the public, and link up with existing trails to Mt. Shaw and Bald Knob (both of which start on private land and ascend onto the LRCT property). The LRCT has published a topographic trail map showing these trails, with colors corresponding to blazes on the trails; it may be purchased at the Castle in the Clouds gift shop and at some area stores. Additional trails are slated to open in the near future; for trail updates, check www.lrct.org. Note that many of the mountain names appearing on this map are not officially recognized and are therefore not used in the following descriptions.

A new trailhead, with a kiosk and parking area well-marked by signs, has been established on LRCT land on the south side of NH 171 in Moultonborough, 0.2 mi. east of the main entrance to Castle in the Clouds and just east of the jct. with Severance Rd. Access to the Castle grounds (for which there is no longer an admission charge, except for a guided tour of the Castle) is provided by the Shannon Brook Trail. From that trail's end at Shannon Pond, several trails lead to the various summits. The LRCT requests that hikers not park on the Castle grounds as the access roads are gated from late afternoon through mid-morning during the summer and fall, and at all times in other seasons. No camping, overnight use, fires or wheeled vehicles are permitted on the LRCT land. Some of the trails receive heavy snowmobile use in winter.

In 2004 the condition of the carriage road trails varied from clear and well-trodden to grassy to partly overgrown with weeds and brambles (particularly at the higher elevations). Trail clearing efforts have been underway, and it is expected that footways will become clearer as the trails receive more use. Hikers looking for challenge or (with the few exceptions noted) views will not find them on the carriage roads, but those seeking longer, easier woods walks very occasionally supplied with views may well find them enjoyable.

Mount Shaw Trail (LRCT trail map, USGS Melvin Village quad)

This trail is the traditional route to Mt. Shaw and uses some of the newly blazed carriage roads in its upper section. The trailhead and lower part of the trail are on private land. Although technically the Mount Shaw Trail now ends where the carriage road portion of the hike begins, for convenience the entire route to the summit is described here as the Mount Shaw Trail. It begins (no sign) as a woods road on the north side of NH 171, 3.9 mi. east of the jct. of NH 109 and NH 171, 3.8 mi. west of Tuftonboro, and 9.7 mi. west of the jct. of NH 171 and NH 28 in Ossipee. The trailhead is just east of the bridge over Fields Brook and nearly opposite Sodom Rd. (the road from NH 171 to Melvin Village). The trail is fairly easy to follow and has been better blazed in recent years, but is not recommended for inexperienced hikers. It must be followed very carefully because it is blazed in dark red, which is sometimes difficult to see. In addition, it may be overgrown in places, which may cause some trail-finding problems from time to time.

The trail follows the dirt road north; avoid two branch roads that diverge right. At 0.3 mi. it curves left to a hemlock grove, where there is a cascade on the left. In another 100 yd., just beyond a second cascade, the trail follows the left-branching road at a fork; red blazes begin here. Be careful to avoid the Tate Mountain Trail, an unofficial path that diverges right and is also marked with red paint; the Mount Shaw Trail follows the brook here. The trail detours above the stream around a washout, then runs along a bank to the left of a gullied section of the old road. Rejoining the road, it passes a jct. with a branch road that diverges sharp right, bears right at a fork at 0.7 mi., then keeps right after passing through an old logging camp clearing. At 0.9 mi. it bears left at a fork and goes through a deep cut, then climbs alongside the brook, bearing left at a fork at 1.1 mi. The trail leaves the road on the right at 1.4 mi., follows the east bank of the brook, and crosses it at a ledgy spot. It climbs away from the brook, then bears right and recrosses it at 1.8 mi. It ascends moderately to the north, with many twists and turns, then swings northeast and climbs steeply to an old carriage road, now part of the white-blazed Black Snout Trail, at 2.5 mi. Here the route turns right and climbs easily to a side trail (also white-blazed) on the right at 2.7 mi.; this carriage road spur leads 0.3 mi. at easy grades to Black Snout, an open knob with a good view out over Lake Winnipesaukee to the west and south.

From the jct. with the spur to Black Snout, the route to Mt. Shaw follows the main Black Snout Trail as it makes a sharp turn to the left (north), passing the yellow-blazed Thunderbird Trail on the right. (This obscure, viewless, and little-used path descends about 2.5 mi. to Canaan Rd.; it is not maintained by LRCT and is not shown on the trail map.) The Black Snout Trail ascends easily to a fork, where it meets the blue-blazed High Ridge Trail at 3.1 mi. Here the route to Mt. Shaw bears right and climbs by switchbacks to a loop around the summit at 3.5 mi., where there are excellent views north and east. (From the east end of the summit loop the yellow-blazed Gorilla Trail, not maintained by LRCT and not shown on the trail map, departs for Camp Merrowvista near Dan Hole Pond.)

Descending, the Mount Shaw Trail leaves the carriage road/Black Snout Trail on the left at a cairn and blazes 0.2 mi. below the spur to Black Snout.

Distances from NH 171 (680')

> *to*   Black Snout Trail/carriage road (2670'): 2.5 mi., 2000 ft., 2 hr. 15 min.

> *to*   Mt. Shaw summit (2990') via Black Snout Trail and High Ridge Trail: 3.5 mi. (5.6 km), 2300 ft., 2 hr. 55 min.

Bald Knob Trail *(LRCT trail map, USGS Melvin Village quad)*

This trail begins on NH 171 at the Moultonborough–Tuftonboro town line, 0.5 mi. west of the Mt. Shaw trailhead at the Fields Brook bridge. There may or may not be trail signs; No Trespassing signs traditionally have not been intended to keep hikers out, and this path receives fairly heavy use. The lower 0.7 mi. is on private land. Two roads lead from the parking area into the overgrown gravel pit; either may be followed to where they rejoin in a small clearing. Continue on the road from the far left side of the clearing, descending and swinging right. At 100 yd. from the clearing, turn left where a grassy path continues ahead. The trail runs nearly level into the woods, where it becomes very well beaten and easy to follow, though markings are sparse up to Bald Knob.

After an initial moderate section, the trail ascends steeply over rough and eroded terrain. At 0.7 mi. it scrambles up a fairly difficult slab (use caution when wet), swings left at the top, and soon reaches an open ledge with an excellent vista south. It goes back into the woods, runs through an area with a number of boulders, and heads generally north, ascending at a less steep grade. The trail then turns west, scrambles steeply up through a wide V in the rock, and enters an old carriage road turnaround at 1.1 mi., just behind the open ledges of Bald Knob with their fine views of Lake Winnpesaukee.

The trail, from here on well-blazed in white, exits the open area via the carriage road leading northwest along the side of the ridge. Open views continue for the first 100 yd. along the carriage road, then the trail descends into the woods. It skirts around the west slope of the high knob unofficially called Turtleback Mtn. at easy grades and ends in 0.7 mi. at the Turtleback Mountain Trail. For Mount Shaw or the Turtleback ledges bear right uphill, or bear left downhill for the Castle in the Clouds area. The ledges at the summit of Turtleback Mtn., which offer good views, can be reached in 2.2 mi. from Bald Knob with only 500 ft. of climbing via the Bald Knob Trail, Turtleback Mountain Trail, and Turtleback Summit Trail.

Distances from NH 171 (700')

   to   Bald Knob (1801'): 1.1 mi., 1100 ft., 1 hr. 5 min.

   to   Turtleback Mountain Trail (1700'): 1.8 mi. (2.9 km.), 1100 ft. (rev. 100 ft.), 1 hr. 25 min.

Shannon Brook Trail (LRCT trail map, USGS Melvin Village quad)

This red-blazed trail is the access route from the LRCT trailhead on NH 171 to the various trails that lead from the Castle in the Clouds area to the higher summits of the Ossipees. It begins as a gated woods road on the north side of NH 171, 0.2 mi. east of the main entrance to the Castle in the Clouds and across from the designated hiker's parking area. It follows the woods road, soon swinging left past a building and approaching Shannon Brook near a small cascade and gorge at 0.3 mi. It climbs moderately, keeping well above the brook, then swings left and descends to cross a branch of the brook on a snowmobile bridge at 0.8 mi. It continues up to a large clearing at 1.0 mi. and turns left to cross the opening (follow markings carefully) with the Castle visible on a knoll up to the left. It re-enters the woods and ascends easily to another clearing at 1.4 mi., where the Turtleback Mountain Trail diverges sharp right. The Shannon Brook Trail continues another 25 yd. to a kiosk and trail map on the east side of Shannon Pond, where it meets the Pond Trail and Oak Ridge Trail.

Distance from trailhead on NH 171 (730')

   to trail junction by Shannon Pond (1230'): 1.4 mi. (2.3 km.), 500 ft., 55 min.

Turtleback Mountain Trail (LRCT trail map, USGS Melvin Village quad)

This yellow-blazed trail follows old carriage roads across the south slopes of the range, connecting the Shannon Pond area with trails leading to Bald Knob, Black Snout, and Mt. Shaw. It leaves sharp right (east) from the Shannon Brook Trail near the shore of Shannon Pond and runs at easy grades through fine woods. It passes branches of the Oak Ridge Trail on the left at 0.4 mi. and 0.5 mi., and at 1.1 mi., after a short moderate ascent, it passes two entrances to the Faraway Mountain Trail, also on the left. It swings around a brook ravine, crosses the stream on a culvert at 1.3 mi., then climbs by easy switchbacks to meet the Bald Knob Trail at 2.0 mi. Here the white-blazed Bald Knob Trail continues ahead 0.7 mi. to Bald Knob, while the Turtleback Mountain Trail (unblazed and occasionally overgrown by weeds from here on in 2004) turns sharp left and climbs by shorter, then longer switchbacks to a height-of-land north of a high knob at 3.0 mi. Here the Turtleback Summit Trail to the summit ledges of the unofficially-named Turtleback Mtn. leaves on the right, while the Turtleback Mountain Trail turns left (north), then swings east again and crosses a branch of Fields Brook on a snowmobile bridge at 3.7 mi. It follows the brook for a short distance, then swings right around a minor ridge, turns sharp left at 4.4 mi., and climbs to the jct. with the Black Snout Trail on the right at 5.0 mi. Here the Turtleback Mountain Trail turns left and ascends gently to meet the High Ridge Trail by a stagnant pool.

Distances from Shannon Brook Trail (1230')

> *to* Bald Knob Trail (1700'): 2.0 mi., 500 ft., 1 hr. 15 min.
>
> *to* Turtleback Summit Trail (2070'): 3.0 mi., 900 ft., 1 hr. 55 min.
>
> *to* High Ridge Trail (2410'): 5.2 mi. (8.4 km.), 1200 ft., 3 hr. 10 min.

Turtleback Summit Trail (*LRCT trail map, USGS Melvin Village quad*)

This spur trail follows an old carriage road from the Turtleback Mountain Trail, at a height-of-land 3.0 mi. from the Shannon Pond trailhead to open ledges at the summit of Turtleback Mtn. It curves left and right, then contours along the west slope of Turtleback Mtn. It swings left at 0.3 mi. and ascends easily by switchbacks to the ledges, where there is a fine close-up view of Mt. Shaw and the main ridge of the Ossipees.

Distance from Turtleback Mountain Trail (2070')

> *to* Turtleback Mtn. summit (2203'): 0.5 mi. (0.8 km.), 150 ft., 20 min.

Oak Ridge Trail (*LRCT trail map, USGS Melvin Village quad*)

This blue-blazed trail makes possible an easy loop over the southern end of a low ridge, passing a good viewpoint over Lake Winnipesaukee. It begins on either of two short branches (each about 100 yd. long) that leave the Turtleback Mountain Trail, 0.4 mi. and 0.5 mi. from the Shannon Brook Trail. From the point where the two branches join, the trail follows a carriage road through several turns and reaches a short loop that leads to Oak Ridge Lookout at 0.4 mi. The main trail crosses the flat crest of the ridge and descends gradually, then moderately on a woods road, making a long curve around to the left (south). At 1.2 mi. it meets the orange-blazed Pond Trail; here it turns left and the two trails coincide to the kiosk and meet a jct. with the Shannon Brook Trail near the east shore of Shannon Pond.

Distances from Turtleback Mountain Trail (1290')

> *to*   Oak Ridge Lookout (1490'): 0.4 mi., 200 ft., 20 min.
>
> *to*   kiosk at Shannon Pond (1230'): 1.3 mi. (2.1 km.), 200 ft. (rev. 250 ft.), 45 min.

Cold Spring Trail (LRCT trail map, USGS Melvin Village quad)

This red-blazed trail follows a paved road and an old bridle path from Shannon Pond to the middle section of the Faraway Mountain Trail. It is part of the shortest route from the kiosk at Shannon Pond to the viewpoints on Faraway Mtn. and Mt. Roberts. From the kiosk, the most convenient route follows the orange-blazed Pond Trail to the right (north) into the woods, passing the jct. with the Oak Ridge Trail on the right and soon bearing left across a bridge over Shannon Brook and reaching paved Cold Spring Rd. at 0.2 mi.; turn right here. (Alternatively, from the kiosk one can bear left and follow roads around the south and west sides of Shannon Pond, then bear right on paved Cold Spring Rd. past a sign for the Cold Spring Trail and a gate, and reach the point on the road where the Pond Trail emerges from the woods at 0.3 mi. By either route one can reach the Mount Roberts Trail, which begins near the stables on the west side of Cold Spring Rd.) Mileages given below start at the kiosk using the shorter route described above.

The Cold Spring Trail follows the road uphill at easy grades. At 0.6 mi. the trail turns right into the woods onto an old bridle path; travel is prohibited on the road beyond this point as it leads to a private inholding. The trail climbs moderately through several turns with occasional wet footing. At 1.0 mi. it bears right at a fork and ascends by long, grassy switchbacks to the Faraway Mountain Trail. Turn left for Faraway Mtn. and Mt. Roberts.

Distances from kiosk at Shannon Pond (1230')

> *to*   right turn off Cold Spring Rd. via Pond Trail (1370'): 0.6 mi., 150 ft., 20 min.
>
> *to*   Faraway Mountain Trail (1840'): 1.9 mi. (3.1 km.), 600 ft., 1 hr. 15 min.

Faraway Mountain Trail (LRCT trail map, USGS Melvin Village and Tamworth quads)

This orange-blazed trail follows an old carriage road and connects the Turtleback Mountain Trail, 1.1 mi. from the kiosk at Shannon Pond, with the High

Ridge Trail, 0.9 mi. east of Faraway Mtn. Lookout. Leaving the Turtleback Mountain Trail by either of two forks, it ascends gently past a jct. with the Oak Ridge Cutoff on the right at 0.5 mi. and turns sharp left across a bridge over a branch of Shannon Brook at 0.8 mi. (This bridge was unsafe to cross in 2004 and was scheduled for repair.) It turns right where the Cold Spring Trail enters on the left at 1.2 mi. At 2.1 mi., in the middle of a long traverse to the left, there is a limited view of the Castle in the Clouds and Lake Winnipesaukee. The trail then climbs by several switchbacks and ends at the High Ridge Trail.

Distances from Turtleback Mountain Trail (1550')

> *to* Cold Spring Trail (1840'): 1.2 mi., 300 ft., 45 min.

> *to* High Ridge Trail (2450'): 2.9 mi. (4.7 km.), 900 ft., 1 hr. 55 min.

High Ridge Trail (LRCT trail map, USGS Melvin Village and Tamworth quads)

This blue-blazed trail follows carriage roads along the crest of the range between Mt. Shaw on the southeast and Faraway Mtn. and Mt. Roberts on the northwest. It is lightly used and apt to be overgrown by weeds and brambles in places, but provides the opportunity for an extended ridge walk through a fine hardwood forest. Grades are easy. From the loop at the summit of Mt. Shaw, it descends south, then makes two switchbacks down to its jct. with the Black Snout Trail at 0.4 mi. Here it turns sharp right as the Black Snout Trail continues ahead. At 0.6 mi. it turns left where a snowmobile trail continues ahead. It descends to a jct. with the Turtleback Mountain Trail on the left by a stagnant pool at 1.1 mi. Here it turns right and meanders along the ridge. At 1.5 mi. it turns sharp right (north) and contours along the west side of a knob, passing a jct. with the Oak Ridge Cutoff on the left at 1.7 mi. After crossing a saddle, it swings left (west) around the north side of a knob, descends to another saddle, and ascends easily to a jct. with the Faraway Mountain Trail on the left at 2.9 mi. It now angles upward along the east side of Faraway Mtn.'s south ridge, then makes a hairpin turn left (south) and curves back to the right, reaching Faraway Mtn. Lookout at 3.8 mi. where there is a good view south over Lake Winnipesaukee. The trail swings back to the north through boreal forest and curves around the ravine at the head of Shannon Brook, passing a bog on the right. At 4.4 mi. it swings right and crosses Shannon Brook on a bridge. It descends to a saddle at easy grades through overgrown stretches, then climbs easily by switchbacks to a 0.1 mi. loop around the summit of Mt. Roberts at 5.0

mi., where it meets the Mount Roberts Trail. A good view north to the Sandwich Range and Mt. Washington seen beyond the northern Black Snout is found by following the left fork of the loop for 60 yd. The upper terminus of the Mount Roberts Trail can be reached by following the right fork of the loop for a short distance.

Distances from summit of Mt. Shaw (2990')

> *to* junction with Turtleback Mountain Trail (2410'): 1.1 mi., 0 ft. (rev. 600 ft.), 35 min.

> *to* Faraway Mountain Trail (2450'): 2.9 mi., 150 ft. (rev. 100 ft.), 1 hr. 30 min.

> *to* Mt. Roberts summit loop (2570'): 5.0 mi. (8.1 km.), 450 ft. (rev. 200 ft.), 2 hr. 45 min.

Mount Roberts Trail (LRCT trail map, USGS Melvin Village and Tamworth quads)

Starting on the Castle grounds, this orange-blazed trail ascends Mt. Roberts (2582 ft.) via its ledgy south ridge. It offers several excellent outlooks and passes through an unusual and extensive forest of scrub oak. The trail begins behind the Castle's horse stable, on the left (west) side of Cold Spring Rd. just above Shannon Pond. It follows an old bridle path through a switchback, then at 0.4 mi. turns right onto an old woods road and ascends gradually to the north. It then climbs steadily up the ridge through oak forest, making several turns and reaching the first outlook south towards Lake Winnipesaukee at 1.3 mi. It continues up the ridge, alternating between grassy oak forest and open ledges; follow the marked route carefully as near this area there are rare, easily damaged plants that must be protected. At 2.0 mi. it emerges on a large open ledge with expansive views to the east and south. The trail descends slightly, then climbs moderately through coniferous woods to the west end of the blue-blazed High Ridge Trail, which makes a 0.1 mi. loop around the summit of Mt. Roberts. The loop can be followed in either direction to a fine north outlook. The other fine outlook in this area, on the slope of Faraway Mtn., can be reached by following the High Ridge Trail for 1.2 mi. with about 100 ft. of descent and 200 ft. of ascent, all gradual.

Distance from stables on Castle grounds (1290')

> *to* Mt. Roberts summit loop (2570'): 2.3 mi. (3.7 km.), 1300 ft., 1 hr. 50 min.

Oak Ridge Cutoff (LRCT trail map, USGS Melvin Village quad)

This white-blazed trail connects the Faraway Mountain Trail, 0.5 mi. north of the Turtleback Mountain Trail, with the High Ridge Trail, 1.7 mi. west of Mt. Shaw. It forms part of the shortest route from the Shannon Pond area to Mt. Shaw and Black Snout. From the Faraway Mountain Trail it climbs moderately northeast along the west side of Oak Ridge on an old woods road, then swings right (east) at 0.5 mi. and continues climbing to meet the High Ridge Trail via either of two short branches.

Distance from Faraway Mountain Trail (1610')

   to High Ridge Trail (2370'): 1.0 mi. (1.6 km.), 750 ft., 55 min.

Black Snout Trail (LRCT trail map, USGS Melvin Village quad)

This white-blazed trail follows carriage roads along the southwest side of Mt. Shaw, connecting with several other trails and providing access (via a spur path) to the fine views from Black Snout. Its west end diverges to the north from the Turtleback Mountain Trail, 0.2 mi. south of the High Ridge Trail. It climbs by switchbacks, then turns right and traverses southeast across the slope, passing the jct. with the red-blazed Mount Shaw Trail on the right at 1.0 mi. At 1.2 mi. the trail swings around to the left; here a spur path on the right follows an old carriage road 0.3 mi. at easy grades to a short loop at the summit of Black Snout, where there are fine views west and south. (At 0.2 mi. from the main trail the spur passes the blue-blazed Ball Mountains Trail on the left. This trail, not maintained by LRCT and not shown on the trail map, and emphatically not for the inexperienced, descends steeply to a col, then rises to the ledgy north summit of a nameless 2070 ft. knob at 1.2 mi., entering private land shortly before reaching the top. Here there are good views west and south. It continues over the south summit of the nameless knob with more views, then descends over a lower knob and ends on Canaan Rd.) A few yards beyond the jct. with the spur the main trail passes the start of the obscure, yellow-blazed Thunderbird Trail (not maintained by LRCT and not shown on the trail map) on the right. It then ascends northwest to its jct. with the High Ridge Trail at 1.5 mi.; continue straight to reach the summit of Mt. Shaw in 0.4 mi.

Distances from junction with Turtleback Mountain Trail (2390')

   to spur path to Black Snout (2730'): 1.2 mi., 350 ft., 45 min.

   to junction with High Ridge Trail (2810'): 1.5 mi. (2.4 km.), 450 ft., 1 hr.

The Belknap Range and Mt. Major

The Belknap Mtns. are a prominent range west of Lake Winnipesaukee in the towns of Gilford, Gilmanton, and Alton. The range and the county in which it rises were named for Jeremy Belknap (1744–1796), author of the first comprehensive history of New Hampshire and a member of one of the early (1784) scientific expeditions to Mt. Washington (though Belknap himself did not reach the summit). The principal peaks on the main ridge, from north to south, are Mt. Rowe (1690 ft.), Gunstock Mtn. (2250 ft.), Belknap Mtn. (2382 ft.), and Piper Mtn. (2044 ft.). A fire tower on Belknap and the cleared summit of Gunstock, as well as numerous scattered ledges on all the peaks, provide fine views of Lake Winnipesaukee, the Ossipee and Sandwich ranges, and Mt. Washington. Principal trailheads are located at the Gunstock Recreation Area (east side) and Belknap Carriage Rd. (west side). The East Gilford Trail also ascends from the east. Paths along the ridge connect all four summits. Mt. Major (1786 ft.), which has excellent views over Lake Winnipesaukee, is located in Alton, east of the main Belknap Mtns. A long, lumpy ridge runs east from Belknap Mtn. to Mt. Major, consisting of Straightback Mtn. (1910 ft.) and several other humps that are officially nameless but have been given local names by the Boy Scouts of the Hidden Valley Reservation: Mt. Klem (2001 ft.), Mt. Mack (1945 ft.), and Mt. Anna (1670 ft.). A parallel ridge to the north is sometimes called the Quarry Mountains. The jewel of this range is Round Pond, a beautiful and secluded mountain pond lying at the foot of Mt. Klem, just south of the main ridgecrest, at an elevation of 1652 ft. Refer to the USGS West Alton and Laconia quadrangles. The trail system has been greatly expanded and improved in recent years, with better blazing and signage, though some trails described below may still require considerable care to follow. A detailed though unofficial map of the Belknap Range may be available for study at the Gilford Public Library and the Belknap Mtn. fire tower; this map shows all the trails described here plus many others that may be extremely obscure or require the permission of the landowner for hiking use, and labels many minor knobs with names that are not recognized by any authority.

Public and quasi-public organizations own most of the peaks and much of the slopes of the Belknap Mtns. In general, camping and fires are prohibited in this area. The public ownership includes Belknap County (the Gunstock Recreation Area), the State of New Hampshire (Belknap Mountain State Forest), and the Town of Gilford. The Griswold Hidden Valley Scout Reservation, owned by the Daniel Webster Council Boy Scouts of America, includes much of the land to the south of the eastern ridge and a considerable portion of the ridge itself, including most of Round Pond (the western shore is part of Belknap Mountain State Forest) and Mts. Klem, Mack, and Anna. A major network of trails has been developed in this reservation, of which the ones on and near the ridgecrest, described below, are open to public use. The trails near the main camp area are not open to the general public without advance permission. A volunteer organization, the Belknap Range Trail Tenders (BRATTs), has recently been established to assume primary responsibility for the maintenance of trails on the Belknap Range; for information on trail maintenance activities contact Hal Graham, 1204 New Hampton Rd., Sanbornton, NH 03268 (603-286-3506).

The Gunstock Recreation Area is a four-season recreation area off NH 11A, operated by Belknap County. It includes a major downhill ski area located on Mt. Rowe and Gunstock Mtn., and a large campground. Ellacoya State Beach on Lake Winnipesaukee is nearby. The chairlift on Gunstock Mtn. operates on weekends and holidays in summer. The ski trails can be used to ascend Gunstock Mtn. and Mt. Rowe, and there is also an extensive network of cross-country ski trails, many of which are available as multi-use trails during the non-winter months. A trail map is available at the information center.

The Belknap Carriage Rd., which provides access to all the trails on the west side of the Belknap Range, is reached by leaving NH 11A at Gilford village and following Belknap Mountain Rd. south, bearing left at 0.8 mi. and right at 1.4 mi. At 2.4 mi. the Belknap Carriage Rd. forks left and leads in 1.5 mi. to a parking area. Various relatively easy loop hikes may be made from this trailhead. For the Green, Red, and Blue trails, follow the road up to the fire warden's garage (signs on wall). The White Trail is a short distance down the road. There is a gate on this road (located 0.3 mi. from Belknap Mountain Rd.) that is locked from 6 PM to 9 AM in the summer and fall and all the time in winter. There is a small parking area on the left just before the gate. Overnight parking is not allowed anywhere in this area.

Blue Trail (USGS Laconia and West Alton quads)

This trail runs from the Belknap Carriage Rd. to the summit of Belknap Mtn. It follows the extension of the carriage road past the garage and the jcts. with the Red and Green trails, descends slightly to cross a brook, then diverges right and climbs to the Belknap–Gunstock col at 0.6 mi. Here the orange-blazed Overlook Trail continues straight and the white-blazed Saddle Trail turns left for Gunstock Mtn. The Blue Trail, now coinciding with the Belknap Range Trail, turns right and climbs, passing an outlook to Gunstock Mtn. at 0.7 mi. and an excellent outlook across Lake Winnipesaukee to the Sandwich Range (and Mt. Washington in clear weather) at 0.8 mi., and continues to the summit.

Distances from Belknap Carriage Rd. parking area (1670')

   to Belknap–Gunstock col (2000'): 0.6 mi., 350 ft., 30 min.

   to Belknap Mtn. summit (2382'): 1.1 mi., 700 ft., 55 min.

Green Trail (USGS Laconia and West Alton quads)

The Green Trail, which starts at the end of the Belknap Carriage Rd., is the shortest route to Belknap Mtn. but is rather steep with ledges that are slippery when wet, particularly when descending. It leaves the carriage road extension behind the garage and ascends on a service road, crossing a telephone line. It continues to climb, passes a well, and reaches the tower at the summit.

Distance from Belknap Carriage Rd. parking area (1670')

   to Belknap Mtn. summit (2382'): 0.7 mi. (1.1 km.), 700 ft., 40 min.

Red Trail (USGS Laconia and West Alton quads)

This trail, less steep and more scenic than the Green Trail but somewhat rough in parts, climbs from the Belknap Carriage Rd. to the summit of Belknap Mtn. It leaves the carriage road extension just beyond the Green Trail jct., climbs past a good outlook to the west at 0.5 mi., and continues to the summit.

Distance from Belknap Carriage Rd. parking area (1670')

   to Belknap Mtn. summit (2382'): 0.8 mi. (1.3 km.), 700 ft., 45 min.

White Trail (USGS Laconia and West Alton quads)

This white-blazed trail ascends to the summit of Belknap Mtn. via the Belknap–Piper col. It begins on the Belknap Carriage Rd. about 0.1 mi. below the parking area, just below the highest bridge. It ascends 0.4 mi. to a point about 50 yd. below the pass between Belknap and Piper where the orange-blazed Old Piper Trail continues straight to the pass and then turns right to Piper Mtn. The White Trail turns left here and winds up a recently relocated section to an outlook to the south and west just off the trail at 0.6 mi. Here the trail turns sharp left and soon reaches an excellent outlook to the southeast. The White Trail continues to climb, passing through some beautiful, shady coniferous woods, to the jct. with the East Gilford Trail, which enters from the right on the ledges at 1.2 mi. The two trails, which also coincide with the Belknap Range Trail in this segment, ascend together at an easy grade to the summit and its fire tower.

Distance from Belknap Carriage Rd. parking area (1670')

> *to* Belknap Mtn. summit (2382'): 1.4 mi. (2.2 km.), 800 ft. (rev. 100 ft.), 1 hr. 5 min.

Old Piper Trail (USGS Laconia quad)

This trail, blazed in orange, ascends Piper Mtn. from the White Trail 50 yd. below the Belknap–Piper col. It turns right on reaching the col, and in 30 yd. it passes a jct. on the left with the blue-blazed Piper Link, which leads to the Belknap Range Trail at the bottom of the Boulder Trail. It ascends at easy grades for 0.2 mi., then climbs moderately through woods and over ledges, passing an excellent outlook east over the Moulton Brook valley at 0.3 mi. It emerges on open ledges by an east-facing rock throne at the north summit of Piper Mtn., where it meets the Piper Mountain Trail and Whiteface–Piper Link.

Distance from Belknap–Piper col (1800')

> *to* north summit of Piper Mtn. (2030'): 0.5 mi. (0.8 km), 250 ft., 20 min.

Whiteface Mountain Trail (USGS Laconia and Belmont quads)

This trail leads from the end of Belknap Mountain Rd. to the open summit of Whiteface Mtn. (1670 ft.) and also provides access to Piper Mtn. via the Whiteface–Piper Link. The trail is unblazed but easy to follow. Its lower part is on land recently acquired by the Lakes Region Conservation Trust (LRCT), while the upper part follows a jeep road that has been heavily impacted by ATV use. To reach the trailhead, continue ahead on Belknap Mountain Rd. past the jct. with the Belknap Carriage Rd. at 2.4 mi. from NH 11A. Turn left at 3.4 mi. and park on the right at the end of the road at 3.8 mi., just before a gate; do not block the gate. Follow the woods road beyond the gate for 130 yds. and turn left onto an older road by a trail map posted on a tree. The trail ascends moderately on the eroded roadbed, passing a LRCT kiosk. At 0.4 mi. it swings right, crosses a small brook, then climbs to the ridgecrest, meeting the Whiteface–Piper Link at 0.7 mi. Here the Whiteface Mountain Trail bears right through a gap in a stone wall and descends slightly, passing an unmarked path that descends left, to an open meadow with a view of the summit ahead. The trail swings right across the meadow, then turns left to join a rocky jeep road badly eroded by ATV use and follows it along the ridge, crossing an intermediate hump with partial views. It makes a short, steep ascent to open ledges on the north side of the summit, with excellent views north and west, then continues to a large clearing at the true summit, where there are views to the south.

Distances from end of Belknap Mountain Rd. (1050')

> *to* Whiteface–Piper Link (1510'): 0.7 mi., 450 ft., 35 min.
>
> *to* Whiteface Mtn. summit (1670'): 1.6 mi. (2.6 km), 700 ft. (rev. 100 ft.), 1 hr. 10 min.

Whiteface–Piper Link (USGS Laconia, Gilmanton Ironworks and West Alton quads)

This trail connects the Whiteface Mountain Trail with Piper Mtn. The footway must be followed with care across the ledges, where it is marked by cairns and faded green arrows. It leaves the Whiteface Mountain Trail on the ridgecrest, 0.7 mi. from the trailhead, and soon begins a steady ascent to the northeast through oak woods. Higher up it crosses semi-open ledges with some views to the south. At 0.5 mi., at the top of a large sloping ledge, there is an excellent outlook south and west. The trail climbs a short distance farther, then bears right into conifers and at 0.6 mi. reaches a posted jct. at the south summit of Piper Mtn. Here the Vista Trail diverges sharp right. The Whiteface–Piper Link bears left, then shortly right across a ledgy area with views of Belknap Mtn. and out to the east. The trail winds across ledges and through scrub along the nearly level ridge, passing to the left of a rock throne; in places the footway is obscure and cairns must be followed carefully. At 0.8 mi. the trail emerges in a large open ledgy area and crosses it to reach two rock thrones on the north summit of Piper Mtn. Here the orange-blazed Old Piper Trail leaves north and the red-blazed Piper Mountain Trail descends northwest.

Distances from Whiteface Mountain Trail (1510')

> *to* Vista Trail (2010'): 0.6 mi., 500 ft., 35 min.
>
> *to* north summit of Piper Mtn. (2030'): 0.8 mi. (1.3 km), 500 ft., 40 min.

Vista Trail (USGS Laconia, Gilmanton Ironworks and West Alton quads)

This trail, blazed in yellow, provides access to open ledges on the southeast ridge of Piper Mtn. It diverges to the east from the Whiteface–Piper Link at the south summit of Piper Mtn., soon swings right, and descends moderately over ledges and through patches of woods, with some views to the southwest. At 0.3 mi. it levels in a spruce grove, then emerges on an expansive area of open ledge with wide views south and east, where blazes end. A line of cairns extending southeast down the ledges marks the beginning of an obscure trail to Swett Mtn., a lower spur along the ridge.

Distance from Whiteface–Piper Link (2010')

> *to* ledges on southeast ridge (1870'): 0.4 mi. (0.6 km), 0 ft. (rev. 150 ft.), 15 min.

Piper Mountain Trail (USGS Laconia quad)

This trail, blazed in red, provides direct access to Piper Mtn. from the lower end of the Belknap Carriage Rd. Grades are mostly moderate. It leaves the Carriage Rd. on the right (south), 0.4 mi. from Belknap Mountain Rd., just beyond a bridge over Gunstock Brook. There is no parking at the trailhead, but parking space is available 0.1 mi. below the trailhead (on the left, just before the gate) or 0.1 mi. above the trailhead (at a pulloff on the right).

Leaving the Carriage Rd., the trail soon swings left and crosses a brook, then ascends rather steeply along the blue-blazed boundary of Belknap Mountain State Forest. At 0.2 mi. the grade eases as the trail enters private land that has been recently logged; follow markings carefully at skid road crossings. At 0.6 mi. it crosses a muddy logging road, leaves the logged area, and ascends through spruce forest. At 0.8 mi. the trail swings left and climbs through a ledgy area, passing an outlook northwest to Mt. Cardigan. The trail continues climbing over ledges and through patches of woods, with several turns; follow blazes and cairns carefully. It passes two views southwest to Mt. Kearsarge and emerges on open ledges at the north summit of Piper Mtn. Here there is a rock throne with a view west. The trail continues another 25 yd. across open ledges to a second rock throne with an excellent view east. Here the orange-blazed Old Piper Trail joins from the left (north) and the poorly-marked Whiteface–Piper Link joins from the right (south). Descending, the Piper Mountain Trail drops northwest into the woods from the west-facing rock throne; look for a finger-like cairn.

Distance from Belknap Carriage Rd. (1030')

> *to* north summit of Piper Mtn. (2030'): 1.3 mi. (2.1 km), 1000 ft., 1 hr. 10 min.

Ridge Trail (USGS Laconia and West Alton quads)

This white-blazed trail, a segment of the Belknap Range Trail, runs from the main parking lot at the Gunstock Recreation Area to the summit of Mt. Rowe, then continues along the ridge to the summit of Gunstock Mtn. The first part was formerly known as the Try-Me Trail. It starts on a gated paved road 100 yd. north of the main base lodge and follows the road uphill. At 0.3 mi. it turns left onto a gravel service road and climbs fairly steeply to a communications tower at 0.8 mi., near the flat summit of Mt. Rowe. The trail continues to the left on a woods road along the nearly level ridge with excellent views. Take care to stay on the blazed route, avoiding side roads and beaten paths. Shortly after some smooth ledges the trail turns left off the road, runs into a small ravine, and then climbs up into blueberry patches. It comes within sight of a ski trail and turns right, staying to the right of (above) the ski trail as it climbs through patches of woods and open places. At 1.7 mi. it joins another road (sign). Turn left and cross over snowmaking pipes to a ski trail, then turn right up the ski trail (which is also the Flintlock Trail) on a service road, continuing on the ski trail when the road swings off to the left. The ski trail curves around to the left and climbs to the summit.

Distances from Gunstock Recreation Area parking lot (930')

> *to* summit of Mt. Rowe (1690'): 0.8 mi., 750 ft., 45 min.
>
> *to* summit of Gunstock Mtn. (2250'): 2.4 mi. (3.9 km.), 1550 ft. (rev. 250 ft.), 2 hr.

Flintlock Trail (USGS Laconia and West Alton quads)

This trail uses ski trails to ascend Gunstock Mtn. from the Gunstock Recreation Area main parking lot. Start by aiming for a large stone fireplace on the lower part of the slopes. This trail (no sign) follows a service road that curves upward to the right and crosses under the chairlift. The Ridge Trail enters from the right at 1.0 mi., and the trails coincide to the summit of Gunstock Mtn., always keeping to the right on ski trails. Descending, keep to the left edge of the ski trails until the Ridge Trail enters (sign), then bear right on the service road.

Distance from Gunstock Recreation Area parking area (930')

> *to* summit of Gunstock Mtn. (2250'): 1.7 mi. (2.7 km.), 1300 ft., 1 hr. 30 min.

Brook Trail (USGS Laconia and West Alton quads)

This trail, blazed in yellow, is the most direct hiking trail from the Gunstock Recreation Area to the summit of Gunstock Mtn. It is rather steep and rough in places. Start by aiming for a large stone fireplace on the lower part of the slopes. This trail (sign) goes to the right of the fireplace and follows the left edge of a ski trail for about 50 yd., then enters the woods and crosses a brook, follows the bank of the brook, and crosses another ski trail. After re-entering the woods, it crosses and quickly recrosses a brook, and soon begins to climb away from the brook as it ascends in the valley. At 0.5 mi. it crosses another ski trail and climbs, steeply at times, until it meets a stone wall, turns left along it, and soon reaches another ski trail at 1.2 mi. It crosses this trail and ascends along the left edge to the jct. with yet another ski trail, which it immediately crosses, entering the woods over snowmaking pipes. It then climbs to a jct. with the Saddle Trail on the ridgecrest at 1.5 mi., where it turns right. From here it is a segment of the Belknap Range Trail. The trail scrambles up a short steep section, then turns left and climbs more gradually, passing two memorial stones and a picnic table and soon reaching the summit.

Distance from Gunstock Recreation Area parking area (930')

> *to* summit of Gunstock Mtn. (2250'): 1.7 mi. (2.7 km.), 1300 ft., 1 hr. 30 min.

Saddle Trail (USGS Laconia quad)

This very short white-blazed trail, also a segment in the Belknap Range Trail, connects the col between Belknap Mtn. and Gunstock Mtn. with the Brook Trail. Leaving the jct. with the Overlook Trail and the Blue Trail in the col, it crosses the flat sag and climbs moderately to the jct. where the Brook Trail enters on the right.

Distance from Belknap–Gunstock col (2000')

> *to* Brook Trail junction (2100'): 0.1 mi. (0.2 km.), 100 ft., 5 min.

Round Pond Trail (USGS West Alton quad)

This trail is a multi-use trail of the Gunstock Recreation Area trail system, running from the main ski area parking lot to Round Pond. In addition to providing access to Round Pond from the recreation area, it connects with the Overlook Trail, the East Gilford Trail, and the Belknap Range Trail (both at the beginning and near Round Pond), making possible a great variety of loop hikes from several trailheads.

There are two ways of starting out from the ski area parking lot. One route follows the access road back past the last of the maintenance buildings, then turns right on the Cobble Mountain Trail (#5). After 70 yd. turn right onto the Maple Trail (#9). After 0.3 mi. turn right at a T intersection for 50 yd., then turn sharp left at the fork where the other access route bears right. The second access route can be found by passing through a gate under a hanging sign ("Cobble Mountain Stables"), then going to the left of the base building of the Pistol chairlift and following a woods road signed "Connector" (#15). In 0.3 mi. from the gate with the hanging sign, this trail reaches the fork (its first significant jct.) and turns sharp right where the first route bears left.

The trail, still a well-defined woods road, climbs to the top of a rise where it crosses a stone wall, bears right uphill on the better road at a fork, and crosses another stone wall. At 0.9 mi. the Oak Trail (#7) diverges right. At 1.0 mi. the woods road turns sharp left at the edge of a small field; it is possible (and easier, though this is not the signed route) to continue straight along the edge of the field and pick up the continuation of this trail—the other (southern) end of the Oak Trail (#7)—next to a bridge over a small brook. The Maple Trail continues along the road about 100 yd. to a T intersection, where another trail (#8) enters on the left and continues across the field to the bridge, where it meets the Oak Trail (#7). In the opposite direction, you have the option of following the edge of the field to the Maple Trail (#9) at its sharp turn, or crossing the field to the other trail (#8), then immediately turning left on the Maple Trail (#9).

From the field, the Round Pond Trail follows the Oak Trail (#7) across the bridge and into the woods, then 30 yd. from the bridge it diverges left onto a footpath (sign). From this point it is marked mostly by black diamonds inscribed "B20." It crosses a stone wall, a small brook, a larger brook with a plank bridge at 1.4 mi., and another small brook. It then enters an old woods road and follows it to the right, then turns left off the end of the road just as it reaches the edge of a swamp. It climbs rather steeply for a short distance, then levels off and reaches the East Gilford Trail at 1.8 mi. Here it turns right and coincides with the East Gilford Trail for 0.2 mi., then leaves it on the left (sign) and runs with minor ups and downs to a woods road at 2.3 mi. It follows this woods road to the left across a brook, and 20 yd. past the brook it turns sharp right on another woods road. (By continuing straight ahead on the first woods road, one can reach the East Gilford Trail in 0.6 mi. at the fork 0.4 mi. from its trailhead.) At 3.0 mi., just before the Round Pond Trail reaches the height-of-land, the blue-blazed Belknap Range Trail enters on the right and diverges on the left 30 yd. farther on. The Round Pond Trail then descends moderately to a beautiful secluded spot on the shore of Round Pond.

Distances from Gunstock Recreation Area parking lot (930')

   to northern junction with Oak Trail #7 (1100'): 0.9 mi., 200 ft., 35 min.

   to lower junction with East Gilford Trail (1200'): 1.8 mi., 400 ft. (rev. 100 ft.), 1 hr. 5 min.

   to Belknap Range Trail (1680'): 3.0 mi., 1000 ft. (rev. 100 ft.), 2 hr.

   to Round Pond (1652'): 3.1 mi. (5.4 km.), 1000 ft., 2 hr. 5 min.

Overlook Trail (USGS West Alton quad)

This orange-blazed trail connects the main parking lot at the Gunstock Recreation Area with the col between Belknap Mtn. and Gunstock Mtn., providing a convenient route to either peak and offering a fine viewpoint along the way. It is also the easiest and most convenient route for ascending either mountain in winter (when the Belknap Carriage Rd. is not open), since it has easier grades than the Brook Trail and does not cross any downhill ski trails. It was opened in November 1998, carefully located to avoid as much as possible steep areas that are vulnerable to damage by erosion.

It leaves the main parking area by following the Round Pond Trail (#9, see above), with which it coincides to the first (northern) jct. with the Oak Trail (#7) at 0.9 mi. Here it turns right onto the Oak Trail (#7) and follows this trail for 0.3 mi. to a point just past a hairpin turn. Here the Overlook Trail diverges right, immediately descends across a branch of Poorfarm Brook, and begins to climb. Constantly winding about to avoid any steep grades, it ascends to the upper edge of a steep slope and, at 1.7 mi. from the parking area, reaches open ledges covered with low juniper bushes where there is a fine outlook to the east across the valley. The trail re-enters the woods, descends through a dip, and resumes the climb. At 2.1 mi. it crosses a small brook that falls in tiny needles of water over a five-foot vertical ledge to the left. After crossing more small brooks the grade becomes easier, then steeper again as the trail enters the main ravine below the ridgecrest. At 2.9 mi. it reaches the col between Belknap Mtn. and Gunstock Mtn. For Gunstock Mtn. turn right on the white-blazed Saddle Trail to the yellow-blazed Brook Trail. For Belknap Mtn. turn left on the blue-blazed Blue Trail. Straight ahead is the Blue Trail to the upper end of the Belknap Carriage Rd.

Distances from Gunstock Recreation Area parking area (930')

  to Oak Trail (#7) junction (1100'): 0.9 mi., 200 ft., 35 min.

  to divergence from Oak Trail (1150'): 1.2 mi., 250 ft., 45 min.

  to overlook (1560'): 1.7 mi., 650 ft., 1 hr. 10 min.

  to Belknap Mtn.–Gunstock Mtn. col (2000'): 2.9 mi. (4.7 km.), 1100 ft., 2 hr.

  to Belknap Mtn. summit (2382') via Blue Trail: 3.4 mi. (5.5 km.), 1500 ft., 2 hr. 25 min.

  to Gunstock Mtn. summit (2250') via Saddle Trail and Brook Trail: 3.3 mi. (5.3 km.), 1350 ft., 2 hr. 20 min.

East Gilford Trail (USGS West Alton quad)

This trail, perhaps the most attractive on the Belknap Range, is also sometimes referred to as the Yellow Trail since it has yellow blazes. To reach it, turn right off NH 11A at a point 1.7 mi. south of the Gunstock Recreation Area road or 2.7 mi. west of NH 11 onto Bickford Rd., then at 0.2 mi. turn left on Wood Rd. and park near the jct. (or—as is recommended by the Gilford police—at the bridge across the small brook in the sag on Bickford Rd.). Do not under any circumstances park near the house at the end of Wood Rd.

The trail (sign) follows a cart track that diverges left at a telephone pole before reaching the white house at the end of the road. It circles around to the right and bears right at a fork at 0.4 mi. (The left branch here immediately crosses the brook and runs 0.6 mi. to a jct. with the Round Pond Trail 0.8 mi. below Round Pond.) At 0.5 mi. the multi-use Round Pond Trail (marked B20) from the Gunstock Recreation Area to Round Pond enters on the right, and at 0.7 mi. it diverges on the left. The trail soon begins to climb more steeply, and at 1.1 mi. it passes to the left of an interesting rock formation where nearly perfectly rectangular blocks of rock have been riven from a ledge by frost action. The trail winds back and forth, angling up the ledgy face of the mountain, and views begin to appear. The ledges are slippery when wet. At 1.6 mi., just above an excellent outlook over Lake Winnipesaukee, the blue-blazed Boulder Trail (part of the Belknap Range Trail) enters on the left (sign). Now coinciding with the Belknap Range Trail, the East Gilford Trail continues across ledges and through patches of woods at a moderate grade and joins the White Trail, which enters from the left at 1.9 mi. The two trails coincide and ascend at an easy grade, passing a communications shed and tower, and reaching the summit at 2.1 mi.

Distances from junction of Bickford Rd. and Wood Rd. (1070')

   to junction with Boulder Trail (2100'): 1.6 mi., 1050 ft., 1 hr. 20 min.

   to summit of Belknap Mtn. (2382'): 2.1 mi. (3.3 km.), 1300 ft., 1 hr.
          40 min.

Piper Link (USGS Laconia and West Alton quads)

This blue-blazed trail links the col between Belknap Mtn. and Piper Mtn. with the lower end of the Boulder Trail (a part of the Belknap Range Trail), giving convenient access to the fine ledges on the east side of Mt. Belknap from the Belknap Carriage Rd. It leaves the Old Piper Trail 30 yd. south of its jct. with the White Trail and descends to a small brook and crosses it, then descends fairly steeply on a rocky slope with loose footing, where the woods were severely damaged by the January 1998 ice storm. At 0.4 mi. it reaches the bottom of the descent and swings left uphill, and at 0.5 mi. it passes a ledge with a good view up to Piper Mtn. It now crosses a minor ridge and descends easily with occasional small ascents to a jct. with the Belknap Range Trail at the foot of the segment called the Boulder Trail. This jct. is well signed. Turn left uphill to ascend Belknap Mtn., or bear right for Round Pond, Mt. Major, or other objectives between those two places.

Distance from Belknap-Piper col (1800')

   to Boulder Trail junction (1550'): 1.0 mi. (1.6 km.), 100 ft. (rev. 350 ft.),
          35 min.

Boulder Trail (USGS West Alton quad)

This trail, a segment of the Belknap Range Trail, ascends the steep east ledges of Mt. Belknap. The trail footway is not well established in several places, and the markings must be looked for and followed with great care. Beginning where the Piper Link enters the Belknap Range Trail at the foot of the east ledges, it climbs over a slope of loose talus blocks and up ledges with partial but ever-improving views, meeting the East Gilford Trail (sign) just above an excellent outlook ledge on that trail. The two trails ascend together, soon joined by the White Trail, to the summit of Belknap Mtn.

Distances from Piper Link junction (1550')

> *to* East Gilford Trail junction (2100'): 0.4 mi. (0.6 km.), 550 ft., 30 min.

> *to* summit of Belknap Mtn. (2382') via East Gilford Trail: 0.9 mi. (1.4 km.), 850 ft., 50 min.

Round Pond Woods Road *(USGS West Alton quad)*

Although on private land and not a maintained trail, this clear, easily followed woods road is the shortest route to beautiful Round Pond. It also provides access to (or a convenient exit from) points on the ridge between Belknap Mtn. and Mt. Major. It begins on Grant Rd., a gravel road that turns south off NH 11A about 2.2 mi. south of the access road to the Gunstock Recreation Area and 0.4 mi. south of Bickford Rd. (the access road to the East Gilford Trail), and 2.3 mi. north of NH 11. The trailhead, with parking for several cars, is on the left 0.2 mi. from NH 11A where the woods road is blocked by a concrete barrier.

The road soon reaches the lower edge of a field; there are views as the road passes the upper part of this field. At a fork at 0.4 mi., take the right branch that runs across the bottom of the upper field. (The left branch runs along the left edge of this field parallel to a stone wall and ends in 250 yd. at the top of the field, from which there are fine views to the north.) The road climbs at a moderate grade to the height-of-land at 1.0 mi., then continues with slight ups and downs to a junction at 1.2 mi. where the blue-blazed Belknap Range Trail (sign: "Mt. Belknap") enters on the right. The road continues as part of the Belknap Range Trail, extending almost to the summit of Mt. Mack.

Distance from Grant Rd. (1200')

> *to* Belknap Range Trail (1670'): 1.2 mi. (1.9 km.), 500 ft., 50 min.

Mount Klem Loop *(USGS West Alton quad)*

This trail runs from the shore of Round Pond to a point just east of the summit of Mt. Mack, missing the wooded, viewless summit of Mt. Klem by about 100 yd. and 50 ft. of elevation. It is a much longer and more strenuous but much more scenic alternative to the Belknap Range Trail between the two end points. It is marked with red wooden diamonds nailed to trees and is fairly easy to follow, although some care is needed, particularly in the open areas.

The northwestern trailhead is on the Belknap Range Trail, in the section where the trail is a woods road running near the edge of the pond, 0.1 mi. east of the point where the Belknap Range Trail enters the woods road and 0.1 mi. west of the Boy Scout camping area. At this jct. it is marked only by two red wooden diamonds (no sign); the diamonds are facing toward a westbound hiker; eastbound, the trail diverges on the left just after the woods road begins to climb away from the edge of the pond. The southeastern trailhead, which is amply signed, is on a ledge just east of the summit of Mt. Mack.

Leaving the shore of Round Pond, the trail climbs steadily through a dense coniferous forest, then levels and passes through a small sag. It then climbs more easily, crossing a stone wall and ascending to a ledgy area where it swings to the left, descending slightly, then ascends slightly across another ledgy outcrop. It then descends slightly through a shallow, flat sag, and runs on contour as it curls around the north end of Mt. Klem somewhat below the true summit at 0.6 mi. At 0.8 mi. it passes a cleared outlook to the northeast and swings right, then runs almost level for some distance, passing a jct. with the white-blazed Quarry Trail (no sign) on the left at 0.9 mi. Finally it begins to descend and crosses an open area with views at 1.0 mi. It descends across another ledgy spot with a view into a sag at 1.3 mi., then climbs up to a rocky knob, crosses a small dip, and climbs to its southeastern jct. with the Belknap Range Trail near the summit of Mt. Mack.

Distance from Round Pond (1652')

   to Mt. Mack (1945'): 1.6 mi. (2.5 km.), 550 ft. (rev. 250 ft.), 1 hr. 5 min.

Mount Major Trail (USGS West Alton quad)

Mt. Major offers views that are among the best in southern New Hampshire for the effort required, but the upper ledges are steep and dangerous in wet or icy conditions. These dangerous ledges and the easy accessibility of the mountain have combined to produce a number of serious injuries, particularly in late fall and winter when ice is present. In such conditions the Brook Trail, an unofficial alternative route described below, is probably safer, and it may also be a better choice for the descent at other times—as well as providing good views from the open west ridge that are not duplicated by the main trail.

This trail begins at a parking area (large sign) on NH 11, 4.2 mi. north of Alton Bay and 1.7 mi. north of the jct. of NH 11 with NH 11D. The trail leaves the right side of the parking area and follows a lumber road west, ascending a steep, severely eroded section where several alternate roads diverge and rejoin; the road farthest to the right (ascending) offers slightly better footing than the others. At the top of this steep section, at 0.3 mi., the road becomes nearly level and smooth. At 0.7 mi. the Mt. Major Trail diverges sharp left on a path marked with dark-blue paint. It climbs steeply through second growth and over ledges, with some steep scrambles near the top. At several points there are one or more alternate paths, all of which rejoin and lead to the summit. The summit, with the ruins of a stone hut, is reached at 1.5 mi. This is also the eastern terminus of the Belknap Range Trail.

For the descent from the summit via the Mount Major Trail, follow blue blazes northeast directly down the ledges towards the southern part of Lake Winnipesaukee. For descent via the alternate route (Belknap Range Trail and Brook Trail), walk southwest down the ledges towards Straightback Mtn.; the blue blazes are sparse for the first 0.1 mi., then become more frequent. At 0.5 mi. from the summit turn right onto the yellow-blazed Brook Trail (sign).

Distances from NH 11 (650')

   to Mt. Major summit (1786') via Mount Major Trail: 1.5 mi. (2.4 km.), 1150 ft., 1 hr. 20 min.

   to Mt. Major summit (1786') via Mount Major Trail, Brook Trail, and Belknap Range Trail: 2.4 mi. (3.8 km.), 1150 ft., 1 hr. 45 min.

   to starting point via complete loop: 3.9 mi. (6.2 km.), 1150 ft., 2 hr. 30 min.

Brook Trail (USGS West Alton quad)

Continue on the lumber road past the jct. where the Mount Major Trail leaves it on the left, 0.7 mi. from the parking area. There are several diverging roads along this route but none of them is nearly as clear and obvious as the correct route, which is blazed in yellow. At 0.5 mi. the road appears to end, but a lesser woods road bears right toward a small brook, crosses it, and continues to climb, with loose footing on some severely eroded sections. At 0.9 mi. it swings left away from the edge of the valley and climbs to the saddle between Mt. Major and Straightback Mtn. at 1.2 mi., where it meets the Belknap Range

Trail. Here the two trails, coinciding, turn left and climb mostly over open ledges with good views to the summit at 1.7 mi.

Distance from junction with the Mount Major Trail (930')

    to summit of Mt. Major (1786'): 1.7 mi., 850 ft., 1 hr. 15 min.

Boulder Loop Trail (USGS West Alton Quad)

This trail provides an attractive route up the south side of the mountain from the trailhead parking area on NH 11. The lower section follows a snowmobile trail that leaves the left side of the parking area (sign: "Trail E"), crosses two plank bridges, and in 30 yd. turns right up a bank past a boulder where a woods road continues ahead. It climbs moderately up a woods road also used as a snowmobile trail to a T-junction at 0.4 mi. Here it turns right, then in 40 yd. bears left at a fork, where orange blazes begin, and ascends south along the woods road. At 0.7 mi., where the road becomes wet and curves to the left, the trail continues ahead into the woods on a footpath.

It ascends steadily through an area strewn with boulders, swings right (west) at 1.0 mi., squeezes between and under boulders at 1.2 mi., then climbs a steep, gravelly pitch. At the top of the pitch it turns right, then left and runs at easy grades through pine and oak woods, then ascends gradually over open ledges, with increasing views east and south, to the summit. To descend by this trail, walk south across the ledges from the hut and look for orange blazes on the rock.

Distance from NH 11 (650')

    to Mt. Major summit (1786'): 1.6 mi. (2.6 km.), 1150 ft., 1 hr. 25 min.

Belknap Range Trail (USGS Laconia and West Alton quads)

This trail (at least in theory) extends from the Gunstock Recreation Area to the summit of Mt. Major, using all or part of several other trails along the way. Sections of this trail, even between Mt. Belknap and Mt. Major, have existed in some form for a number of years, but only very recently has it been possible for the average hiker to have any hope of following large segments of this route. Much of the trail between the Gunstock Recreation Area and Mt. Anna is easy to follow, and the rest requires only reasonable care. Between Mt. Anna and Mt. Major following some parts of this trail requires a substantial amount of care, though considering the constant improvement of this trail as a whole in the last few years, significant improvement in the less well-defined sections may be hoped for in the near future.

Leaving the Gunstock Recreation Area main parking lot, the Belknap Range Trail follows the Ridge Trail over Mt. Rowe to the summit of Gunstock Mtn. at 2.4 mi. It then descends on the Brook Trail and Saddle Trail to the Belknap–Gunstock col at 2.8 mi., and follows the Blue Trail to the summit of Belknap Mtn. at 3.3 mi. It then descends on the combined Boulder Trail, East Gilford Trail, and White Trail, following the Boulder Trail as the others diverge and becoming quite steep until it reaches the sag where the Piper Link enters on the right at 4.1 mi.

From here on, the Belknap Range Trail, which is mostly blazed in blue, no longer coincides with other trails. It climbs over several small humps and through the sags between them, then climbs with two short steep pitches up a larger hump. It then runs along the north side of the ridge with minor ups and downs, and meets the Round Pond Trail coming up from the left (north) at 4.9 mi. It turns right on this trail, then diverges left off it in 30 yd. (From this jct., the Round Pond Trail descends gradually 0.1 mi. to a secluded spot at the shore of the pond.) The Belknap Range Trail ascends easily over a knoll, descends and crosses a moist flat sag, and then, with the pond in sight on the right, swings left, climbing briefly to the Round Pond Woods Road at 5.2 mi. To the left it is 1.2 mi. to Grant Rd., 0.2 mi. from NH 11A. The Belknap Range Trail follows the road to the right, passing a side path on the right leading to the pond and then descending to the edge of the pond. The Mount Klem Loop, a longer and more scenic alternate route between Round Pond and Mt. Mack, diverges left at 5.4 mi., just after the road begins to climb gradually away from the pond. Then the road swings away from the pond and at 5.5 mi. enters a small clearing among the pines—an outpost campsite of the Hidden Valley Reservation. (To the right at this campsite, a trail marked by red wooden diamonds continues near the pond, crosses an inlet brook in 100 yd., and reaches a jct. in another 100 yd. Here this trail continues straight ahead to Hidden Valley, while a branch trail turns left and climbs 0.2 mi. to rejoin the Belknap Range Trail 0.3 mi. above the campsite.)

From the campsite, the Belknap Range Trail continues straight ahead (away from the pond) on the woods road. At 5.8 mi. the branch trail enters on the right, and the Belknap Range Trail continues to climb, passing a ledge with a wide view south and west to the Uncanoonuc Mtns., Crotched Mtn., the Pack Monadnocks, and Monadnock at 6.0 mi. It crosses over the ledgy summit of

Mt. Mack, passing a communications tower and an apparently defunct windmill, and reaches the jct. with the Mount Klem Loop just beyond at 6.1 mi. From this jct. the trail turns right but soon swings back to the left and descends at easy to moderate grades. In all it descends over 500 feet—the last part with several minor ups and downs—until it reaches its low point at a mossy brook at 6.8 mi. It begins to climb a bit, crossing a stone wall that is the Gilford–Gilmanton town line, and then climbs more seriously, although descending briefly at one point to cross a brook, to the flat ledgy summit of Mt. Anna, where views are restricted. At 7.5 mi., in the flat summit area, a trail jct. is reached; the trails to the right and straight ahead descend toward Hidden Valley, while the Belknap Range Trail turns left and starts a mild descent.

At 7.6 mi. the trail reaches the top of a short steep, rocky pitch, then makes numerous small ascents and descents with occasional slightly obscure places. At 8.2 mi. it bears left at a small rock face, and at 8.4 mi. it enters an open ledgy area with views ahead to part of Straightback Mtn. and, higher up, back to Belknap Mtn. The general route across this area is obvious, but it is poorly marked; there is little problem in clear weather, but in fog it could be very difficult to cross this area correctly without following a compass course. The trail climbs past a jct. with the Quarry Trail on the left at 8.6 mi., and reaches a point just north of the south summit of Straightback Mtn. at 8.7 mi., where it turns sharp left. The various ledges and open areas of this summit repay exploration; an obscure trail continues ahead (east) across the ledges, eventually descending the southeast side of the mountain. The main trail now descends, mostly in the woods, often angling to the left, passing a jct. with a branch of the Quarry Trail on the left at 9.0 mi. At 9.1 mi. it crosses a ledge with a glimpse of Lake Winnipesaukee, then descends again to the col between Straightback Mtn. and Mt. Major, reaching a trail jct. just on the Mt. Major side of the col at 9.3 mi. The path on the left here is the Brook Trail, which descends to the parking lot on NH 11 in 1.9 mi. The Belknap Range Trail now ascends the ridge, soon coming into the open, passing a jct. on the right with the obscure Beaver Pond Trail at 9.5 mi., and following a somewhat poorly marked but fairly obvious route up to the summit of Mt. Major at 9.8 mi., where there are magnificent views and the remains of a stone hut.

Distances from Gunstock Recreation Area parking area (930')

> *to* summit of Gunstock Mtn. (2250'): 2.4 mi., 1550 ft. (rev. 200 ft.), 2 hr.
>
> *to* summit of Belknap Mtn. (2382'): 3.3 mi., 1950 ft. (rev. 250 ft.), 2 hr. 40 min.

    to Round Pond Trail junction (1680'): 4.9 mi., 2200 ft. (rev. 950 ft.), 3 hr. 35 min.

    to summit of Mt. Mack (1945'): 6.1 mi., 2550 ft. (rev. 100 ft.), 4 hr. 20 min.

    to summit of Mt. Anna (1670'): 7.5 mi., 3050 ft. (rev. 750 ft.), 5 hr. 15 min.

    to high point on Straightback Mtn. (1880'): 8.7 mi., 3450 ft. (rev. 200 ft.), 6 hr. 5 min.

    to summit of Mt. Major (1786'): 9.8 mi. (15.8 km.), 3650 ft. (rev. 300 ft.), 6 hr. 40 min.

Quarry Trail (USGS West Alton quad)

This white-blazed trail provides an interesting ridge traverse from the south peak of Straightback Mtn. to Mt. Klem, passing several viewpoints and crossing over or near the summits of the north peak of Straightback Mtn. (1910 ft.) and several other officially unnamed humps sometimes called the Quarry Mountains. It makes possible various loop hikes over the east–central section of the range. There are several short steep, rough stretches, and other sections may require care to follow, though the trail has been improved in recent years and is now well-blazed.

At its east end, it diverges north from the Belknap Range Trail at an open ledgy area 0.1 mi. west of the south summit of Straightback Mtn. It descends into the woods, then ascends easily through the woods and across open areas where it must be followed with care. At 0.4 mi. a white-blazed branch path (no sign), 0.3 mi. long, diverges right, descending and then climbing to the Belknap Range Trail at a point 0.3 mi. west of the Straightback–Major col. The main trail continues over the wooded north summit of Straightback Mtn., where it turns left and descends steeply to a saddle. It next ascends the south slope of the long low ridge northwest of Straightback, and at 0.9 mi. turns sharp left at a ledge with a view northeast. In another 50 yd. it turns right and makes a short, steep drop to a sign where a steep, rough side path descends 50 yd. to the right to some boulder caves in a rockfall (use caution). Here the main trail turns left and emerges on a ledge at the top of the rockfall with a fine view east. The trail makes a tricky scramble up a ledge with a drop-off on the right (this spot should be avoided in wet weather or by hikers uncomfortable with exposure) and then loops back up to the left into the woods. (The short loop down to the outlook and back up can be bypassed by bushwhacking 15 yd.

straight ahead, up and across a wooded ledge, at the point where the trail turns right to descend to the cave side trail.)

The trail climbs through spruces, with one short scramble, to a wooded summit at 1.1 mi, then descends a short, steep pitch to a ferny sag. It ascends across a knob through several open, brushy areas where the blazes must be carefully followed, descends slightly, and swings left (south) across a plateau where the footing may be wet. At 1.6 mi. it swings left to a ledge overlooking a beaver pond at the base of Straightback Mtn., climbs over a second wooded summit (1894 ft.) at 1.7 mi., then descends and bears right (northwest) past an outlook on the left towards Mt. Mack and Mt. Klem. It continues down through old-growth spruces to an informational sign and left turn at 2.0 mi. Here a less steep bypass path, marked with yellow flagging, continues ahead while the main trail descends a very steep pitch, soon swinging right across exposed sloping ledges with a view west; this spot is potentially dangerous if wet. It descends another steep pitch over mossy ledges, and the bypass path joins from the right at 2.1 mi. The trail now swings left and descends to an old quarry site on the left, and continues down to a saddle at 2.3 mi. It ascends, crossing a logging road, crosses a third wooded summit (1883 ft.) at 2.7 mi., then turns sharp left and winds down to a right turn and a fine outlook south at 2.8 mi. The trail descends and ascends briefly, then drops very steeply to a notch where there is a small, stagnant brook. It climbs steadily up the east slope of Mt. Klem, crossing a stone wall, then eases and runs through an open area to meet the Mount Klem Loop just east of the wooded summit. Turn left for Mt. Mack or right for the most direct descent to Round Pond.

Distances from Belknap Range Trail near south summit of Straightback Mt. (1830')

   to   first summit (1890'): 1.1 mi., 250 ft. (rev. 200 ft.), 40 min.

   to   second summit (1894'): 1.7 mi., 350 ft. (rev. 100 ft.), 1 hr. 5 min.

   to   third summit (1883'): 2.7 mi., 650 ft. (rev. 300 ft.), 1 hr. 40 min.

   to   Mount Klem Loop (1970'): 3.3 mi. (5.3 km), 950 ft. (rev. 200 ft.), 2 hr. 10 min.

Copple Crown Mountain (USGS Wolfeboro quad)

This mountain (1868 ft.) rises south of Lake Winnipesaukee in the towns of Brookfield and New Durham. The summit area is within a large tract of land owned by the Lakes Region Conservation Trust. The ledgy summit offers fine views over low brush to Lake Winnipesaukee and the mountains beyond: the Belknap, Squam, and Sandwich Ranges. There is also a beautiful clifftop outlook on the slightly lower east knob, which provides views of the gentler, more pastoral region to the south. To reach the trailhead, follow NH 109 west 1.2 mi. from its jct. with NH 16, then turn left onto Governors Rd. Follow this for 0.4 mi., then turn right onto Mountain Rd. and follow it for about 1.5 mi. to the end of the pavement. Bear left at a fork—this road is rough and may not be passable to all vehicles—and continue 0.4 mi. to the parking area for Jones Brook Wildlife Management Area, past which the road is gated.

The trail follows a gravel road to a jct. where it joins another gravel road that comes in from the right—this is the road that bears right at the fork 0.4 mi. before the parking area, so if the road is not passable past the fork one could park near there and follow the right branch to this point. The woods road continues from the jct., ascending gradually. At 1.3 mi. it passes a woods road leaving on the left and shortly reaches the LRCT kiosk on the left, where a trail map is posted and copies are sometimes available.

The trail (blue blazes) runs through the woods for a short distance and joins the woods road just mentioned; if this jct. is missed on the descent there is no problem, since the woods road leads to the gravel road at virtually the same point as the trail. The woods road climbs gradually, then more steeply, with some poor footing on the steepest, eroded sections, through dense second growth hardwoods in a logged-over area. At 1.9 mi. it emerges from the logged area into fine conifer woods where it climbs the steep, rocky slope by switchbacks at easy grades. At 2.3 mi. a side trail enters on the right a few steps before a sharp left turn; take care not to follow this trail on the descent—it leads to the private Copple Crown Community and is not open to the public. The trail now ascends easily with mostly excellent footing through beautiful woods to a jct. at 2.5 mi. Here a side path diverges left, descends through a small col, and then climbs easily to the excellent clifftop viewpoint on the east knob at 0.2 mi. The main trail bears right here and soon comes to another fork, where the left branch leads about 100 yd. to a restricted outlook to the south. The right branch continues a short distance to the summit and the ledgy viewpoint a few steps beyond.

Distances from Jones Brook Wildlife Management Area parking lot (860')

   to the LRCT kiosk (1100'): 1.3 mi., 250 ft., 45 min.

   to summit of Copple Crown Mtn. (1868') including side trip to east knob outlook: 3.0 mi. (4.8 km.), 1100 ft., 2 hr. 5 min.

Devils Den Mountain (USGS Wolfeboro and Alton quads)

The summit of this small mountain (1110 ft.) in the town of New Durham is an interesting rock formation with an excellent view of the White Mtns. over Lake Winnipesaukee, with rugged Rattlesnake Island in the foreground. There is no official trail, but the mountain is easy to climb. From New Durham village, off NH 11, take the road to Powder Mill Fish Hatchery and Merrymeeting Lake to a jct. where the pavement on the main road ends and North Shore Rd, (which is paved) enters on the right. Follow the dirt road ahead (which is too rough for most ordinary cars), bearing uphill to the right at a fork at 0.8 mi. The road continues at easy grades, then makes a fairly steep and rough descent into a dip where there is a beaver pond on the left at 1.3 mi. The road next ascends to a height-of-land at 1.5 mi., where a woods road turns left (faint arrow on a rock), runs past the end of a stone wall and swings right, then continues to the foot of the summit ledges at 1.8 mi. Here one can go straight up the rock face by means of a short crack with excellent hand- and footholds, or bear left and follow a beaten path that swings around the side of the ledge and climbs it from the back side over easy ledges. Note carefully the ascent route for use on the descent—there is a confusing network of beaten paths on the summit ledges.

Distance from road junction at northwest end of Merrymeeting Lake (690')

>   *to* summit of Devils Den Mtn. (1110'): 1.9 mi. (3.0 km.), 600 ft. (rev. 150 ft.), 1 hr. 15 min.

Section 5
Southeastern New Hampshire

SUGGESTED HIKES

Easy Hikes

Stonehouse Pond [rt: 0.5 mi., 200 ft., 0:20]. This beautiful small pond with an interesting rock formation that can be ascended for views. The Blue Job Mtn. Trail **[lp: 1.3 mi., 350 ft., 0:50]** climbs a small mountain with ledgy views and an operating fire tower (in season).

South Pawtuckaway Mtn. [lp: 2.3 mi., 500 ft., 1:25]. This loop hike, via Tower Trail Connector, Mountain Trail, South Ridge Trail, South Ridge Connector, and Tower Rd., makes a fine traverse of this small, ledgy mountain, with many interesting rock formations and boulders and good views.

Moderate Hikes

Fundy Trail [rt: 3.4 mi., 0 ft., 1:40]. The Fundy Trail passes an interesting swamp and traces of an old farming village.

North Pawtuckaway Mtn. with the boulders and the Devils Den [lp: 4.9 mi., 750 ft., 2:50]. This loop hike, via North Mountain Trail, Boulder Trail, and North Mountain Bypass, offers fine views, many interesting rock formations and an unusual assembly of large glacial erratic boulders. The distance given is for the approach from the south (Reservation Rd.); the distance for the loop with an approach from the north (Round Pond Rd.) is 1 mi. (30 min.) less.

LIST OF TRAILS

This section covers the southeastern portion of New Hampshire, extending from the seacoast to the first significant ranges of hills—the Pawtuckaway Mtns., which rise to just short of the 1000-foot level in Nottingham and Deerfield about 25 miles from the Atlantic Ocean, and the Blue Hills, which reach an elevation of 1400 feet in Strafford and Farmington about 30 miles inland.

New Hampshire's coastline totals only 18 miles—the least of any state that has a coastline at all—but it provides a fine variety of scenery and terrain, from rocky headlands to salt marshes to the fine harbor at the mouth of the Piscataqua River, shared between Portsmouth NH and Kittery ME. This harbor and other areas near the Piscataqua were the site of much of New Hampshire's early settlement, and of the renowned shipbuilding industry that developed at Portsmouth in early colonial times, which provided the central symbol of a ship under construction for the state flag. But the two most significant features of the New Hampshire seacoast area are not on the coastline itself: about ten miles out to sea the picturesque Isles of Shoals rise a few dozen feet above the weather-driven surf, while just a few miles inland lies what is perhaps the crown jewel of the area, the 4500-acre tidal estuary called Great Bay, which may well be the most important ecosystem in the state.

Behind the coastal area the land is only rarely flat, being mostly low rolling hills consisting largely of piles of gravel left behind by retreating glaciers. Many of the more prominent hills are drumlins, heaps of gravel usually about a mile long and a quarter-mile wide, oriented parallel to the track of the glacier in a northwest–southeast direction and rising 100 to 150 feet above the surrounding countryside. Perhaps the most prominent and accessible of these hills—as well as one of the most finely formed—is Stratham Hill in Stratham, south of Great Bay. Continuing inland, hills become higher, and some of them are formed by bedrock with occasional rocky outcrops. Eventually the first real ranges—the Pawtuckaways and the Blue Hills—are encountered.

Included in this section are the trail network on the Pawtuckaway Mtns. and near Pawtuckaway Lake in 5535-acre Pawtuckaway State Park, and a number of scattered hills and other natural features that offer interesting walks, including the Isles of Shoals, Odiorne Point State Park, Great Bay, Stratham Hill, Rock Rimmon Hill, Stonehouse Pond, Garrison Hill, Parker Mtn. and Blue Job Mtn. in the Blue Hills Range, and Teneriffe Mountain and Preserve.

Isles of Shoals

This small group of picturesquely rocky, windswept islands lies about 10 miles southeast of Portsmouth Harbor, divided between New Hampshire and Maine. Though the islands are generally considered to amount to nine—Duck, Appledore, Smuttynose, Malaga, and Cedar in Maine, and Star, White, Seavey, and Lunging in New Hampshire—there are many other rocks and ledges, and White and Seavey Islands are joined at low tide. Appledore is the largest at 95 acres and rises over 60 ft. above mean sea level, making it also the loftiest of the Isles. Refer to the USGS Isles of Shoals quadrangle.

These islands have a history that is much greater than their small size might suggest, and that history and a general aura of romance have led to the publication of an unusual number of books about them (several of which are available at the Star Island bookstore). Although they had been sighted no later than 1603, it was probably Capt. John Smith's visit to the islands in 1614 that most effectively brought them to the attention of the British seafaring men as a potentially valuable base near highly productive fishing grounds. In early colonial times a very prosperous industry developed around the fisheries, and the Isles became particularly noted for the production of a premium grade of dried fish called dunfish. In 1767 the population of the village of Gosport on Star Island was reported as 284—a fairly large number of inhabitants on a 40-acre island. At the time of the Revolutionary War, however, the islanders were forcibly evacuated because their suspected sympathy with the British could not be tolerated in such a potentially strategic location; most did not return after the war, and the fishing industry slowly declined.

But the Isles were merely entering another era. Thomas Laighton arrived on White Island in 1839 with his family to operate the lighthouse there, and in 1848 he opened a hotel on Appledore. His daughter Celia Laighton Thaxter became a well-known poet throughout New England, adding to the appeal of the place. That hotel no longer exists, but a hotel built on Star Island in the 1870s still stands and has been a home for religious conferences for more than a century.

At present, several of the smaller islands are owned by individuals or families. Duck Island, once used as a bombing target, is now maintained as a sanctuary for waterfowl, and unauthorized visits are not allowed. Appledore and Star, the two largest islands, are owned by the Star Island Corporation, which is composed of representatives of the Unitarian-Universalist and Congregationalist religious groups. Star Island is managed as a home for religious conferences, while Appledore is managed primarily as the site of a marine biology laboratory operated by Cornell University with the cooperation of the University of New Hampshire.

The most convenient access to the Isles of Shoals for the general public at the present time is provided by the Isles of Shoals Steamship Co. (Barker Wharf, 315 Market St., Portsmouth, NH 03801; 800-441-4620, 800-894-5509 in NH; www.islesofshoals.com). They operate a daily cruise during the summer season that provides a three hour stopover on Star Island, allowing ample time to explore the points of interest on the island, such as the rugged, rocky headlands, Betty Moody's cave (a traprock dike with a cave formed by boulders that have fallen from its sides), the John Smith Monument, and a number of old or historic buildings. A map of Star Island showing all principal points of interest is available at the Barker Wharf office. This stopover cruise is limited to 100 visitors per day, so reservations are highly recommended. Visitors to Star Island should comply with the owners' regulations for use of the island, and be careful to avoid the abundant poison ivy.

Odiorne Point State Park

Located in the town of Rye along the edge of the southern part of Portsmouth Harbor, in the area where the Piscataqua River merges into the Atlantic Ocean, Odiorne Point State Park contains the Seacoast Science Museum and offers fine opportunities for walking along the shore in the transition zones between land and water, an area where resident plants and animals must be able to deal with significant regular fluctuations in the salt content of the water as the tides rise and ebb. Once an area of fine summer homes that was taken over by the military during World War II to provide protective fortification for the harbor, it was given to the state after the war to be turned into a park; some of the former Fort Dearborn's gun emplacement earthworks still exist. The park has two entrances from NH 1A, the main one being near the science museum and the secondary one somewhat farther to the north just before the bridge over Berrys Brook. In addition to the shoreline, the area is crisscrossed by old roads and paths that offer a variety of interesting walks, with the longer loops around the area reaching a length of 1.0 mi. to 1.5 mi. depending on the route chosen. Visitors should take care to avoid the plentiful poison ivy. Refer to the USGS Kittery quadrangle.

Great Bay

Great Bay is a 4500-acre tidal estuary, the largest inland tidal bay on the east coast of the United States, furnishing an ecosystem that is particularly notable for the constant, rhythmic changes in the conditions that confront resident plants and animals. At low tide much of the bay becomes exposed mud flats, while at high tide most of these flats are covered by water. Numerous rivers and brooks constantly feed the bay with fresh water, while the high tides of the Atlantic, coming twice each day, cause salt water to flow up the Piscataqua River and into the bay. Thus the salinity of the water varies from place to place and is constantly fluctuating with the tides. At low tide, minerals and organisms flow out of the bay and down the Piscataqua to the coastal region. This constant bi-directional flow of nutrients and organisms contributes to the importance of Great Bay as a habitat that nurtures many forms of life, both resident and visitor. The bald eagle is a particularly notable example of the many kinds of wildlife that find a bountiful food supply here.

Hiking opportunities around Great Bay are relatively limited, but there are several areas where visitors can enjoy short, easy walks while learning about this magnificent resource. Poison ivy may be present in these areas and care should be taken to avoid it.

Great Bay National Wildlife Refuge

This area was once occupied mainly by farms with pastures, orchards, and woodlots before it became part of Pease Air Force Base. After the base was closed, the 1054-acre portion on and near Great Bay was turned into a national wildlife refuge. Most of the area is not open to the public; public access is confined to designated trails, and this restriction is strictly enforced. At present trails consist of (1) the *Ferry Way Trail*, about 1.5 mi. long, which runs past a former weapons-storage complex to an old field and apple orchard, then makes a loop out to the edge of the bay and back to the field; and (2) the *Peverly Pond Trail*, a loop about 0.3 mi. long that leads to the shore of Upper Peverly Pond. Other trails may be open, at least on a seasonal basis. To visit Great Bay National Wildlife Refuge, take US 4/NH 16 (the Spaulding Turnpike) to the Pease International Tradeport (Exit 1), then follow "Great Bay Refuge" signs to the parking area. Trail maps are usually available here. Further information can be obtained from the Refuge Manager, Great Bay National Wildlife Refuge, 336 Nimble Hill Rd., Newington, NH 03801 (603-431-7511).

Adams Point

Located on the west shore of the north arm of Great Bay—known as Little Bay—Adams Point is almost directly opposite the less prominent point reached by the Ferry Way Trail in the Great Bay National Wildlife Refuge. The large field and shoreline offer interesting views, including one across Great Bay with two small, photogenically placed islands in the foreground. Adams Point, now almost reverted to nature except for the UNH Jackson Estuarine Laboratory, has at various times supported a farm, a hotel, a brickyard, and a shipyard. The Evelyn Browne Trail, about a mile long, makes a loop through the eastern part of the point; another path, also about a mile long, circles the south and west perimeter of the point and connects back into the Evelyn Browne Trail. The shoreline is accessible from this trail at several points. A trail map is usually available at the trailhead, which is reached by following NH 108 south (toward Newmarket) from Durham. At a point 1.1 mi. from the intersection of NH 108 and Main St. in Durham, bear left on Durham Point Rd. After 3.9 mi. on Durham Point Rd., turn left through a gate with a sign for the Jackson Estuarine Laboratory, and proceed for 1.2 mi. past a boat launch area to the parking area at the trailhead.

Sandy Point

Sandy Point, at the southwest corner of Great Bay, offers short interpretive trails and a small but excellent discovery center where many exhibits help to reveal the importance of Great Bay as a habitat and ecosystem. It is reached from NH 33, 0.3 mi. west of Stratham Hill Park (0.4 mi. west of the New Hampshire Technical Institute), by taking Sandy Point Rd. for 1.0 mi., then turning left at a T intersection and continuing 0.1 mi. to the end of the road.

Stratham Hill (USGS Newmarket quad)

Located in Stratham, Stratham Hill (290 ft.) is a textbook example of a drumlin, a pile of gravel left by the continental glacier. It is about 150 ft. high and a half-mile long by a quarter-mile wide, oriented in the direction of the glacier's travel—northwest to southeast. There are good views to the north and east from the summit, and in almost all directions from the former fire tower, which has an open observation deck built to replace the cab. Refer to the USGS Newmarket quadrangle. Access is from Stratham Hill Park on NH 33, 0.1 mi. west of the New Hampshire Technical Institute. Park in the large parking area and enter the fenced inner area through a gate. There are a number of other trails not described here, which may be used to provide longer walks; they are shown on a trail sign at the entrance to the recreation area from the parking area.

The summit can be reached by a direct trail 0.2 mi. long from the northwest and by a woods road 0.5 mi. long that makes a gentler ascent along the southwest slope. The structure of the drumlin is revealed more clearly from the walk along this road. A loop hike ascending by the northwest ridge trail and returning by the woods road is recommended here, but it is equally convenient to ascend and return by either route or make the loop in the opposite direction. The trail along the northwest ridge turns left just before the second building on the left beyond the gate. It ascends a gravel path, and in about 100 yd. it passes a plaque to the right of the trail that commemorates the spot where Robert Lincoln, son of Abraham Lincoln, declaimed the Declaration of Independence as a student at Philips Exeter Academy on July 4, 1860. Just before reaching the summit tower, the path passes a circular viewfinder dated 1881 that helps identify visible locations, though some no longer exist and many are no longer visible, at least from ground level. To return via the woods road, continue southeast along the grassy ridge until the unmistakable road swings right into the woods.

In order to use this woods road as an ascent route, its lower end can be reached from the parking area by continuing straight on the path from which the direct trail diverges. At a point just before a gate surrounded by boulders, where the path leads out of the park toward a farmhouse, the summit road turns left.

Distances from gate in Stratham Hill Park (160')

> *to* summit of Stratham Hill (290') via northwest ridge: 0.2 mi. (0.4 km.), 130 ft., 10 min.

> *to* starting point (160') via woods road: 0.7 mi. (1.2 km.), 130 ft. (rev. 130 ft.), 25 min.

Rock Rimmon Hill (USGS Kingston quad)

This small hill (345 ft.) on the Kingston–Danville town line is unusual for this part of the state because it is formed by a rocky outcrop, with a very steep, south-facing ledge about 150 ft. high. The former fire tower has been removed and the summit has been abused by visitors (litter, much broken glass, etc.), but the outlook across Long Pond to the low, rolling hills stretching southward is one of the few such views available in this area, and Rock Rimmon Hill itself is interesting as a rock formation. Refer to the USGS Kingston quadrangle. The easiest access is from a new housing development at the hill's northwest foot. From NH 111A, 2.7 mi. north of its jct. with NH 111 near South Danville or 3.5 mi. south of its jct. with NH 107 near Fremont, follow Long Pond Rd. east for 0.6 mi., then turn left on Rock Rimmon Rd. and follow it 0.5 mi. to a T intersection. Turn right here onto Emerald Drive and follow it for 0.7 mi. until the pavement ends where Opal Drive enters on the left. Continue straight about 40 yd. to a crossroads. Most vehicles should park here. The road on the right (south) at this crossroads descends gently, then climbs, becoming steadily rougher, to the summit of Rock Rimmon Hill at 0.4 mi. This crossroads also can be reached from the east, from Kingston village just off NH 125. From the village green, next to the fire station, follow Rock Rimmon Rd. Pavement ends at 1.0 mi., and after the last house at 1.5 mi. the road becomes too rough for most vehicles. The crossroads is reached at 2.1 mi., where the road to the summit is on the left.

Distance from Rock Rimmon Rd. (212')

    to summit of Rock Rimmon Hill (345'): 0.4 mi. (0.7 km.), 150 ft., 15 min.

Pawtuckaway State Park

The Pawtuckaway Mtns. in Nottingham are a series of three parallel ridges— North Mtn. (995 ft.), Middle Mtn. (845 ft.), and South Mtn. (885 ft.)—all contained within Pawtuckaway State Park (5535 acres), the finest natural area in southeastern New Hampshire. The valley east of North Mtn. contains an extraordinary collection of huge boulders and several other unusual and interesting rock formations, designated as the Boulder Natural Area. While the mountains are small and provide only a few sweeping viewpoints, they offer a variety of rugged, rocky scenery that surpasses even some of the four-thousand-foot peaks of the White Mtns. For a trail map, go to www.nhstateparks.org. Refer also to the USGS Mt. Pawtuckaway quadrangle.

The mountains can be reached from NH 107 between Deerfield and Raymond, 3.2 mi. north of its jct. with NH 101 Business Loop, where there is a fire lookout sign. The road, called Reservation Rd., leads east, becoming gravel after 0.9 mi. Bear right at 1.2 mi. and reach a jct. at 2.3 mi. From this point the roads make a loop through the heart of the Pawtuckaway Mtns.; the road to the left at this jct., the western branch of the loop (which continues on beyond the north end of the loop for some distance), is known as Round Pond Rd. The eastern branch of the loop, which meets Reservation Rd. 0.2 mi. farther east, is called Tower Rd. These roads are rough and eroded at times, but walking distances to most objectives from the loop are relatively short. The eastern branch of the loop (Tower Rd.) has received the majority of the traffic in the recent past, since the west branch (the southern part of Round Pond Rd.) has sometimes been under more than a foot of water from a beaver flowage near its midpoint, which makes it a problem to pass through either in a car or on foot. Reservation Rd. is now plowed in winter to the jct. of Reservation Rd. and Tower Rd., and on to the houses on the road that runs south from this jct., but parking may be limited.

For the trails to the three main mountains, continue on Reservation Rd. to the jct. with Tower Rd., then turn left (sign: "Lookout Tower") on Tower Rd. and follow it for 0.8 mi. Here on the left is a small clearing, the former location of the ranger's cabin, where there is a tiny old graveyard in the woods at the edge of the clearing. A few cars can be parked here. The Tower Trail Connector to the Mountain Trail from the main part of the state park enters about 50 yd. beyond here at a small parking area on the right, and the short path to the South Mtn. tower leaves the same parking area on the right in another 50 yd. The Middle Mountain Trail begins about 50 yd. below (south of) the ranger's cabin site. Location #7, where the South Ridge Connector leads to the Shaw Trail and the South Ridge Trail, is 0.2 mi. farther along the road beyond the Tower Trail. The north end of the loop (the jct. of Tower Rd. and Round Pond Rd.) is about 1.8 mi. from the jct. of Tower Rd. with Reservation Rd. This point (the north end of the loop) also can be reached directly from Reservation Rd. by Round Pond Rd. in about 1.3 mi. when that road is passable. The Boulder Trail to the Boulder Natural Area and North Mtn. begins on Round Pond Rd. 0.4 mi. north of the north loop jct. The other end of the Boulder Trail, which gives access to the boulders and North Mtn. via the Lower Slabs, begins at the edge of Round Pond 0.6 mi. farther along this road (this section may not be passable for ordinary cars).

The easiest road access to the mountains is from the state park off NH 156, but walking distances are much longer—though in winter, access to some of the trails on the mountains may be more convenient from this side. Reach the trails by following the road toward the swimming beach, passing a tollbooth (fee charged in summer), and then passing a pond on the left. The park furnishes trail maps that are usually available at the visitor center; most trailheads and important jcts. are numbered, with small signs that are keyed to locations on the map. The trails in the eastern part of the park are maintained for multiple use, and are particularly favored by trail bikers in summer and snowmobilers in winter. These trails are sometimes muddy in places and offer few long-range views, but they frequently traverse interesting woodlands and pass near extensive swamps. They will probably appeal most to hikers looking for pleasant but not spectacular walks fairly close to home.

Boulder Trail

This scenic short trail runs through the principal boulder field and passes the Lower Slabs as well as several other interesting rock formations. It provides access to the northern terminus of the North Mountain Trail and to Round Pond Rd. at Round Pond (the northern terminus of the South Ridge Trail), and also makes possible several interesting loops in the Round Pond and North Mtn. areas.

The trail leaves Round Pond Rd. at the hairpin turn 0.4 mi. north of Tower Rd. at Location #11 and 0.6 mi. west of Round Pond at Location #9. It descends on an old woods road through a dense hemlock forest, swings right and then left, and meets the northern terminus of the North Mountain Trail in 0.2 mi. at Location #10, in the midst of an impressive boulder field of large moss-covered glacial erratics. Here the trail turns sharp right (east), becoming a footpath, and passes through a stone wall, then skirts the northern side of an attractive open marsh. At 0.5 mi. the trail reaches a clearing at the base of an impressive set of nearly vertical ledges next to the marsh and immediately passes beneath several overhanging boulders (arrow). It passes several slabs and ledges in a hemlock grove (a mecca for local rock climbers) and soon reaches a jct. (marked by a trail sign for the Lower Slabs) next to a seasonal stream. Here there is a side path to the left, shown on the park map as a link between the Boulder Trail and Round Pond Rd. just north of Round Pond but no longer officially maintained; it can be followed for about 100 yd. to some interesting rock formations. The main trail passes a beaver dam (right) that partially obstructs the brook connecting the marsh with Round Pond, swings left and then right, and descends to the Round Pond Rd. at the northwest corner of Round Pond at Location #9, directly opposite the northern terminus of the South Ridge Trail.

Distances from Round Pond Rd. (450')

   to   North Mountain Trail (400'): 0.2 mi., 0 ft. (rev. 50 ft.), 5 min.
   to   Round Pond Rd. at Round Pond (350') at Location #9: 0.7 mi. (1.1 km.), 0 ft. (rev. 50 ft.), 20 min.

North Mountain Trail

This recently lengthened trail, which traverses North Mtn. from north to south, is the longest in the park and provides the most scenic trip. Of particular note among the features passed along the way are the collection of large glacial erratic boulders in the valley at the east end of the mountain, and the Devil's Den, a cave formed by the removal of a large fragment of rock by frost action, located in the wild, boulder-strewn eastern promontory. North Mtn. has many interesting and striking vistas along its ridge, and the hemlock groves on the north side of the mountain are among the finest in the park.

The northern end of this trail is on the Boulder Trail near the boulder field at Location #10, 0.2 mi. from Round Pond Rd. via the boulders and 0.5 mi. from Round Pond Rd. at Round Pond (the northern trailhead of the South Ridge Trail) via the Lower Slabs. The southern trailhead is on Reservation Rd., 1.8 mi. east of NH 107 and 0.5 mi. west of Round Pond Rd., at a sharp turn in the road where there is a small area for parking directly opposite the extension of Snowmobile Route 17W. Since the greatest amount of use is on the section between the boulders and the summit of North Mtn., this trail is described in the north-to-south direction.

From the jct. at Location #10 the trail climbs at a moderate grade through a beautiful hemlock forest to Dead Pond at 0.6 mi., then turns left and climbs steeply up a boulder-strewn promontory, which is covered with lichens and moss and contains many boulder caves, and soon reaches the Devil's Den (a crevice cave in the rocks to the left of the trail); nearby there is an outlook to the right across Dead Pond. From here the trail angles steeply up the north side of the ridge and, marked with cairns, continues near the ridgecrest to a small notch below another set of boulder cliffs. It then climbs by a switchback in beautiful hemlock woods to an excellent outlook to the east (including Middle Mtn. and South Mtn.) on a bluff where there is a large green Public Service Company communications reflector. It then continues along the ridge to the overgrown summit at 1.2 mi. from Location #10. The ledgy summit is marked by a cairn, and there is a limited view west toward Fort Mtn.

The trail continues along the ledgy ridgecrest, descending easily with occasional short ascents, passing through patches of hemlock woods and encountering the blue-blazed park boundary line. At 1.9 mi. the trail reaches the shoulder of the ridge at a rocky outlook next to an old stone fireplace, then begins a steeper decent down the rocky ridge over scattered ledges, passing several easterly views toward Middle Mtn. over a large marshy area. At the foot of the steep section, at 2.2 mi., the trail meets an intersection of several roads. The better woods road ascends on an angle from the left and continues roughly straight ahead; the North Mountain Bypass follows the section of road that ascends from the left here, Snowmobile Route 17W also enters here on a woods road from the right. The North Mountain Trail continues on the road nearly straight ahead, coinciding with the continuation of Snowmobile Route 17W as it descends gradually, swinging left, then right, and passing an old road that diverges on the right. It crosses a stream near several stone walls, then ascends gradually, passes through a clearing where another old road enters on the right, and continues to Reservation Rd.

Distances from Boulder Trail at Location #10 (400')

   to North Mtn. summit (995'): 1.2 mi., 600 ft., 55 min.
   to North Mountain Bypass (700'): 2.2 mi., 700 ft. (rev. 400 ft.), 1 hr. 25 min.
   to Reservation Rd. (600'): 2.7 mi. (4.3 km.), 700 ft. (rev. 100 ft.), 1 hr. 40 min.

North Mountain Bypass

This trail mostly follows woods roads, connecting Round Pond Rd. with the North Mountain Trail at the south end of North Mtn., and provides a return route for a loop hike over North Mtn. It is easy to follow for most of its length and has good footing with easy to moderate grades. Since the south end of the loop has the easiest vehicular access, this trail is described as a return route from north to south.

The trail leaves Round Pond Rd. at a point about 0.3 mi. north of its jct. with Tower Rd. at Location #11 and about 0.1 mi. south of the southern terminus of the Boulder Trail. It ascends on an old road through pine and hemlock forest, heading generally southwest. It soon bears right onto an old road coming in from the left, then swings sharp right to reach a viewpoint overlooking a large clearing (left). It descends gradually, skirts the north end of a large bog, then ascends gradually through mixed forest. The trail swings left, then right, and at 0.8 mi. it enters another old road (which is also used as a snowmobile trail) and follows it to the right. To the left, this road leads in 0.3 mi. to Round Pond Rd. at a point 0.4 mi. south of Tower Rd. at Location #11 and 0.9 mi. north of Reservation Rd.

The trail swings left, then right twice along a stone wall as it ascends gradually along the southeast slope of North Mtn. After two more bends, it meets the North Mountain Trail 0.5 mi. north of Reservation Rd. and 1.0 mi. south of the summit of North Mtn. Here the North Mountain Trail to Reservation Rd. continues on the woods road, bearing left and heading south, or, for the summit of North Mtn., it follows a footpath to the right. At this jct. Snowmobile Route 17W comes in from the left, coinciding with the North Mountain Trail, and descends straight ahead on another road.

Distance from Round Pond Rd. (500')

    to North Mountain Trail (700'): 1.4 mi. (2.3 km.), 200 ft., 50 min.

Distance from Reservation Rd. (600')

    to starting point by complete loop via North Mountain Trail, Boulder Trail, and North Mountain Bypass: 4.9 mi. (7.9 km.), 750 ft., 2 hr. 50 min.

South Mountain Tower Trail

Probably the most popular hike in the park, this trail ascends South Mtn. directly from the north and provides access to the fine views from the fire tower and nearby ledges for a modest effort. The extensive views include Mt. Wachusett, Monadnock, Sunapee Mtn., Lovewell Mtn., Mt. Kearsarge, Blue Job Mtn., and Fort Mtn. The trail begins on Tower Rd. 0.8 mi. north of Reservation Rd., just north of Location #6, where the Tower Trail Connector from the Mountain Trail reaches Tower Rd. The trail ascends by switchbacks through a pine grove on a white-blazed trail; in the lower part there is a steep direct route and a less steep route to the left. The trail passes several boulder caves (left) and the grade eases temporarily, then the path ascends granite steps and climbs by switchbacks again to the open ledges near the summit of South Mtn., where the South Ridge Trail is reached.

Distance from Tower Rd. (540')

    to South Mtn. summit (885'): 0.4 mi. (0.6 km.), 350 ft., 25 min.

South Ridge Trail

This trail traverses South Mtn., giving access to its fire tower and far-reaching views. Most hikers approach the mountain from Tower Rd. to the west, although ambitious hikers may wish to approach it from the State Park Rd. to the east via the less-traveled Mountain Trail or Round Pond Trail. The southern terminus of the South Ridge Trail is near the height-of-land on the Mountain Trail (Location #5), 1.8 mi. west of State Park Rd. at Mountain Pond (Location #2) and 0.6 mi. east from Tower Rd. at the trailhead for the South Mountain Tower Trail (Location #6) via the Tower Trail Connector.

The trail ascends an old road past several stone walls before entering a hemlock grove with several scattered boulders and ledges. At 0.6 mi. it emerges onto semi-open ledges with increasing views to the west and soon arrives at the summit of South Mtn. Here the South Mountain Tower Trail comes up from the north (left). From the top of the lookout tower the views to the west are extensive, running from Mts. Wachusett and Monadnock to Mt. Kearsarge and beyond.

From the summit, the trail descends northward on a rocky ridge into a hemlock forest with occasional minor ascents, then swings left across the ridgecrest and descends sharply past several interesting rock formations. At 1.0 mi. it swings left, then right, past a beaver pond (left) as the grade eases. The trail continues through a wet area, crosses a small stream next to a small beaver pond (left), and ascends gradually to an old road at Location #8. From here the old road (the South Ridge Connector) leads left 0.2 mi. to Tower Rd. at Location #7, 0.2 mi. north of the trailheads of South Mountain Tower Trail and the Tower Trail Connector. The South Ridge Trail turns right onto this old road and descends along the stream past a cellar hole (right), which is the foundation of an old mill. In a short distance, the western terminus of the Shaw Trail is reached at a dilapidated bridge (right). This trail leads 2.5 mi. to the Fundy Trail at Fundy Cove.

The South Ridge Trail continues straight and descends sharply by a series of switchbacks through a hemlock grove, away from the stream and down to the southwest shore of Round Pond. Here it swings left and follows the south shore of the pond with undulating grades to the Round Pond Rd. opposite the Boulder Trail at Location #9.

Distances from Mountain Trail (500')

>   *to*   South Mtn. summit (885'): 0.6 mi., 400 ft., 30 min.

> *to* South Ridge Connector at Location #8 (480'): 1.3 mi., 450 ft. (rev. 400 ft.), 50 min.
>
> *to* Shaw Trail (480'): 1.4 mi., 450 ft., 55 min.
>
> *to* Round Pond Rd. at Location #9 (350'): 2.0 mi. (3.2 km.), 450 ft. (rev. 150 ft.), 1 hr. 15 min.

Middle Mountain Trail

The trail to Middle Mtn. begins on an old woods road that leaves the west side of Tower Rd. just south of the site of the old fire warden's camp, a bit over 100 yd. south of the trailhead for the short trail to the South Mtn. tower. The trail rises on the old road at a moderate grade along a stone wall, passes a small pond (right), then turns sharp left and climbs a steep, badly eroded section to reach the upper shoulder of the mountain in a pine grove. From there the trail ascends with gentle grades over the almost imperceptible summit at 0.8 mi., then descends gradually to a ledge overlooking ponds and swamps, and affording distant views to the southwest.

Distance from Tower Rd. (500')

> *to* Middle Mtn. outlook (845'): 1.0 mi. (1.6 km.), 350 ft., 40 min.

Mountain Trail

This trail connects State Park Rd. near the main east park entrance off NH 156 with Tower Rd. just north of its jct. with Reservation Rd. in the western part of the park. It is the major access route from the eastern park facilities to the hiking areas surrounding North, Middle, and South Mtns. It is the preferred route for hikers planning to traverse between the eastern and western sections of the park, because a section of the principal alternative, the Shaw Trail, is often submerged in several feet of water (see trail description). The Mountain Trail is a wide woods road for its entire length, easy to follow and often packed down by snowmobiles during the winter months.

The trail begins on State Park Rd. at Location #2, 0.4 mi. north of the tollbooth and main parking area. There is no parking available at the trailhead; hikers are required to park in the main parking area. A new trail called the Woronoco Trail, recently cut by the New England Mountain Bike Association, also leaves this trailhead and runs roughly north, then roughly east for about 2.5 mi. to the Fundy Trail, just north of the point where that trail crosses the first brook north of its trailhead. The trail follows an old road along the northern shore of Mountain Pond in a hemlock forest, coinciding with the Round Pond Trail. The trail passes the west end of the pond, enters a wet area in a mixed forest, and at 0.5 mi. turns right at an intersection where the Round Pond Trail continues straight ahead.

After the intersection, the trail descends gradually past a stone wall and small frog pond (right), ascends gradually and crosses a large brook, parallels a stone wall, then descends again into a hemlock and pine forest. The trail swings left near a stone wall, crosses a small stream, then begins to ascend the south flank of South Mtn., which is seen across a beaver bog (right). At 1.6 mi. the trail reaches the height-of-land, then descends gradually to the jct. with the South Ridge Trail (right) at Location #5 at 1.8 mi. The trail then swings right by a frog pond, passes a stone wall, and almost immediately reaches the Tower Trail Connector (right), which runs north parallel to Tower Rd. for 0.6 mi. to the South Mountain Tower Trail. Within another 0.1 mi. the trail reaches Tower Rd. just north of its intersection with Reservation Rd. in a small grassy clearing (no sign, limited parking).

Distances from State Park Rd. at Location #2 (250')

   to Round Pond Trail junction (350'): 0.5 mi., 100 ft., 20 min.

   to height-of-land (550'): 1.6 mi., 300 ft., 55 min.

   to South Ridge Trail (500'): 1.8 mi., 300 ft. (rev. 50 ft.), 1 hr.

   to Tower Rd. (450'): 1.9 mi. (3.1 km.), 300 ft. (rev. 50 ft.), 1 hr. 5 min.

   to South Mtn. (885') via South Ridge Trail: 2.4 mi. (3.9 km.), 700 ft., 1 hr. 35 min.

Round Pond Trail

This trail connects State Park Rd. near the main east entrance with Round Pond Rd., just north of its jct. with Reservation Rd. near the west entrance to the park. It is a major access route from the eastern park facilities to the hiking areas surrounding North, Middle, and South Mtns. In winter, it forms the major snowmobile route through the park as it continues north on Round Pond Rd. to Round Pond. In summer, various connecting roads may be used to link the Round Pond Trail with routes up Middle Mtn., North Mtn., and South Mtn. It is a wide woods road for most of its length and easy to follow.

The trail begins at the State Park Rd. (Location #2), 0.4 mi. north of the toll-booth and main parking area. There is no parking available at the trailhead; hikers are required to park in the main parking area. Coinciding with the Mountain Trail, it follows the old woods road along the northern shore of Mountain Pond in a hemlock forest. After passing the west end of the pond, the trail enters a wet area in a mixed forest, and at 0.5 mi. the route continues straight ahead where the Mountain Trail turns right toward South Mtn.

The trail then ascends 0.4 mi. to a height-of-land and descends to a beaver pond with a dam and lodge (right), where the footway may be flooded during the spring. The trail ascends again through wooden gateposts to Location #14, where another old road continues straight and the trail turns right and emerges in an open area with juniper bushes. The trail then descends past an old stone wall and turns sharp left where another old road continues straight. After crossing a gravel road (the southern extension of Tower Rd.) next to a private home, the trail passes yet another old road, and at 1.6 mi. reaches a jct. marked by snowmobile signs. (Straight ahead here, Snowmobile Route 17W follows an old road over a small ridge, then down past several stone walls to end at Reservation Rd. in 0.9 mi., directly opposite the southern end of the North Mountain Trail.)

The Round Pond Trail turns right at this jct. and descends to an intersection at Location #13 in a small pine grove and clearing, where an old road continues straight 0.1 mi. to the intersection of Tower Rd. and Reservation Rd. Here the main route swings left, then right, descends past a beaver pond (left), and crosses Reservation Rd. next to the outlet of the pond at 2.0 mi., 0.1 mi. west of its jct. with Tower Rd. and 0.1 mi. east of its jct. with Round Pond Rd. The trail ascends an old road, swings left past an old cellar hole, runs through a pine plantation, and ends at the Round Pond Rd., about 75 yd. north of its jct. with Reservation Rd. and 2.2 mi. south of Round Pond.

Distances from State Park Rd. at Location #2 (250')

> *to* Mountain Trail junction (350'): 0.5 mi., 100 ft., 20 min.
>
> *to* height-of-land (450'): 0.9 mi., 200 ft., 35 min.
>
> *to* Reservation Rd. (450'): 2.0 mi., 250 ft. (rev. 50 ft.), 1 hr. 10 min.
>
> *to* Round Pond Rd. (450'): 2.2 mi. (3.5 km.), 250 ft. (rev. 50 ft.), 1 hr. 15 min.
>
> *to* Round Pond (350') via Round Pond Rd.: 4.4 mi. (7.1 km.), 500 ft. (rev. 350 ft.), 2 hr. 25 min.

Fundy Trail

This scenic trail connects the State Park Rd. with the boat launch parking area at the northern tip of the northwest arm of Fundy Cove on Lake Pawtuckaway, reached in just over 0.5 mi. by a good gravel road from Deerfield Rd. (There are plans to create a new trail from this location east along the northern shore of Lake Pawtuckaway toward Nottingham Square.) The Fundy Trail is easy to follow with gentle grades and mostly dry footing, passing Burnham's Marsh, Fundy Cove on Lake Pawtuckaway, and the remnants of a nineteenth-century farming community. There is ample opportunity to observe waterfowl and other birds, particularly during the migration season. This marshy lowland contrasts sharply with the small but rugged rocky hills of the western section of the park, and this trail affords an ideal walk for young families, though hikers should be well prepared during mosquito season. The trail leaves the State Park Rd. at Location #3, 1.4 mi. north of the entrance tollbooth and 1.0 mi. north of the trailhead for the Round Pond Trail and Mountain Trail. Parking is available across the road in the group picnic and camping area. Please do not block the trail entrance.

The trail follows a gravel road north between two wooden stakes, turns left onto an old road (arrow), passes through a small clearing, and enters a pine and hemlock forest. The trail soon crosses a small stream on a snowmobile bridge; on the far side the Woronoco Trail diverges, leading roughly west then roughly south 2.5 mi. to the Mountain Trail trailhead. The Fundy Trail follows the western shore of Burnham's Marsh (right), where waterfowl and other birds may be readily observed. The trail curves several times, crosses a stream that runs through a culvert, then enters the woods and passes the northwest corner of Burnham's Marsh just before reaching the southwest shore of Fundy Cove. This quiet and sheltered area is connected by a narrow passage to the main body of Lake Pawtuckaway, which dominates the eastern boundary of Pawtuckaway State Park. There are many views across the cove toward the northern side of the lake.

The trail enters an attractive hemlock forest, crosses an outlet brook on a snowmobile bridge next to a beaver bog and dam (left), and reaches the eastern terminus of the unmaintained Shaw Trail (left) at Location #4. If conditions allow (a section is frequently flooded), the Shaw Trail affords access to the western trail network near Round Pond and South Mtn. (see trail description). The Fundy Trail continues straight along the western shore of Fundy Cove, past numerous unmarked old roads. Soon several old stone walls, cellar holes, and unmarked paths are visible on both sides of the trail. This marks the site of an early farming community that flourished more than 150 years ago. The trail bears away from the lake into the forest past several other stone walls and unmarked paths, crosses a bridge over an inlet to the north arm of Fundy Cove, and reaches the boat launch parking area.

Distances from State Park Rd. (250')

>   *to*   Shaw Trail (250'): 1.0 mi., 30 min.

>   *to*   boat launch (250'): 1.7 mi. (2.7 km.), 50 min.

Shaw Trail *(AMC Pawtuckaway State Park Map)*

This trail connects the Fundy Trail near the southwest corner of Fundy Cove with the South Ridge Trail south of Round Pond. It begins at Location #4 on the Fundy Trail, 1.0 mi. north of the State Park Rd. and 0.7 mi. south of the boat launch parking area. At present it is not officially maintained and may be very wet in places.

The trail follows an old road west, first along the north side of a beaver swamp (left), then along the south side of an open marsh (right). At 0.4 mi. it passes through a stone wall and crosses an outlet brook that emerges from a beaver pond (right) and flows into a flooded beaver swamp (left). The trail swings sharp left (south), crosses an outlet stream along the western shore of the large beaver swamp (left), passes two large glacial erratics, crosses a small stream, and at 1.0 mi. makes a 180° hairpin turn to the right (north). In another 0.3 mi., the trail swings left (west) and maintains this general direction for the remainder of its course. It passes a small frog pond (left), descends into a hemlock forest with several wet areas, passes a stone wall, crosses a stream, then swings right and ascends an ill-defined ridge skirting several wet areas. The trail makes several left turns past stone walls, crosses another small stream, swings right near the height-of-land on the northern slope of South Mtn., and descends gradually to cross a partially collapsed bridge over a small brook just before ending at the South Ridge Trail. From here, it is 0.1 mi. south to the South Ridge Connector leading to Tower Rd. and 0.5 mi. north to Round Pond Rd. and the Boulder Trail at the western end of Round Pond.

Distances from Fundy Trail (250')

>   *to*   the hazardous swamp crossing (260'): 0.4 mi., 0 ft., 10 min.

>   *to*   South Ridge Trail (480'): 2.5 mi. (4.0 km.), 250 ft., 1 hr. 25 min.

Stonehouse Pond

This small, attractive pond in the town of Barrington is dominated by a prow-like ledge that rises about 150 ft. from the water's edge on the southwest shore, forming an unusual and picturesque combination of rock and water. There are interesting views from the top of the ledge down to the pond and out across nearby hills. Refer to the USGS Barrington quadrangle. Access is by means of a side road 0.3 mi. long to a public boat launch (street sign: Stonehouse Pond) that leaves US 202/NH 9 2.0 mi. west of the point where these routes divide west of Barrington village, or 3.2 mi. east of where they join US 4 in North-wood. There is a good view of the Stonehouse from ledges near the launching area. There are no official, marked paths around the pond, but beginning on the far side of the outlet brook there are several beaten paths just above the shore-line that can be followed fairly easily in a clockwise direction to the foot of the Stonehouse, where a steep path ascends a gully and continues across ledges through sparse woods to the summit and the viewpoints down to the pond. The easiest route of return is back along the ascent route, but it is also possible (and quite interesting) to complete the circuit of the pond. The paths on this route are less well beaten, and on the descent from the Stonehouse to the shore of the pond one must use care to stay back from the ledges that drop toward the pond. On reaching the pond, one will encounter the swampy western arm of the pond, with much evidence of beaver activity. It is possible to cross this arm (though probably not with dry feet), but it is better to continue around the periphery of the arm through open woods and return from there along the shore to the boat launch area. From the boat launch to the Stonehouse and back—either by retracing the ascent route or by continuing around the pond—is roughly 0.5 mi.

Garrison Hill

This small hill (290 ft.) on the Dover–Rollinsford town line boasts what is probably the most elaborate observation tower in New Hampshire, which provides excellent views of southeastern New Hampshire and southwestern Maine. The Pawtuckaways and Blue Hills are prominent, and Mt. Washington can be seen in clear weather, particularly during the months when it has a snow cap. The tower can be reached very easily (during daylight hours) by driving up Abbey Sawyer Memorial Highway, which leaves NH 16 north of the center of Dover and just south of Wentworth-Douglass Hospital. It is also possible to make a short but brisk ascent on foot. Take Old Rollinsford Rd., which runs between the hospital on the north and a group of professional buildings on the south. Vehicle travel ends in a short distance at a gate. Continue on the road for about 0.2 mi., then ascend one of several steep, rough beaten paths on the trails of an abandoned ski area, reaching the summit in another 0.2 mi.

Blue Hills Range

The Blue Hills are a small but prominent range of hills in the towns of Strafford and Farmington, consisting of (from west to east) Evans Mtn. (1232 ft.), Parker Mtn. (1410 ft.), Mack Mtn. (1170 ft.), Blue Job Mtn. (1357 ft.), Nubble Mtn. (1030 ft.), Hussey Mtn. (1204 ft.), and Chesley Mtn. (1035 ft.). Trails on Parker Mtn. and Blue Job Mtn. offer interesting walks; the best views in the range are obtained from the fire tower on Blue Job Mtn.

Blue Job Mountain Trail (USGS Baxter Lake quad)

Blue Job Mtn. (1357 ft.) is located in Farmington near the Strafford town line. There are excellent views from the fire tower on the summit. Refer to the USGS Baxter Lake quadrangle. There are several paths on the mountain; the official hiking trail (orange blazes) is a loop consisting of the longstanding fire warden's trail and a new route to the north of the old one, made up of a combination of woods roads and new sections of foot path. In addition to these trails, there is also a beaten path that runs north to the currently active blueberry fields on the north shoulder of the mountain; this path should be noted and avoided by hikers attempting to follow the trail described here. The trailhead is on First Crown Point Rd., which leaves NH 202A 5.3 mi. east of its jct. with NH 126 in Center Strafford, or 2.8 mi. west of its jct. with US 202 near Rochester. (Note that there is also a Crown Point Rd., which leaves NH 202A about 1.7 mi. west of First Crown Point Rd. and runs roughly parallel to it; Blue Job can also be approached by this road but the route is more complicated.) The trailhead is about 5.5 mi. from NH 202A, just past the height-of-land at a point where there are two gates close together on the right (east) side of the road. There are plans to construct a new parking area a short distance farther along the road; this would probably place the loop jct. somewhat to the north (clockwise) along the loop but should have no significant effect on distances.

The trail begins at the right-hand gate and runs 30 yd. to the loop jct. The loop is described here in the counter-clockwise direction, since most hikers will probably find the footing on the steep, badly-eroded fire warden's trail easier for ascent than for descent. The fire warden's trail to the summit continues straight at the jct., while the other section of the loop turns left here. (Note that if the path from the new parking area does move the loop junction to the north, this part of the loop will probably turn right, then left onto the fire warden's trail.) From the loop jct. the fire warden's trail climbs a rough, rocky path, rather steeply at times, to a point just east of the summit where there is a ledge with a restricted view on the right; here the trail swings left and climbs the last pitch to the summit at 0.5 mi.

The loop descends from the summit roughly southwest and then west at first, following a jeep road with fairly steep sections that are ledgy or occasionally paved to minimize erosion. After 0.3 mi. the road reaches a point just above the edge of an open field, with a communications tower visible through the trees. From this point downward public use is prohibited on the jeep road; here the trail turns off the road to the right and follows a footpath. In about 100 yd. it meets the blue-blazed state forest boundary and runs near it for another 60 yd. It crosses a small brook and at 0.9 mi. turns sharp left, almost immediately crossing through an opening in a stone wall which has been visible on the left, following a woods road that is not obvious at first but becomes gradually more well-defined. (At this sharp left turn there is a sign "To Blue Job Fire Tower" for ascending hikers, who turn sharp right here just after crossing through the stone wall.) The trail recrosses the small brook in a soggy spot, then soon diverges to the right off the now-obvious woods road. It crosses a stone wall, and then a bit farther on turns left and parallels First Crown Point Rd., crossing a gravel road that is closed to public use and soon reaching the loop jct.

Distances from First Crown Point Rd. (990')

> *to* Blue Job Mtn. summit via fire warden's trail (1357'): 0.5 mi. (0.8 km.), 350 ft., 25 min.

> *to* starting point via loop path: 1.3 mi. (2.0 km.), 0 ft. (rev. 350 ft.), 50 min.

Parker Mountain Trails (USGS Parker Mtn. quad)

Parker Mtn. (1410 ft.) in the town of Strafford is a long, fairly flat-topped ridge running southwest to northeast, with gentle slopes on the northwest but steep ones on the southeast. Refer to the USGS Parker Mtn. quadrangle. The main trail, the Spencer Smith Trail, ascends from the east (NH 126) and follows the ridgecrest to the summit. It is also possible to make a loop via the Mooers Loop Trail, the Link Trail, and the Spencer Smith Trail; this loop is better done in the sequence mentioned, since the Link Trail is somewhat obscure on the ledges just under the ridgecrest, but the route in this direction is obvious even if the trail is lost. In addition to the trails mentioned here, there are others connected to the summer camps on the ponds at the northwest foot of the mountain.

The Spencer Smith Trail begins at a wide turnout on NH 126 just south of its height-of-land, 7.4 mi. south of its jct. with NH 28 in Center Barnstead and 2.5 mi. north of the northern jct. with NH 202A in Center Strafford. The two trailheads for the Mooers Loop Trail are located 0.2 mi. and 1.1 mi. south of the trailhead for the Spencer Smith Trail; the southern trailhead is located in a field just south of a white farmhouse and opposite a brick house, marked by a Mooers Loop Trail signpost and a plaque for the Strafford Town Forest mounted on a large rock.

The ridgecrest route, the Spencer Smith Trail, passes a gate and follows a red-blazed woods road uphill. At 0.3 mi. several very short unmarked side paths lead left to a ledge with good views to the south, with nearby Blue Job Mtn. just barely visible to the far left—perhaps the best outlook on the trail. The old woods road continues to climb fairly steeply, rather eroded with less than ideal footing, until it reaches the shoulder of the ridge at 0.4 mi. From there on it follows the ledgy ridgecrest with generally easy grades. At 0.8 mi. it crosses an open ledgy area with views through and over trees, where there is a crudely built stone enclosure. Here the blue-blazed Link Trail enters from the south. The Spencer Smith Trail continues across ledges and through minor sags, passing a sparsely blazed path that runs off to the north. At 1.1 mi. the trail reaches the true summit, where there is a large cairn under a pine tree with a small spruce intertwined and a ledge with old inscriptions nearby. From here a path continues to the northwest, descending across several ledges that provide glimpses through the trees, tantalizing a hiker with the unfulfilled promise of wide views.

To make a loop hike via the Mooers Loop Trail and the Link Trail in the recommended direction, follow the wide gravel shoulder of NH 126 downhill for 0.2 mi. from the trailhead for the Spencer Smith Trail, then follow a woods road, marked with a trail sign, that runs along the base of the steep southeast slope of Parker Mtn. for 0.6 mi. to a jct. with the Link Trail (sign). The Link Trail, blazed in blue, ascends at a moderate grade for 0.6 mi. to a ledge 0.3 mi. southeast of the true summit. Blazing is adequate but there is little footway in many places, so the blazes must be followed with care. At the ridgecrest ledges one can go left to the true summit or right to return to NH 126. (Beyond the jct. with the Link Trail, the Mooers Loop Trail climbs briefly on the woods road, then diverges left and follows a route with adequate red blazes but little foot-way—follow with care. The trail swings back toward NH 126, enters another woods road, and passes a route that leaves on the right, profusely blazed in white but not cleared, which runs around the south shore of a small unnamed pond. The Mooers Loop Trail, now mostly blazed in white, descends across a wet sag at the end of the pond, passes through some ruins of an old farm, then diverges left off the woods road to climb over a small knoll, descend past a small old cemetery, and cross a field to its southern trailhead NH 126, 0.9 mi. south of its northern trailhead.)

Distance from NH 126 (907')

    to summit of Parker Mtn. (1410') via Spencer Smith Trail: 1.1 mi. (1.8 km.), 500 ft., 50 min.

Distances from NH 126 (907')

    to summit of Parker Mtn. (1410') via Mooers Loop Trail, Link Trail, and Spencer Smith Trail: 1.6 mi. (2.5 km.), 600 ft., 1 hr. 5 min.

    to starting point by complete loop via Spencer Smith Trail: 2.7 mi. (4.4 km.), 600 ft., 1 hr. 40 min.

Appendix A

Leave No Trace

The Appalachian Mountain Club is a national educational partner of Leave No Trace, a nonprofit organization dedicated to promoting and inspiring responsible outdoor recreation through education, research, and partnerships. The Leave No Trace Program seeks to develop wildland ethics—ways in which people think and act in the outdoors to minimize their impacts on the areas they visit and to protect our natural resources for future enjoyment. Leave No Trace unites four federal land management agencies—the U.S. Forest Service, National Park Service, Bureau of Land Management, and U.S. Fish and Wildlife Service—with manufacturers, outdoor retailers, user groups, educators, organizations such as the AMC and the National Outdoor Leadership School (NOLS), and individuals.

The Leave No Trace ethic is guided by these seven principles:
* Plan ahead and prepare
* Travel and camp on durable surfaces
* Dispose of waste properly
* Leave what you find
* Minimize campfire impacts
* Respect wildlife
* Be considerate of other visitors

The AMC has joined NOLS—a recognized leader in wilderness education and a founding partner of Leave No Trace—as a national provider of the Leave No Trace Master Educator course. The AMC offers this five-day course, designed especially for outdoor professionals and land managers, as well as the shorter two-day Leave No Trace Trainer course, at locations throughout the Northeast.

For Leave No Trace information and materials, contact:
Leave No Trace Center for Outdoor Ethics
PO Box 997, Boulder, CO 80306
800-332-4100; 303-442-8222; Fax: 303-442-8217
www.lnt.org

Appendix B

Accident Report

Incident Location:_____ Date:_____ Time:_____

Description of Lost or Injured Person:

Name_____ Age/Sex_____

Address_____ Phone_____

Reporting Person:

Name_____

Address_____ Phone_____

1. INCIDENT SUMMARY

_____

_____

2. PATIENT INFORMATION

Allergies_____

Medication_____

Previous Injury/Illness_____

Last 24 Hr. Food/Water Intake_____

Medical Conditions/Other_____

Experience_____

Physical/Mental Conditions_____

Patient Clothing (color/style/size):

Jacket_____ Shirt_____ Shorts/Pants_____

Hat/Gloves_____ Pack_____ Footgear_____

Patient Gear (circle all that apply):

Map	Sleeping Bag	Tent/Bivy	Rain/Windgear
Flashlight/Batts	Extra Clothing	Food/Water	Ski Poles/Ice Axe

3. PATIENT EXAMINATION

Problem Areas/Injuries (circle all that apply):

Head	Face	Eyes	Mouth	Neck
Shoulder	Chest	Stomach	Upper Back	Lower Back
Upper Leg (R)	Knee (R)	Lower Leg (R)	Ankle (R)	Foot (R)
Upper Leg (L)	Knee (L)	Lower Leg (L)	Ankle (L)	Foot (L)
Upper Arm (R)	Elbow (R)	Lower Arm (R)	Wrist (R)	Hand (R)
Upper Arm (L)	Elbow (L)	Lower Arm (L)	Wrist (L)	Hand (L)

4. VITAL SIGNS

| Time | Essential | | | Helpful | | |
	Level of Consciousness	Breathing Rate	Pulse	Blood Pressure	Skin	Pupils

5. NOTES/PLAN

_____

_____

_____

Glossary

blaze trail marking on a tree or rock, painted and/or cut

blazed marked with paint (blazes) on trees or rocks

bluff high bank or hill with a cliff face overlooking a valley

boggy muddy, swampy

boulder large, detached, somewhat rounded rock

bushwhack to hike through woods or brush without a trail

buttress rock mass projecting outward from a mountain or hill

cairn pile of rocks to mark trail

cirque upper end of valley with half-bowl shape (scoured by glacier)

cliff high, steep rock face

col low point on a ridge between two mountains; saddle

crag rugged, often overhanging rock eminence

flume ravine or gorge with a stream running through it

grade steepness of trail or road; ratio of vertical to horizontal distance

graded trail well-constructed trail with smoothed footway

gully small, steep-sided valley

height-of-land highest point reached by a trail or road

knob rounded minor summit

lean-to shelter open on one side

ledge large body of rock; or, but not usually in this book, a horizontal shelf across a cliff

ledgy having exposed ledges, usually giving views

monadnock isolated peak above a level plain

outcrops large rocks projecting out of the soil

plateau high, flat area

potable drinkable

ravine steep-sided valley

ridge highest spine joining two or more mountains, or leading up to a mountain

runoff brook brook usually dry (intermittent), except shortly after rain or snowmelt

saddle lowest, flattish part of ridge connecting two mountains; col

scrub low trees near treeline

shelter building, usually of wood, with roof and three or four sides, for camping

shoulder point where rising ridge levels off or descends slightly before rising higher to a summit

slab (n.) smooth, somewhat steeply sloping ledge

slab (v.) to travel in a direction parallel to the contour of a slope

spur minor summit projecting from a larger one

spur trail side path to a point off a main trail

strata layers of rock

summit highest point on a mountain; or, a point higher than any other point in its neighborhood

switchback zigzag traverse of a steep slope

treeline elevation above which trees do not grow

Index

Boldface denotes only trails fully described.

Get Out & Get Active with the AMC

Become an AMC Member!

With the AMC, you can participate in a wide variety of outdoor activities, connect with new people, and help to protect the natural world you love. Join us and each year you'll receive 10 issues of our member magazine, AMC Outdoors, which will keep you informed of environmental issues and outdoor recreation opportunities—including hiking, paddling, biking, and snowshoeing—across the Appalachian region. You'll also enjoy discounts on AMC skills workshops, lodging, and books. You can also join our Conservation Action Network (CAN) and help increase public influence on critical conservation issues today at www.outdoors.org/conservation/can.

AMC Outdoor Adventures

Develop your outdoor skills and knowledge through AMC Outdoor Adventures and Workshops! Learn to rock climb, snowshoe, or navigate by map and compass. From beginner backpacking and family canoeing to dogsledding and guided winter camping trips, you'll find something for any age or interest at spectacular locations throughout the Appalachian region, including the Maine Woods, White Mountains, Adirondacks, Catskills, and the Delaware Water Gap. For a full listing and to make your reservations, go to www.outdoors.org and click on Education.

AMC Books & Maps: Explore the Possibilities

AMC's hiking, biking, and paddling guides lead you to the most spectacular destinations in the Appalachian region. We're also your definitive source for how-to guides, trail maps, and adventure books. Explore the possibilities at www.outdoors.org /publications.

AMC Destinations: Be Our Guest

From the North Woods of Maine to the White Mountains to the Delaware Water Gap, AMC offers a wide variety of accommodations, from full service lodges to backcountry huts, shelters, and campsites. Experience outdoor adventure at its best as our guest. Get trip suggestions, check lodging availability, and make reservations at www.outdoors.org.

Contact Us Today

Appalachian Mountain Club
5 Joy Street
Boston, MA 02108
617-523-0636

www.outdoors.org

236

AMC Book Updates

AMC Books strives to keep our guidebooks as up-to-date as possible to help you plan safe and enjoyable adventures. If after publishing a book we learn that trails arc relocated or route or contact information has changed, we will post the updated information online. Before you hit the trail, check for updates at www.outdoors.org/publications/books/updates.

While hiking or paddling, if you notice discrepancies with the trail description or map, or if you find any other errors in the book, please let us know by submitting them to amcbookupdates@outdoors.org or in writing to Books Editor, c/o AMC, 5 Joy Street, Boston, MA 02108. We will verify all submissions and post key updates each month.

AMC Books is dedicated to being a recognized leader in outdoor publishing. Thank you for your participation.

AMC Books & Maps
Appalachian Mountain Club
5 Joy Street
Boston, MA 02108

Notes

Notes

Notes

Notes

Notes

Notes

Also Available from the AMC Hiking Series

White Mountain Guide, 27th edition
Edited by Gene Daniell and Steven D. Smith
1-929173-22-9

Mount Washington and the Presidential Range Trail Guide, 7th edition
Edited by Gene Daniell and Steven D. Smith
1-929173-25-3

High Huts of the White Mountains, 2nd edition
By William E. Reifsnyder
1-878239-20-1

Maine Mountain Guide, 9th edition
1-929173-69-5

Massachusetts Trail Guide, 8th edition
Compiled and edited by Charles W. G. Smith
1-929173-44-X

Catskill Mountain Guide
By Peter W. Kick
1-929173-16-4

North Carolina Hiking Trails, 4th edition
By Allen de Hart
1-929173-47-4

West Virginia Hiking Trails, 2nd edition
By Allen de Hart
1-878239-56-2

AMC BOOKS
EXPLORE THE POSSIBILITIES

917.42　28 day

Get ready for
adventure.

Cardigan Lodge offers access to miles of hiking and skiing trails, perfect for families, individuals, and groups.

For 70 years, Cardigan Lodge has been a year-round destination for the whole family and a great escape for anyone who enjoys outdoor adventure. At our doorstep, you'll find miles of hiking, skiing, and snowshoeing trails. Stay in the comfort of our newly renovated lodge or High Cabin retreat. Spend an evening by the fire and relax with old friends or meet new ones. Conveniently located only 2.5 hours from Boston and near the Lakes Region of New Hampshire, your next adventure is closer than you think. Make a reservation at Cardigan Lodge today.

Photo Credits: Paul Mozell, Marny Ashburne

Cardigan
LODGE & RESERVATION

Get ready for adventure. For information and reservations, call (603) 466-2727 or visit www.outdoors.org.

AMC destinations
Wake up to a World of outdoor adventure.

Appalachian Mountain Club • Cardigan Lodge • 774 Shem Valley Road, Alexandria, NH 03222 • (603) 466-2727 • www.outdoors.c

The Appalachian Mountain Club is an equal opportunity service provider.